ESSENTIAL STUDY SKILLS
THE COMPLETE GUIDE TO SUCCESS AT UNIVERSITY

SECOND EDITION

ESSENTIAL STUDY SKILLS
THE COMPLETE GUIDE TO SUCCESS AT UNIVERSITY

SECOND EDITION

TOM BURNS AND SANDRA SINFIELD

Los Angeles • London • New Delhi • Singapore

First published 2008

SAGE Publications Ltd
1 Oliver's Yard
55 City Road
London EC1Y 1SP

SAGE Publications Inc.
2455 Teller Road
Thousand Oaks, California 91320

SAGE Publications India Pvt Ltd
B 1/I 1 Mohan Cooperative Industrial Area
Mathura Road
New Delhi 110 044

SAGE Publications Asia-Pacific Pte Ltd
33 Pekin Street #02-01
Far East Square
Singapore 048763

Library of Congress Control Number: 2007939032

British Library Cataloguing in Publication data

A catalogue record for this book is available from the British Library

ISBN 978-1-4129-4584-4
ISBN 978-1-4129-4585-1 (pbk)

Typeset by **Keyword Group**
Printed in Great Britain by Cromwell Press, Trowbridge, Wiltshire
Printed on paper from sustainable resources

Contents

'The effect on our students was like star dust!'

Anne Schofield, Director of Social Work Studies, Ruskin College, Oxford, commenting on the authors' teaching

About the Authors

Tom Burns is a Senior Lecturer in Learning Development at London Metropolitan University, specialising in devising and delivering study and academic skills programmes, resources and staff development sessions. He has been a lecturer in education, literature, media and sociology and a producer of high quality teaching and learning resources (his video 'Take Control' won the IVCA gold award for education).

Sandra Sinfield is Coordinator of Learning and Language Development at London Metropolitan University. She has developed a range of study and academic skills courses and teaching and learning resources, is a moderator for the Open College Network London Region, is a founder member of the Learning Development in Higher Education Network and is part of the Learn Higher Centre for Excellence in Teaching and Learning (www.learnhigher.ac.uk).

This second edition of *Essential Study Skills* has two guest chapters – 'How to use computers and e-learning' and 'How to make the most of PDP', by **Debbie Holley** of London Metropolitan University, and **Christine Keenan** of Bournemouth University, respectively.

Acknowledgements

The authors would like to thank all the students with whom they have worked, with a special thank you to Kate Hoskins who read the manuscript for this second edition and, hopefully, improved it. They would also like to thank Dr James Bentley Philip, an exceptional scholar, teacher and friend for his support and encouragement.

A huge thank you goes to our colleagues, Debbie Holley of London Metropolitan University and Chris Keenan of Bournemouth University, for contributing their chapters on 'How to use computers and e-learning' and 'How to make the most of PDP'. It was wonderful for us to be able to draw on their special expertise and in-depth insight and knowledge in this way.

We would also like to acknowledge the Centres for Excellence in Teaching and Learning (CETLs) Learn Higher, Write Now and RLO-CETL. We are part of Learn Higher and we work with Write Now and RLO-CETL, and we have found this collaboration inspiring and energising.

We are very grateful to our friends and colleagues for their input into this text.

Finally, a very special thank you goes to our families, whose love and support has made everything possible.

Guided tour

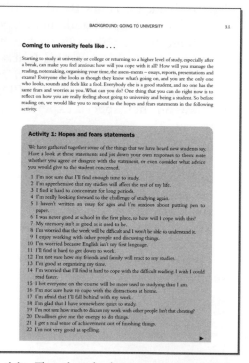

1

Going to University

AIMS

To examine what it feels like to be a student, and to outline our SOCCER or 'six steps to success' strategy that informs this book and the activities and information that we cover within it.

LEARNING OUTCOMES

After reading this section and engaging with the activities, you will have:
- reflected on what it feels like to be a university student
- gained an understanding of the premise of the book
- been introduced to the characteristics of successful study that inform the rest of the book.

Coming to university feels like . . .

Starting to study at university or college or returning to a higher level of study, especially after a break, can make you feel anxious: how will you cope with it all? How will you manage the reading, notemaking, organising your time, the assess-ments – essays, reports, presentations and exams? Everyone else looks as though they know what's going on, and you are the only one who looks, sounds and feels like a fool. Everybody else is a good student, and no one has the same fears and worries as you. What can you do? One thing that you can do right now is to reflect on how you are really feeling about going to university and being a student. So before reading on, we would like you to respond to the hopes and fears statements in the following activity.

Activity 1: Hopes and fears statements

We have gathered together some of the things that we have heard new students say. Have a look at these statements and jot down your own responses to them: note whether you agree or disagree with the statement, or even consider what advice you would give to the student concerned.

1. I'm not sure that I'll find enough time to study.
2. I'm apprehensive that my studies will affect the rest of my life.
3. I find it hard to concentrate for long periods.
4. I'm really looking forward to the challenge of studying again.
5. I haven't written an essay for ages and I'm anxious about putting pen to paper.
6. I was never good at school in the first place, so how will I cope with this?
7. My memory isn't as good as it used to be.
8. I'm worried that the work will be difficult and I won't be able to understand it.
9. I enjoy working with other people and discussing things.
10. I'm worried because English isn't my first language.
11. I'll find it hard to get down to work.
12. I'm not sure how my friends and family will react to my studies.
13. I'm good at organising my time.
14. I'm worried that I'll find it hard to cope with the difficult reading. I wish I could read faster.
15. I bet everyone on the course will be more used to studying than I am.
16. I'm not sure how to cope with the distractions at home.
17. I'm afraid that I'll fall behind with my work.
18. I'm glad that I have somewhere quiet to study.
19. I'm not sure how much to discuss my work with other people. Isn't that cheating?
20. Deadlines give me the energy to do things.
21. I get a real sense of achievement out of finishing things.
22. I'm not very good at spelling.

▶

Aims: An outline of the main aims discussed throughout the chapter.

Learning Outcomes: A useful and quick guide as to what you will have learnt by the end of the chapter.

Activity: Throughout the chapter, activities are supplied to offer a hands-on approach to understanding the concepts discussed.

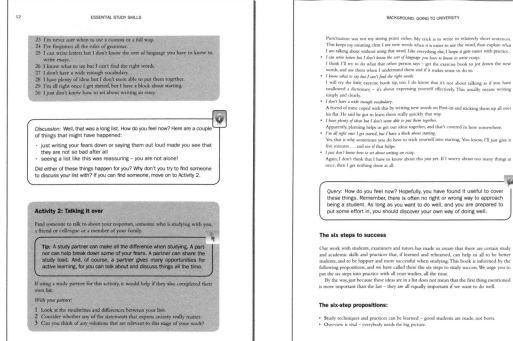

23 I'm never sure when to use a comma or a full stop.
24 I've forgotten all the rules of grammar.
25 I can write letters but I don't know the sort of language you have to know to write essays.
26 I know what to say but I can't find the right words.
27 I don't have a wide enough vocabulary.
28 I have plenty of ideas but I don't seem able to put them together.
29 I'm all right once I get started, but I have a block about starting.
30 I just don't know how to set about writing an essay.

Discussion: Well, that was a long list. How do you feel now? Here are a couple of things that might have happened:

· just writing your fears down or saying them out loud made you see that they are not so bad after all
· seeing a list like this was reassuring – you are not alone!

Did either of these things happen for you? Why don't you try to find someone to discuss your list with? If you can find someone, move on to Activity 2.

Activity 2: Talking it over

Find someone to talk to about your responses, someone who is studying with you, a friend or colleague or a member of your family.

Tip: A study partner can make all the difference when studying. A partner can help break down some of your fears. A partner can share the study load. And, of course, a partner gives many opportunities for active learning, for you can talk about and discuss things all the time.

If using a study partner for this activity, it would help if they also completed their own list.

With your partner:

1 Look at the similarities and differences between your lists.
2 Consider whether any of the statements that express anxiety really matter.
3 Can you think of any solutions that are relevant to this stage of your work?

Punctuation was not my strong point either. My trick is to write in relatively short sentences. This keeps my meaning clear. I use new words when it is easier to use the word, than explain what I am talking about without using that word. Like everything else, I hope it gets easier with practice.

· *I can write letters but I don't know the sort of language you have to know to write essays.*
I think I'll try to do what that other person says – get the exercise book to jot down the new words, and use them when I understand them and if it makes sense to do so.

· *I know what to say but I can't find the right words.*
I will try the little exercise book tip, too. I do know that it's not about talking as if you have swallowed a dictionary – it's about expressing yourself effectively. This usually means writing simply and clearly.

· *I don't have a wide enough vocabulary.*
A friend of mine coped with this by writing new words on Post-its and sticking them up all over his flat. He said he got to learn them really quickly that way.

· *I have plenty of ideas but I don't seem able to put them together.*
Apparently, planning helps us get our ideas together, and that's covered in here somewhere.

· *I'm all right once I get started, but I have a block about starting.*
Yes, that is why sometimes you do have to trick yourself into starting, You know, I'll just give it five minutes . . . and see if that helps.

· *I just don't know how to set about writing an essay.*
Again, I don't think that I have to know about this just yet. If I worry about too many things at once, then I get nothing done at all.

Query: How do you feel now? Hopefully, you have found it useful to cover these things. Remember, there is often no right or wrong way to approach being a student. As long as you want to do well, and you are prepared to put some effort in, you should discover your own way of doing well.

The six steps to success

Our work with students, examiners and tutors has made us aware that there are certain study and academic skills and practices that, if learned and rehearsed, can help us all to be better students, and to be happier and more successful when studying. This book is informed by the following propositions, and we have called these the six steps to study success. We urge you to put the six steps into practice with all your studies, all the time.

By the way, just because these ideas are in a list does not mean that the first thing mentioned is more important than the last – they are all equally important if we want to do well.

The six-step propositions:

· Study techniques and practices can be learned – good students are made, not born.
· Overview is vital – everybody needs the big picture.

Discussion: Promotes the understanding of concepts through discussion with a partner.

Tip: Assist with the understanding of ideas with helpful pieces of information.

Query: Prompts to assist in the understanding and contemplation of important points that are raised throughout the chapter.

Learning and remembering are not necessarily automatic or simple, but we can learn how to do these effectively, and we have structured the book to reinforce this. To explore this in more depth, go to:

10 How to be a reflective learner
15 How to write a great reflective essay
19 How to build your memory and revise effectively
20 How to understand and pass exams
21 How to make the most of Personal Development Planning

'I love doing my learning logs, as it helps me make sense of what I'm doing. If I didn't do my logs, I don't think I'd understand anything at all.'

Conclusion

In this brief chapter, we have covered your hopes and fears about becoming a university student, our six-step propositions and the six steps to success. We have argued that good students, like you, are made, not born. If you build SOCCER into your study habits every day, you will have real progress in your study habits.

Review points

By reading this six-step chapter, you should now have an:

■ awareness of your own hopes and fears about becoming a student
■ awareness that developing your potential as a student will involve you in change
■ awareness of the six steps to success, the propositions that shape and inform the rest of the book itself.

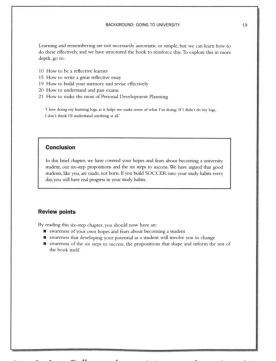

Tips checklist

□ Look forward to becoming a student. Enjoy being a student.
□ Help your family and friends to see how important being a student is to you.
□ Have a regular place to study: when you sit there, your body will learn to work.
□ Make some time to study every day: turn off the phone, don't answer the door. Focus.
□ Concentrate for 15-minute blocks at first and build up.
□ Move out of your comfort zone.
□ Practise writing every day.
□ Develop your memory with the revision cycle (pages 274–5).
□ Discover if you like working alone or with other people.
□ Discover if you like working with noise or quiet.
□ Discover if you like working in the morning, afternoon, or evening, or at night.
□ Buy an English dictionary, a subject dictionary and a dictionary of sociological terms.
□ If English isn't your first language, join an academic English class.
□ Buy an exercise book and make your own list of all the new words that you encounter.
□ Buy an exercise book and make your own subject dictionary. Put in the key people of your subject. Put in new theories. Put in the key words, phrases and terms that you will have to use.
□ When you encounter new theories, theorists, words and phrases, write them on Post-its and stick them up all round your home. Take them down when you know them.
□ Practise organising your time: prioritise, make lists, use a diary, use a 24/7 timetable. Sometimes be very organised, and sometimes sit amongst a pile of work and plunge in.
□ Find a study partner, or use online discussion boards.
□ Enjoy studying – do not see it as 'work'.
□ Use deadlines to keep you on track.
□ If unhappy with your spelling, punctuation or grammar, buy a simple grammar book and use it.
□ Keep a small notebook with you at all times. When you have a bright idea or an insight into your subject, write it down.

Conclusion: Pulls together and discusses the main points of a chapter, as well as offering some further reading ideas that can help develop your knowledge further.

Review Points: All the main issues and points that have been discussed in the chapter are summarised.

Checklist: Many chapters feature checklists which will help collate and understand all the relevant factors, which you can tick off as you proceed.

List of Tables

List of Figures

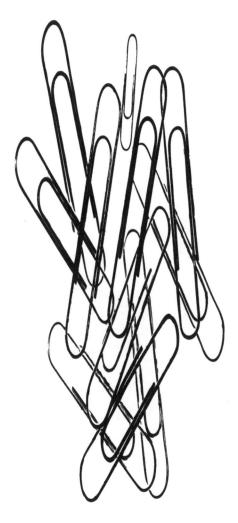

SECTION 1

Background

Introduction

AIMS

To welcome you to the second edition of *Essential Study Skills* (*ESS2*) and to explain its aims and intentions, and to help you get the most from this book by giving information on 'how to use this book'.

LEARNING OUTCOMES

That after reading this section and engaging with the activities, you will have:
- gained a sense of how this book 'works'
- considered how to get the most from this book.

Welcome

Welcome to *ESS2*. This book is designed to help you become a more effective and happier student, by uncovering the mysteries of Higher Education (HE) so that you can understand the 'what, why and how' of university as quickly as possible. Once you know this, you can get on with the business of enjoying your studies and making the progress that you want to make.

Both of this book's authors were the first in their families to go to university and, as is still true for many of our students today, we found many aspects of university life strange at first. Obviously, if you do not know how universities 'work' and what you are supposed to do once you are there, you will not perform to your best ability. That is why we have produced this book – it is designed to be a guide to universities and what you can do to succeed as a student.

We have tried to adopt a user-friendly tone without over-simplifying or, worse, being patronising. But this is difficult. There is no one writing style or way of explaining university life that will work for everybody. We may explain something in great detail that to you is already obvious, and this may annoy or frustrate you. Try to relax when this happens, for that means you already understand a tricky aspect of university life. However, for another student this might be the key to solving a mystery about HE that would otherwise have defeated them.

Another factor for you to consider when using this book is the time that you have to invest in order to actually become an effective and successful student. This may be felt more sharply if you, too, are the first in your family to go to university, and you feel that there is not enough time to do your course, let alone 'do' a study skills book as well.

The only reassurance we can offer is that if you do invest time to develop and refine your study and academic skills and practices, it will save you time in the long run; you will be studying so much more efficiently and effectively.

It will take time and commitment

The secret to becoming an effective and successful student, as with many of the things that we do in life, is twofold – first, you must *want* to develop the relevant skills, strategies and techniques necessary for your success; and second, you must be prepared to practise, practise, practise. Nothing that we want to do just happens. It all takes time and practice.

Compare becoming a successful student with learning to drive. If this were a driving theory book, it would not mean that you would read it once and then expect to rush out and drive a car perfectly. You would expect to have many practical driving experiences as well. In these practice sessions, you would be putting driving theory into practice. You would expect to make many mistakes as you practised, but over time you would expect to sort them out and get better at driving.

Even when you passed your test, you would still realise, hopefully, that you are always developing as a driver. There would never be a moment when you thought, 'Now I am a perfect driver!' Each time you got into the car, you would be practising and enhancing your driving skills. The more you made yourself aware of that ('today I learned a better way of entering and leaving a roundabout – I'll do that again'), the better a driver you would become.

It is the same with being a student – you will need to actually practise and use the techniques suggested here for them to work for you. There may be days when we slip back into old, less effective habits, but we can always refine our techniques and develop. The writers of this book have been students and teachers for more than 50 years between them. We both still expect to pick up new tips and tricks that will help us become even more effective. We still expect to refine our academic practice.

The aim of this book is to pass on successful techniques to you, the reader. But remember, this is not a one-stop quick fix. The study and academic skills and practices that are covered here will, hopefully, be part of your life for some time, and they will be things that you rehearse and develop over time. So, make your study techniques conscious, and keep practising, refining and reviewing your techniques. This way, you will be able to keep improving as a student.

> **Tip:** Read Chapter 15 on the reflective essay which looks at the student as a reflective practitioner. It also gives an example of an essay plan for a reflective essay on developing your study and academic skills as a student.

Out of your comfort zone

We would like to ask you to be prepared to make mistakes and learn from them. This is the way that we learn as human beings. Often, it feels uncomfortable to make mistakes; it can make us feel foolish and, typically, we do not like to feel this way. However, as a student, if you do not take risks, if you are not prepared to make mistakes and learn from them, you will find that your progress is very slow. Yet, if we can get over those feelings of discomfort, if we can force ourselves out of our comfort zones, and consciously decide to take risks, make mistakes and improve, everything else gets better. There are only two big mistakes:

1 To be so frightened of making mistakes that we do nothing.
2 Not to learn from our mistakes.

So, good luck with this book. And remember, before you work through each of the sections, think first:

- What do I already know about this topic?
- What do I want from this section?

And, at the end, pause and reflect:

- What have I learned?
- How will it help me?

Pens and paper at hand

We recommend that you work through sections of the book with notepad and pens to hand. Before you start to work through a chapter, set yourself goals – know why

▶

Pens and paper at hand—Cont'd

you are reading that chapter and what you want from it (e.g. for Chapter 12 'I want to develop effective notemaking strategies'; for Chapter 16, 'I want the structure of the report, rather than the essay'). Briefly remind yourself of what you already think, believe or know about the topic to get yourself tuned in. Fill in questionnaires and perform the activities as you go. Once you have finished a section of the book, reflect on what you have read and done, asking yourself, what does this tell me? How will knowing this make me a more successful student? In this way, you will get the most from the book as you go through it, and in the long term.

How to use this book

This is the sort of book that you can work through step by step if you want to, but it has also been designed so that you can dip into different sections of the book, as and when you feel they will be useful to you. The trick is to know what *you* want from each section of the book at any particular time.

Each chapter looks like this

Each chapter in this book has an overall theme, and while there might be some slight changes in the presentation of material, certain things will recur throughout the book. Typically there will be:

- aims and learning outcomes that clearly state what we think the chapter will achieve
- an introduction to and presentation of information, coupled with, variously:
  - activities for you to do
  - questions to answer
  - student and staff quotes
  - commentary and discussion points
  - further reading and guides to resources
- a conclusion that draws the chapter together and to a close
- reflection points.

Tip: The online companion to this book will have hypertext links to key URLS, so that you can just click and go. Go to www.sagepub.co.uk/burnsandsinfield

All the activities and suggestions in this book, while supported by research, have arisen out of our practical work with students and lecturers. Students, tutors and course examiners have commented on the effectiveness of the information and activities suggested in this book:

Students: 'This was the best piece of learning I have ever done!'
Examiners: 'This changes students' lives, not just their study skills.'
Tutors: 'The effect on our students was like stardust.'

Activity 1: How to use this book

Reading an academic text is not like the reading that we do for pleasure – we typically have to be more strategic and more effective than that, as there is so little time and so much to do! In this activity, we are attempting to take you through an active reading strategy (see also Chapter 11), so that you are in a position to get the most from this book as quickly as possible. So please follow the instructions below, and see if using this active approach really does help you to get more out of this book.

Read the Contents of the book, asking yourself the following questions:

- Which sections look useful right now? Why is that?
- Which sections will you look at at a later date?
- When will you do this reading? Make a note on a calendar.

Now scan the Index pages of the book (these are at the back and they highlight key words that appear throughout the book, and tell you the pages on which they can be found):

- What words look interesting to you? Make a note – that is, note the topics and note the pages on which they can be found.
- Have a quick look at some of those pages.
- What have you discovered?
- What does this tell you?

Query: Is this the way that you normally approach a book?

Discussion: Reading for academic purposes is usually very different from reading for pleasure. When we read for pleasure, many of us read from cover to cover. We enjoy working through the book from beginning to end. We want to know 'what happens next'. We do not rush to the ending as that might spoil our fun.

▶

Reading for study is different to this. Typically, we do not ever read a book from cover to cover. We dip into books looking for specific bits of information. We do not need to read the whole book – we might not even need to read a whole chapter.

However, this can feel very uncomfortable. On the one hand, we can feel that we are cheating if we do not read the whole book, or we might feel that we will not understand the subject properly, or that we will be missing something. But it is important to remember that we will have to change the way we normally do things in order to succeed in education.

Things to note:

1 What we have tried to do is to very quickly demonstrate to you that there are some successful academic strategies around that help us to study (here it was getting more out of this book). These techniques can help everyone to become a better student; however, they might require us to change some of our behaviours.

2 You might have noticed already that some of these changes are a little uncomfortable. Change is often uncomfortable, and that can be one reason why sensible and intelligent people sometimes refuse to adopt successful study practices – it just feels too uncomfortable. But the uncomfortable feelings do pass, so when you practise some of the activities suggested in this book, be prepared for discomfort and tell yourself that it will pass.

3 Finally, we have tried to help you become more in control of your own learning, and to become an active learner, with respect to this book. Throughout this text, we will argue that we learn more when we take control of our studies, when we recognise what we want ('I'll read that chapter first because . . .'), and when we plan when we will do it ('I'll do it on the bus tomorrow on my way to uni'). All of the advice, strategies, guidelines, tips and tricks in this book are designed to help you become an active learner and an active student. Good luck and enjoy the book!

How to approach each chapter

1 Before you read, set your own goals – know why you are reading a section of this book. Know what you want to get from it.

2 While reading, keep asking questions – what is going on here? What does this tell me? Why are they telling me that? How will knowing this help me?

3 After reading, take the time to reflect on what you have read, and make a few notes to make your learning conscious.

Tip: Have a look at the first part of Chapter 11: How to research and read academically.

And students have said:

'This really sets students up to succeed!'
'It opened up different strategies, learning strategies, . . . and now I don't feel inferior.'
'And you go, *yes*, and it really spurs you on!'

Conclusion

In this first chapter, we have said that we want to demystify the university system, such that you can be as successful as you want as quickly as possible. We did point out that in order for you to develop your study and academic skills and practices, you must be prepared to invest real time, to make mistakes and learn from them, to take risks and move out of your comfort zone, but we argued that all this would pay off in terms of more effective and efficient use of your time in the future. We truly believe that this will also make you a happier and more successful student, with a more positive approach to studying and learning. We explained the structure of the chapters in this book, and took you through a practical (university) reading activity that was designed to help you make the most of this book, and give you a practical demonstration of how to make the most of any book that you read from now on. Good luck with *ESS2* and with all your studies.

Review points

By reading this introductory chapter – and engaging with the activities set – you should now have:

- a sense of the purpose of the book
- some idea of what you want from the book, in both the short and long term
- an understanding of how to approach this, and any, book such that you get the most from it
- an awareness that developing your potential as a student will involve you in change vand will require a commitment of your time, but that this will be worth it.

Tip: If you are the first in your family to go to university, or if you are a little unsure about what to expect and what to do at university, you might like to continue through this background section and look at Chapters 1, 2 vand 3, which give an overview of learning and studying at university.

1

Going to University

AIMS

To examine what it feels like to be a student, and to outline our SOCCER or 'six steps to success' strategy that informs this book and the activities and information that we cover within it.

LEARNING OUTCOMES

After reading this section and engaging with the activities, you will have:
- reflected on what it feels like to be a university student
- gained an understanding of the premise of the book
- been introduced to the characteristics of successful study that inform the rest of the book.

Coming to university feels like . . .

Starting to study at university or college or returning to a higher level of study, especially after a break, can make you feel anxious: how will you cope with it all? How will you manage the reading, notemaking, organising your time, the assess-ments – essays, reports, presentations and exams? Everyone else looks as though they know what's going on, and you are the only one who looks, sounds and feels like a fool. Everybody else is a good student, and no one has the same fears and worries as you. What can you do? One thing that you can do right now is to reflect on how you are really feeling about going to university and being a student. So before reading on, we would like you to respond to the hopes and fears statements in the following activity.

Activity 1: Hopes and fears statements

We have gathered together some of the things that we have heard new students say. Have a look at these statements and jot down your own responses to them: note whether you agree or disagree with the statement, or even consider what advice you would give to the student concerned.

1 I'm not sure that I'll find enough time to study.
2 I'm apprehensive that my studies will affect the rest of my life.
3 I find it hard to concentrate for long periods.
4 I'm really looking forward to the challenge of studying again.
5 I haven't written an essay for ages and I'm anxious about putting pen to paper.
6 I was never good at school in the first place, so how will I cope with this?
7 My memory isn't as good as it used to be.
8 I'm worried that the work will be difficult and I won't be able to understand it.
9 I enjoy working with other people and discussing things.
10 I'm worried because English isn't my first language.
11 I'll find it hard to get down to work.
12 I'm not sure how my friends and family will react to my studies.
13 I'm good at organising my time.
14 I'm worried that I'll find it hard to cope with the difficult reading. I wish I could read faster.
15 I bet everyone on the course will be more used to studying than I am.
16 I'm not sure how to cope with the distractions at home.
17 I'm afraid that I'll fall behind with my work.
18 I'm glad that I have somewhere quiet to study.
19 I'm not sure how much to discuss my work with other people. Isn't that cheating?
20 Deadlines give me the energy to do things.
21 I get a real sense of achievement out of finishing things.
22 I'm not very good at spelling.

▶

23　I'm never sure when to use a comma or a full stop.
24　I've forgotten all the rules of grammar.
25　I can write letters but I don't know the sort of language you have to know to write essays.
26　I know what to say but I can't find the right words.
27　I don't have a wide enough vocabulary.
28　I have plenty of ideas but I don't seem able to put them together.
29　I'm all right once I get started, but I have a block about starting.
30　I just don't know how to set about writing an essay.

Discussion: Well, that was a long list. How do you feel now? Here are a couple of things that might have happened:

- just writing your fears down or saying them out loud made you see that they are not so bad after all
- seeing a list like this was reassuring – you are not alone!

Did either of these things happen for you? Why don't you try to find someone to discuss your list with? If you can find someone, move on to Activity 2.

Activity 2: Talking it over

Find someone to talk to about your responses, someone who is studying with you, a friend or colleague or a member of your family.

Tip: A study partner can make all the difference when studying. A partner can help break down some of your fears. A partner can share the study load. And, of course, a partner gives many opportunities for active learning, for you can talk about and discuss things all the time.

If using a study partner for this activity, it would help if they also completed their own list.

With your partner:

1　Look at the similarities and differences between your lists.
2　Consider whether any of the statements that express anxiety really matter.
3　Can you think of any solutions that are relevant to this stage of your work?

Discussion: Has your discussion helped at all? Why don't you now look at some responses collected from other students?

Hopes and fears statements and responses

- I'm not sure that I'll find enough time to study.
  I realise that I will have to be very organised in order to work, study and maintain my family and friends. I will look at the Study Techniques section of the book.
- *I'm apprehensive that my studies will affect the rest of my life.*
  Well, being a student is going to have a dramatic impact on my life, I can see that. I will not have as much time for friends and family, nor to do the other things that I really like doing perhaps. But, there again, life does change; it's about changes and changing. I can see why they say that change can be very uncomfortable, as it already is.
- *I find it hard to concentrate for long periods.*
  I shall start by concentrating for short periods and try to build up to longer study periods. I don't have to get it all right straight away.
- *I'm really looking forward to the challenge of studying again.*
  So am I! It makes me feel good about me.
- *I haven't written an essay for ages and I'm anxious about putting pen to paper.*
  But that's why I'm using this book.
- *I was never good at school in the first place, so how will I cope with this?*
  I know what you mean, but I didn't like school – maybe that's why I didn't do well there. It's different now.
- *My memory isn't as good as it used to be.*
  I've heard that this isn't really true. As we get older, we pay more attention to what we forget. Apparently, we should notice what we are getting right instead. However, when it comes to studying, I have never realised before how much effort I will have to put in to remembering things. I thought that the brain just remembered stuff or it didn't. I can see now that I have to choose what to remember and how to remember it. It's different, but I hope that I can learn to do that.
- *I'm worried that the work will be difficult and I won't be able to understand it.*
  I noticed the point about being prepared to get things wrong, so I am going to try to be brave and be prepared to learn from my mistakes. I'm also going to ask questions if I don't understand. And I've bought an English dictionary and a subject dictionary to help me cope with the language of my subject.
- *I enjoy working with other people and discussing things.*
  I'm going to have to find a study partner, because I really do like talking things over. I've done some of my best learning in the canteen once class is over.
- *I'm worried because English isn't my first language.*
  My daughter is better at English than I am and she has said that she will help me. She also thinks that I'm being very brave studying in English, which makes me feel strong instead of foolish.

- *I'll find it hard to get down to work.*

  It is hard to study – for everybody. I have a special place to sit, and when I am there, I 'feel' like a student. Sometimes I trick myself into sitting there – I say, just sit there for five minutes and see what happens – before I know it, I have started to work and it is all right after all.

- *I'm not sure how my friends and family will react to my studies.*

  Yes, this can be a problem. I do know people who have a really hard time: their friends think they'll become snobs, or their children start to play up every time they try to get some work done . . . I guess if we want them to understand what we are doing – and support us – we have to explain what we are doing, and build some time for them into our study timetable.

- *I'm good at organising my time.*

  I find I have two approaches: one is to be very organised – I make lists of all the things that I have to do and I work through them. The other system is where I sit down amongst a pile of work, and just plunge in and get on with it. Both systems seem to work sometimes. This tells me that there is no one right way to do anything, but that I do have to keep on top of things or else everything feels worse!

- *I'm worried that I'll find it hard to cope with the difficult reading. I wish I could read faster.*

  I've heard that academic reading does get easier with practice – I certainly hope so. Still, I suppose it's got to take up some time – it's not a detective story, is it?

- *I bet everyone on the course will be more used to studying than I am.*

  I also bet that I'm the only one who's frightened, and I'm the only one whose family doesn't understand them . . . It's not true really, is it?

- *I'm not sure how to cope with the distractions at home.*

  Well, I've got a friend who works from home, so I know it can be done. She puts the answerphone on; she does not open the door, and things like that. The problem arises when we actually want to be distracted, because that is easier than doing the work.

- *I'm afraid that I'll fall behind with my work.*

  I'm hoping the section on organising my time will help me with that.

- *I'm glad that I have somewhere quiet to study.*

  Lucky you – I don't! Anyway, I've heard that this is another case where there is no one right way of working. Some people work best in the quiet, while others like noise.

- *I'm not sure how much to discuss my work with other people. Isn't that cheating?*

  I know the answer to this one. Talking isn't cheating, it's active learning. I like the sound of that.

- *Deadlines give me the energy to do things.*

  Without deadlines, I do find it difficult to finish things. At the same time, I know that I mustn't leave it all till the last minute – I must pace myself through an assignment.

- *I get a real sense of achievement out of finishing things.*

  I love it when I hand a piece of work in on time. But I do know other people who hate finishing things off. They just keep on reading and reading. I guess that sometimes it's difficult to know when you've done enough work.

- *I'm not very good at spelling.*

  I'm going to use the spell checker on my computer. I've also heard that it is a good idea to build up your own dictionary of difficult words. I've already bought a small exercise book to do this.

- *I'm never sure when to use a comma or a full stop.*

- *I've forgotten all the rules of grammar.*

Punctuation was not my strong point either. My trick is to write in relatively short sentences. This keeps my meaning clear. I use new words when it is easier to use the word, than explain what I am talking about without using that word. Like everything else, I hope it gets easier with practice.

- *I can write letters but I don't know the sort of language you have to know to write essays.*
  I think I'll try to do what that other person says – get the exercise book to jot down the new words, and use them when I understand them and if it makes sense to do so.
- *I know what to say but I can't find the right words.*
  I will try the little exercise book tip, too. I do know that it's not about talking as if you have swallowed a dictionary – it's about expressing yourself effectively. This usually means writing simply and clearly.
- *I don't have a wide enough vocabulary.*
  A friend of mine coped with this by writing new words on Post-its and sticking them up all over his flat. He said he got to learn them really quickly that way.
- *I have plenty of ideas but I don't seem able to put them together.*
  Apparently, planning helps us get our ideas together, and that's covered in here somewhere.
- *I'm all right once I get started, but I have a block about starting.*
  Yes, that is why sometimes you do have to trick yourself into starting, You know, I'll just give it five minutes . . . and see if that helps.
- *I just don't know how to set about writing an essay.*
  Again, I don't think that I have to know about this just yet. If I worry about too many things at once, then I get nothing done at all.

Query: How do you feel now? Hopefully, you have found it useful to cover these things. Remember, there is often no right or wrong way to approach being a student. As long as you want to do well, and you are prepared to put some effort in, you should discover your own way of doing well.

The six steps to success

Our work with students, examiners and tutors has made us aware that there are certain study and academic skills and practices that, if learned and rehearsed, can help us all to be better students, and to be happier and more successful when studying. This book is informed by the following propositions, and we have called these the six steps to study success. We urge you to put the six steps into practice with all your studies, all the time.

By the way, just because these ideas are in a list does not mean that the first thing mentioned is more important than the last – they are all equally important if we want to do well.

The six-step propositions:

- **S**tudy techniques and practices can be learned – good students are made, not born.
- **O**verview is vital – everybody needs the big picture.

- Creativity is essential – and can be developed.
- Communicate effectively – in the correct form.
- Emotions rule – dealing with your emotions is crucial.
- Review – without reflection there is no learning.

You might trace the letters in bold, above, that take us from the six-step propositions to the mnemonic designed to help you remember these six steps – SOCCER:

> **S** – Study techniques and practices
> **O** – Overview
> **C** – Creativity
> **C** – Communicate effectively
> **E** – Emotions
> **R** – Review, review, review

We discuss these six steps briefly here, and refer to other sections of this book that develop the ideas even further.

Study techniques and practices can be learned – good students are made, not born

It is all too easy to think that we are not 'cut out' for studying. Often, negative experiences at school can lead many people to believe that studying is not for them – they are just not good students. Our work with students of all ages and 'abilities' leads us to believe that most of us can learn to become good students – what gets in the way is the belief that it should all come naturally, that if we don't just know what to do, then something is wrong with us.

Why should you think that you 'ought' to know how to study effectively? If you wanted to be a fire fighter or a farmer or a chef or a carpenter, you would know that you would have to learn how to be one. You would guess that you could also learn certain tricks of the trade that would make the job easier or more effective. If we think of studying like this, it can become easier. All the way through this book we will look at the constituent study and academic skills that can help you to succeed.

In terms of developing your study techniques, consider:

4 How to learn effectively
5 How to organise yourself for independent study
6 How to use computers and e-learning . . .
7 How to succeed in group work
11 How to research and read academically
12 How to make the best notes
20 How to understand and pass exams.

'Why didn't they tell us this before? I left school feeling like a complete failure, but it was just that I didn't know how to learn. These techniques have given me such a boost. I feel really confident now.'

Overview is vital – everybody needs the big picture

While it is true that we tend to learn things in pieces, one step at a time, this process is helped if we have the big picture first: if we know what we are learning and how the subject area will be covered. To use a simple analogy, it is like a jigsaw puzzle – it is much easier to put the pieces together if we have the picture on the box to guide us.

The institutions in which we study have specific shapes and functions – they are organised and work in particular ways. If we can understand how universities work, we will be able to negotiate our time at university more successfully, and more swiftly.

Further, programmes of study – from GCSE to university courses – have all been designed to have an overall shape and structure. If we can understand the structure of our courses, if we work to get the big picture before we start, this will help us as students to make sense of our learning. Our argument is that each lecture and each piece of reading that we encounter will make more sense if we fit them into a picture of the course as a whole.

In order to get an overview of your university and of your course, have a look at:

2 How universities work
3 How to understand your course.

'I really hated school, not knowing what was going on and why. Using the "overview" has made all the difference. I'm on top.'

Creativity is essential – and can be developed

There is a lot of 'common sense' about being a successful student – it is common sense to have resources to hand, to be well organised, to make time each day for study and so forth. We do not want to criticise common sense, as we know students who have gained good 2:1 degrees with common sense and sheer hard work. However, if you want to do that little bit more, if you want studying to be a little bit easier and more interesting, then a touch of creativity is needed.

If you give back to lecturers what they have told you, if you just use their examples and read the books that they recommend, then you will be a strong, average student. To get a little further, you have to be creative, you have to go somewhere or think something different, but how can you do that? We discuss creativity generally, and explore creative ways to approach assignments and notemaking in *ESS2*, as ways of bringing creativity into learning and studying. These are techniques that in their various ways encourage a different or more original approach to your studies. Look at:

8 How to be creative in your learning
12 How to make the best notes (especially the section on pattern notes).

'At school, I was told to go away and get a job in a shop [sorry, shop workers!], that I would never be able to learn anything. Putting colour and life into my university work has made all the difference; now I get As for my assignments.'

Communicate effectively – in the correct form

Just as we cannot 'know' how to study, we cannot 'know' what an essay, report or presentation is. These things have specific shapes to them (what), they have specific learning and assessment purposes (why), and there are tried and tested ways of approaching them that can be developed (how). In order to help you develop successful assessment techniques, we devote a whole, long section to effective communication, where we look at essays, reports, presentations and seminars and other assessment engines.

> **Tip:** See Chapters 13–18 for coverage on how to prepare successful assignments.

'They used to write things like "there's no introduction" or "there's no conclusion" on my essays. But no one ever told me what these were, or why they wanted them. Now, I only have to worry about my ideas; I know how to present them.'

Emotions rule – dealing with your emotions is crucial

Studying and learning may be cognitive or intellectual activities, but for most of us, they are also fraught with emotion. Typically, when we first start a course or go to a new college, we are apprehensive, nervous or even terrified. Certain tasks exhilarate us while others will bore us. If we do not acknowledge and address our own emotional responses to the different things that we encounter as students, we will never be able to benefit from our positive responses or overcome our negative ones.

We explore the emotional dimension of study and the roles of fear and self-confidence in the academic environment, in order for you to think about your own emotional highs and lows as a student, and what you intend to do about them. Note that positive thinking is useful for all our studying and learning activities, but you may draw on positive thinking tips and tricks even more when approaching your first presentation and your exams. If this is a big issue for you, first read:

9 How to deal with your emotions.

'You ask what the first day was like? I was het up, frightened, terrified . . . I thought "Why the hell have I done this to myself?" I just wanted to run away . . . Oh I love it now, I don't want to leave!'

Review – without reflection there is no learning

There is much evidence to suggest that learning involves an active selection of what to learn, and how to learn it. Throughout the book, we will be examining different revision and review strategies: memory and revision strategies, reflective learning logs and Personal Development Planning (PDP). You might also notice that each chapter ends with 'Review points' that encourage you to explore not only what you have learned but how you learned it.

Learning and remembering are not necessarily automatic or simple, but we can
do these effectively, and we have structured the book to reinforce this. To explore this
depth, go to:

> 'I love doing my learning logs, as it helps me make sense of what I'm doing. If I didn't do my logs,
> I don't think I'd understand anything at all.'

Conclusion

In this brief chapter, we have covered your hopes and fears about becoming a university
student, our six-step propositions and the six steps to success. We have argued that good
students, like you, are made, not born. If you build SOCCER into your study habits every
day, you will have real progress in your study habits.

Review points

By reading this six-step chapter, you should now have an:
- awareness of your own hopes and fears about becoming a student
- awareness that developing your potential as a student will involve you in change
- awareness of the six steps to success, the propositions that shape and inform the rest of
  the book itself.

learn how to ... in more ...

...ing a student. Enjoy being a student.

...nds to see how important being a student is to you.

... study: when you sit there, your body will learn to work.

... study every day: turn off the phone, don't answer

- □ ... 5-minute blocks at first and build up.
- □ Move ... comfort zone.
- □ Practise writing every day.
- □ Develop your memory with the revision cycle (pages 274–5).
- □ Discover if you like working alone or with other people.
- □ Discover if you like working with noise or quiet.
- □ Discover if you like working in the morning, afternoon, or evening, or at night.
- □ Buy an English dictionary, a subject dictionary and a dictionary of sociological terms.
- □ If English isn't your first language, join an academic English class.
- □ Buy an exercise book and make your own list of all the new words that you encounter.
- □ Buy an exercise book and make your own subject dictionary. Put in the key people of your subject. Put in new theories. Put in the key words, phrases and terms that you will have to use.
- □ When you encounter new theories, theorists, words and phrases, write them on Post-its and stick them up all round your home. Take them down when you know them.
- □ Practise organising your time: prioritise, make lists, use a diary, use a 24/7 timetable. Sometimes be very organised, and sometimes sit amongst a pile of work and plunge in.
- □ Find a study partner, or use online discussion boards.
- □ Enjoy studying – do not see it as 'work'.
- □ Use deadlines to keep you on track.
- □ If unhappy with your spelling, punctuation or grammar, buy a simple grammar book and use it.
- □ Keep a small notebook with you at all times. When you have a bright idea or an insight into your subject, write it down.

2

How universities work

AIMS

To prepare you for success at university by exploring the nature of academic communities and how universities work.

LEARNING OUTCOMES

That after reading through this chapter and engaging with the activities, you will have:
- gained an understanding of academic communities
- considered the sorts of activities that go on in universities
- engaged with various activities that have reinforced your understanding of the different parts of the chapter.

Introduction

In this chapter, we present a brief portrait of what being at university means. We will look at places to go and people to see at your university, and we will conclude with a few words about moving on and preparing to leave university. Before you read on, remember – be that active, questioning student we recommend and:

- Ask yourself why this section is in the book.
- Think briefly – what do you already know on the subject?
- What do you want to find out?
- How will knowing those things make you a better student?

Studying at university

Deciding to go to university is a big decision for anyone – it involves changing your life, even yourself. It means that your time is no longer available for other people. Obviously, for such a huge commitment, you will want to make sure that you understand what it is that you have joined and what it is that you are doing.

In this section, we are going to have a quick look at just who goes to university these days. We will move on to consider what it means to go to university, with a special emphasis on joining academic communities. Finally, we shall give advice on how to get the most out of your time at university by exploring teaching and learning at university, and by listing the various things to do and people to see in your university.

Who goes to university?

Previously, only five to seven per cent of the English population went to university. This is a very small proportion of the population of the whole country. Critics of this argued that the education system in England was geared up not to educate but to prevent people from getting up the education ladder. The old O Levels, they argued, were designed to stop people from doing A Levels; and A Levels, in their turn, were designed to stop people from going to university. This is, of course, a contested claim.

This was exacerbated by a classical degree structure that did not encourage flexibility and choice. For example, if you wanted to study English Literature at degree level, you would have needed O Levels (equivalent to GCSE grade C and above) in French and Latin and possibly in classical Greek also. Not only would this be a mysterious practice for most, but many of these subjects were not even taught in state secondary schools.

This system became self-perpetuating – children of graduates went on to become graduates themselves, while others found it more difficult.

All change

There have been changes to university recruitment recently, and it is now expected that upwards of 50 per cent of 18 year olds will be attending university in England in the future.

This book is designed to make university study easier for everybody, but it might be especially useful for you, if you are the first in your family to go to university, if you are unsure of exactly what it means to be a student and if you are slightly unsure of what to do at university, why to do it, and when.

Am I at the right university?

Basically, everyone should consider his or her own reasons for actually going to university in the first place. What is it for you: convenience, money or fun? Many students these days choose the university closest to home – this is either convenient, because you do not have to move, or economic, because you do not have to feed yourself, as your parents will do that. The fun reason might be that you have heard that Manchester, say, has a good nightlife, so Manchester University seems like a good idea.

These may not seem like world-shattering reasons to go to university, but they are the reasons that real students give, and they illustrate a point. You have to choose your university by thinking about why you are going to university in the first place. So what about you:

- are you at a high status institution that will plug you into a high powered network of contacts?
- are you studying a subject because of personal interest?
- are you studying in the hope of getting a better job?
- do you want to plug into up-to-the-minute research?
- or are you more interested in an emphasis on supportive teaching?

Maybe none of these things seems important to you, but you have found a very interesting course and you are happy with that? Well, that's fine, too. The point is to know why you are where you are.

Tip: Not really sure what your university is good at? Use university websites to search for information. Note what post-graduate courses they offer – this will indicate the specialist subjects.

And the winner is?

Throughout this book, we try to stress that there are no rigid right or wrong choices for many of these things. There is only your set of reasons and your choices. But whatever your reasons for going to university – and whichever university you are attending – you will have to work at making it a successful venture for yourself.

Networking at university

If you do want to make contacts at university that could help you throughout your working life, you will have to make the effort to meet the people who will make this happen for you.

Even if this idea does not appeal to you, as perhaps it is not how your community normally operates, you should still invest effort into making the most of yotur time at university. Typically, the graduates who make the most of their working lives are not just the ones that have good degrees; they are the students who were student representatives for courses or on university committees. They are the students who did volunteering or work placements. They were the students who joined clubs or societies, or who set them up.

The biggest secret of university life is that it should involve your whole life while you are there – it should be a 40-hour-per-week commitment! University is a full-time occupation. It is studying, yes – it is reading and talking and writing – and more than that, it is meeting people, it is joining clubs and societies and it is doing things that you would not have been able to do anywhere else.

> 'When I first got here, I kept thinking that I would be "found out", that someone would realise that I didn't belong and throw me out. I don't think that any more, as I know I can do it now.'

Universities are changing:
- Five per cent of the population used to go to university.
- Fifty per cent of 18 year olds are expected to go to university.
- There has been a rise in mature students at some universities.
- Some universities have many overseas students.

All these things represent change and opportunity! Remember, whatever the make-up of the student population at your university, this is going to be the percentage that will earn more, live longer and be healthier. Being a student does open doors for you, and it allows you to meet people and make contacts that you could not make in any other way. Grab the opportunity.

Joining academic communities

Of course, university is more than just joining societies and going to the best nightclubs. You will also be joining an academic institution. So, whatever your previous opinions about yourself – jock, ladette, housewife and mother, wage slave, entrepreneur – it is now time to see yourself as an academic.

When you go to university, whether you are aware of it or not, you are joining an academic community. Often, you are actually joining several academic communities. These might be the community of:

- the whole university
- your department, school or faculty
- your discipline or subject
- your module choices.

As with other communities, academic communities have ground rules, traditions and a sense of self. These will inform and influence the ways that you are expected to behave as a student generally, but more importantly as a student of a particular subject. History, Business, Pharmacology, Computing – all the subjects that you can study – have specific academic practices, that is, particular ways of being researched and of being studied and understood. As well as knowing how to learn and how to study generally, you will need to know how to study your subject, that is, you will have to become familiar with the academic practices of your subject.

Epistemology

Knowledge of academic practices is sometimes called developing your academic literacy or developing an awareness of the epistemology, or theory of knowledge, of the subject, and typically this means knowing the 'what, why and how' of your subject. That is, you must know what counts as argument and evidence in your subject. By argument, we do not mean the everyday use of the term – to disagree or fight – we are talking about how propositions are put together, how knowledge claims are put together, how one gets to say that something is 'so' in your subject. This will also mean that you will have to make an effort to learn how to communicate in your subject.

The communication strategies – and the epistemology – will be slightly different, depending on whether you are a biologist or an historian, a student of film or English literature. But one basic principle will be the same for all subjects: you must develop an understanding of what has gone before (the existing literature) before you will be expected to move on. And moving on will involve engaging analytically and critically with what has gone before.

The first year

Hence, the first year of most degree programmes is designed to lay a good foundation in your subject, by introducing you to the existing literature and the key people and the major knowledge claims of your subject, thus helping you get to grips with the epistemology of your discipline. Often, you will not be told that this is what is happening, but it is what is happening. So, in the first year, you will be introduced to the theories, the people and the dates that have traditionally held significance in your subject. Notice these! You will be building on them throughout your time as a student of that subject and beyond.

In the first year, you will be expected to learn how to 'argue' in the way that you have to in your subject. This means that this is the year where you will have to learn to use argument and evidence like an historian or a biologist, like a philosopher or an educationalist. You will have to notice the rules of your subject, and you will be expected to follow those rules.

Degrees are awarded according to your marks, as follows:
First class – 70% or more
Upper second (2/1) – 60–69%
Second class (2/2) – 50–59%
Third class – 40–49%
Generally, the marks for your first year are not included in your mark average, while the second and third year marks are aggregated.

> **Tip:** Find out what combination of course units or modules will actually be included in your final degree classification at your university.

Make an impact

Further, although the first year, as a foundation year, will generally not count towards the class (level) of your degree, it is the year when many of your tutors will be meeting you for the first time and making up their minds as to what sort of student you are. So, do not treat the first year as a throw-away, casual year. This is the year when you start to make the tutors notice you.

On the whole, tutors will be hoping for – and noticing – students who are interested in the subject, who are motivated and who are prepared to think. They will want to see that you contribute to class discussion and that you put effort into tasks. The opinion they form of you in the first year may have a big impact on your later success.

If a tutor begins to see you as a good student, they will treat you as one. They will see your work as the work of a good student. Conversely, if you come across as a casual student, not really interested in the subject and not prepared to make an effort, this may well be how they receive and mark your work.

So, the first year is the year to definitely start seeing yourself as a successful student, as an academic, even if you are the first person in your family to have gone to university. And as you gain the foundation knowledge of your subject, and lay the foundations of yourself as a student, be interested and do think, and learn how to communicate that in the right way.

And remember, the things that you are interested in at university will most probably be the threads that you follow as you take up a career and work in the related industries or services afterwards. You will do better at both university and work if you have chosen a subject that you enjoy and that does actually interest you.

Teaching and learning at university

As we have mentioned above, when we come to university, we join academic communities that have established ways of teaching and learning already in place. It is very important for you to understand the various teaching and learning systems, so that you can make the most of the opportunities they offer you. Here, we are going to explore the most common teaching and learning systems, and at the same time we will give you some things to think about as you go.

> **Tip:** University is supposed to be a full-time occupation – it is supposed to occupy at least 40 hours a week, every week. Even if the taught part of your course only occupies 10–12 hours, you are expected to fill the other 28–30 hours with reading, talking and writing. You are supposed to be studying and learning full time.

Lectures

Usually, a lecture involves one lecturer plus a large group of students – this can be 150 or more. The lecturer is an expert, often a researcher at the cutting edge of the subject. A lecture is supposed to seed independent research, and thus acts as a starting point – not an end point – for student thought and understanding. The lecturer speaks, and students should listen and note down key points. The purpose of the lecture is to give a shortcut to information, though never 'all you need to know' on the subject. Further, students get to hear the language of their subject being used, thus this models argument and evidence for that subject. Sometimes the lecturer is repared to answer questions, so make sure that you do ask useful questions when the opportunity arises.

> **Tip:** Always prepare before you attend a lecture. Think – what is it about? Why are they giving it? How will it help you gain an understanding of the subject? How will it help you with your assignment?

Seminars

A seminar usually consists of a lecturer (or a research student) plus 10–30 students. The name comes from semen or seed, as it is supposed to seed your thinking and give you ideas. The seminar (and tutorial) system has developed from the Platonic idea that students can be led towards learning by informed discussion with a sage (wise person). Thus, the idea is that student thinking is encouraged through tutor-led discussion.

A seminar is often linked to a lecture programme, and is designed to extend or deepen the knowledge previously covered in the associated lecture. Here, ideas introduced in the lecture might be returned to, explored in associated reading (relevant journal articles) and discussed further. Here, you will be expected to notice the 'big ideas' of the key people in your subject area, and the differing theories that they offer.

Sometimes, the seminar programme is designed to complement the lecture programme rather than to extend it. Here, the lecturer may not even know what you have covered in individual lectures, but is offering a series of activities that are meaningful in a way that works alongside the overall range of lectures. Here, you are expected to make the connections between the ideas in the lecture and seminar for yourself.

Students may be asked to lead seminars of their own (see Chapter 18) or to prepare for seminars in specific ways: for example, by reading a particular article or chapter prior to attending the seminar. You should always do the preparation before a seminar. Be warned – you are expected to participate in discussion and to benefit from that discussion. Be ready to talk and to listen to what is going on.

> **Tip:** Be an active learner – join in the discussions and, as with lectures, prepare before you attend so you know what you are supposed to be doing – and do it. Learn seminar survival strategies: know how to present your opinions assertively, not aggressively; learn how to interrupt the person who never stops talking; and learn how to draw out quiet people who may actually have much to offer.

Tutorials

The tutorial appears to be less common now, though some universities are reintroducing them to encourage a sense of 'belonging'. The typical tutorial structure is one tutor plus two to five students, though some institutions do make time for one-to-one tutorials. Tutorials may be based around a topic or theme or an activity. You might be asked to read an article and comment upon it. You may be expected to deliver a short presentation on a topic (see Chapter 17). As with the seminar, the tutorial is designed to get the student learning, by actively engaging with the ideas and information that are considered vital to the subject.

Often, there is no 'right' answer to a particular issue, and you will be encouraged to think for yourself and to weigh up contradictory arguments (analytical and critical thinking) on your way to synthesising information from various sources, and thus forming your own opinion (moving from surface to deep learning and integrating knowledge with your self). This might feel very uncomfortable. Often, students want the tutor to give them the 'right' answer, but the tutor is trying to encourage the students to think for themselves.

> **Tip:** There is definitely no hiding place in the tutorial. If you do not attend, you are missed: if you do attend, your contributions or lack of them will be noted. Be prepared to join in.

Independent learning

No one thing is ever designed to give you 'all you need to know' on a topic. Lectures, seminars, tutorials and all the reading that you could possibly do are all designed to spur you on to further thought, activity or reading – even designing an experiment or a piece of independent research. Thus, there is much emphasis placed on independent learning. That is, you will be expected to follow up ideas in various ways, including 'reading around a subject', on your own and on your own initiative.

Some people are now using the term interdependent learning – this indicates that we cannot learn in a vacuum, but that all that we encounter comes in a human context. That is, we could not have access to useful texts (books, journals, Internet material) without the librarian, and we could not have meaningful discussions without other people – we are interdependent, social beings and we can benefit from this interdependency if we use it actively. Below, we cover the information sources with which you are expected to engage as an independent learner.

> **Tip:** See Chapter 5 on organising yourself for study and 11 on research and reading. Work with another student (get a study partner), and see the section on group work in Chapter 7.

Information everywhere

As an independent or interdependent learner, you will be expected to make use of the following:

The library – find your university library. Find where the books for your subject are kept. Make a habit of spending some time there every week. Notice the books that are available on your subject, and notice when new books come in. Have a look at the books that are available on other subjects. Ideas can be interdependent as well. Thus, if you are studying sociology, you might find useful material in the psychology section of your library. If studying literature, you might try some chemistry!

> **Tip:** Check out your reading list. Typically, a course or module comes with a reading list that the tutor has put together. This list is often divided into essential and recommended reading. Essential is that which you *should* read for any assignment question. The recommended list might be extensive, and you have to make connections between the question you have decided to answer and the books on the list.

The key text area or **counter loans** section – many libraries acknowledge that there could never be enough books to satisfy all their students. So, what they often do is have a special mini-library within the library proper. This may be called the Key Text Area (KTA), counter loans or something similar. Find this section of the library and see what books are kept there on your subject. Many universities operate such that essential books on a module's reading list will be retained here.

> **Tip:** If there are books that you need that are always out on loan, request that at least one copy be placed within the KTA.

Books – become aware of the most up-to-date and useful texts on your subject. Get used to picking these off the shelves and having a quick look in the index – what is in the book? Anything useful? When will you read it?

Journals (periodicals) – the most up-to-date books are always several months old by the time they are actually written and published – to keep really up to date with your subject, you need to read the latest journals or periodicals.

> **Tip:** Find your subject librarian and ask them to recommend the best journals for you. Make a habit of reading them. When reading the journals, look at how arguments are constructed and look at how articles are written – this will be a model for your writing.

Quality press – many subjects are covered in the quality papers in sections headed Education or Financial Issues or the Media and so on. While such articles may not be academic enough for direct use, they do keep you abreast of current thought on your subject. There will be names dropped that you can then research in the books and journals.

> **Tip:** Start a press cuttings file for your subject. Get into the habit of looking in the papers every week and of putting relevant cuttings into your file. Always source your cuttings: put the date and the name of the paper.

Electronic information systems – accessing information through the computer. You will be aware that search engines can get you to useful information on the Web. You will also need to discover the best search engines and the best sites for your subject. Again, if in doubt, ask your subject librarian. Make a habit of checking the best sites and seeing what's new. (See also Chapter 6: How to use computers and e-learning to support your learning.)

Networked information and VLEs (Virtual Learning Environments) – many university libraries have networked computers and/or intranet systems – this will be where certain key CD-ROMs and other key course materials and resources can be accessed. Many of the journals and the quality press can also be found more easily online than in paper-based format. Again, it is helpful to discover your subject librarian or your course tutor and ask them about these things. Once you have discovered which of your journals are online, or which key resources you can access through your VLE, make a habit of dipping into them and seeing what's new.

> **Tips:** Do a quick journal search, putting in key words from your assignment question and see what happens. Every time you start a new course or module, check what resources and materials are in the related VLE.

Other sources – television, radio, films, video tapes and audio-cassettes – all have a role to play in your learning. Your university library may well offer access to a whole catalogue of useful material that comes in special forms. Don't limit yourself to electronic- or paper-based approaches – explore all the sources of information that your institution offers.

> **Tip:** Do a quick search of the television pages – what programmes are there that might support your studies? BBC2's 'Working Lunch' might help business students, various culture or film programmes might help film or literature students, Teachers' TV might help education students, and so forth. Make a habit of viewing these programmes or channels.

'My development plan is to read broadsheet newspapers like the *Guardian, The Times* and the *Independent*, and I'm currently working on it. If I compare me now to when I got here, I have improved my communication skills already.'

People to see and things to do – useful people and places at university

From reading the above section, you might now be aware that your subject librarian is a person to get to know. There are other useful people to discover at university: here we have listed some of them.

Personal tutor: Many universities still appoint a personal tutor, who is someone designated to give you pastoral support, and someone who has your best interests at heart, as a person. Usually, you find out who your tutor is by looking for a list on the department noticeboard. Once you have a name, make an appointment, go along and introduce yourself. Find out what being a personal tutor means at your university. This person can be your advocate if things go wrong for you. And they can write that glowing job reference if they know who you are. But if you have not approached them when things are going well for you, it will be difficult to approach them if things do go wrong.

> **Tip:** Meet your personal tutor before a problem arises. Help them get to know you. Help them know what to say in a job reference.

Academic tutor: The academic tutor appears to be replacing the personal tutor in many insitutions. The intention is still that this tutor will get to know you and will keep an eye on you. But now he or she may be responsible for helping you develop your academic literacy. Therefore, formal meetings may be timetabled with this tutor, and you will be expected to attend. There may be specific activities set for these meetings. These activities will be designed in order to develop your familiarity with academic practices, work towards specific assignments, or just so that the tutor gets to know more about you as a student. In any case, this means that this tutor will be in a position to represent you at Academic Boards, if there is ever any doubt about your grades, and they will be in a position to write good references for you, either for work placement or for work proper.

> **Tip:** Again, our advice is to get to know your academic tutor: do not put it off – do it now!

Subject librarian: Universities usually appoint subject specialists as librarians, and they have a much more important role than just putting the books back on the shelves. The subject librarian is a specialist in his or her own right. They have knowledge of the subject and they will be able to direct you towards useful books, journals and websites. Some universities offer special drop-in times with the subject librarians. Find out if your university does this, and make a date to go to a session as soon as possible to see what goes on, and how to benefit from them.

> **Tip:** Go to your subject librarian and ask them about the books, journals, websites and CD-ROMs that will be most useful to you.

Learning or writing development and support: Many universities these days realise that students benefit from specific advice on when, where and how to study. They may have a study skills collection in the library, or they may actually have study skills, writing development or learning development units. Some of these offer drop-in or appointment-based sessions where students can get one-to-one guidance with their assignments. They may also offer study skills and other courses, where students can learn and practise all the constituent skills they will need to succeed on their programmes of study. Find out if your university does this and see what they offer. Make a date to use the services and see what they can do for you. (Yes, this sounds like even more work. Well, what we have found is that this sort of investment on your part pays dividends in terms of time saved in other ways, improved grades and the ability to get more benefit from the time and effort that you are prepared to put in.)

Student support services: There are usually several ancillary services built around student life. These could be welfare, chaplaincy, careers, counselling, dyslexia, disability, volunteering, peer support or mentoring and work placement. Find out just exactly what your university offers and find out how you could benefit. Listed below is some information on the most common student support people.

Careers: The careers people have up-to-date information on career opportunities, job requirements and how to plan and prepare a curriculum vitae (CV). One of the most useful things that you could do would be to make an immediate appointment with the careers people – we are talking in your first year, here, not three weeks before the end of your degree programme! Find out what employment opportunities are open to you, now. Get advice about how best to tailor your degree programme to the sort of career you are likely to take up. If you are on a modular degree programme, this will help you choose the best modules for the career that you want.

> **Tip:** Start collecting information for your final CV the moment you read this. Have a folder where you keep key bits of information about yourself – jobs you have held, your responsibilities and how you developed; courses that you have taken and how you have utilised the information learned; modules that you took, and how they fit you for a specific job. Go through this file every so often, so that you always keep it up to date.

Work placement or volunteering: The Work Placement or Volunteering Officers are the ones who find placements for students while they are still on their degree programmes. Once you know what career avenue seems best for you, get into work placement (where you are paid) or volunteering (which is unpaid). Find out how to get a placement in a suitable organisation. This is the best way of finding out whether or not you actually like the work. This gives you great experience to use both in your degree and in your CV and if you make a good impression, you may even find you have a job lined up while you are still taking your degree.

Peer support or mentoring: Many universities now make it possible for students to support other students (their peers). This should interest you in two ways: one, you may want to access support, advice or guidance from another student who just may understand how you feel better than a member of staff. Two, after you have been a student yourself for a while, you may wish to become a peer mentor. This is exactly the sort of university extra-curricular activity that will build your confidence and communication skills, and will look great on your CV as it will involve you with other students in a very rewarding way.

Counselling services: Most universities offer some form of confidential counselling service. If you find that you are having problems adjusting to being a student, if you are incredibly homesick or if you feel overwhelmed by things, go and see a counsellor.

Student Union: Typically, it is the Student Union (SU) at any institution that runs the clubs and societies that serve the extra-curricular needs of the students. Remember, we have strongly advised that if you really want university to work for you, you should join a club or society and, even better, get involved in your SU. Why don't you think about standing for office? As far as we know, Ricky Gervais became a success, not on the back of his degree, but because he was involved in the entertainments side of his SU.

Discussion: How much of the above was new information to you? How much were you aware of already? Has any of the information changed your mind about anything? What are you going to do now?
Remember: The point with learning is that you use information in some way. You might use that information to form an opinion. Here, we are hoping that this information will form or inform your behaviour. We hope that you will do something with and about the above information.

Activity 1: Do something with the information

It is not enough just to notice bits and pieces of information – you must do something with it. Here are some suggestions about what to do with the information above:
1 Make a list of the key points noted above.
2 Make a list of the key people.
3 Set aside time in your schedule to go and do something – find the Key Text Area of the library or find the Learning Development Unit; make appointments with some of the key people noted above.

▶

Activity 1: Do something with the information—cont'd

4 Set goals for each activity that you plan – why are you going to the Key Text Area or Learning Development Unit? What will you ask the person that you have booked an appointment with? How will you know that you have got what you wanted?

5 Complete the checklist at the end of this chapter, noting what you have done, who you have seen, and what you got from the experience.

Moving on – careers, CVs and all that

In the list above, we mentioned the Careers service and we stressed the importance of you making contact with that service as soon as possible. This is such an important point that we have drawn it out into this separate segment. You may already know what you intend to do after you leave university. But we have found in our work with students, especially those that are the first in their family to go to university, that this can vary. Some come to university and tacitly expect that a career will just sort of manifest itself at the end of their degree. Others may have had a particular career or goal in mind, but over time this changes, and they eventually want something very different. Either way, it is in your interest to make an appointment with Careers as soon as possible. Find out what they will do for you, find out if they link with Work Placement and/or Volunteering – go and see these people also, and see what you cando to either find out about the sort of employment you might like, or to make yourself more employable while you are still at university. These days, most universities do not leave employability completely up to student motivation and initiative. Rather, you will be expected to engage in employability activities across your time at university, and usually these will articulate with PDP (Personal or Professional Development Portfolio or Process). This is such a key issue that we have a whole chapter on this, so please also look at Chapter 21. However, this is too important to leave for your university to organise, or to wait until the last few weeks of your degree, before you actually make your thoughts about your future a reality. Talk to Careers early and this may give you clues as to which modules to choose, which societies to join or what volunteering activity to get into, in order to make the most of your time at university and beyond.

Tips: **Go to Careers:** see what jobs are available to someone on your degree programme. **Look up a job advert** in your possible career – see what sorts of skills and experience you will need to get such a job. Discuss with Careers how you can get that experience while at university.

Write your CV and take it to Careers for feedback. Give the same time to writing your CV that you give to your assignments – it's that important.

Practise job interviews with other students: predict questions from the job description, and then rehearse how you would handle yourself in a real job interview.

Conclusion

In this chapter, we have attempted to paint a picture of university, including noting some of the changes that have occurred recently. We have also considered the implications of joining an academic community, paying particular attention to the importance of noting the epistemology of your subject, and making an impression in your first year. We have also sketched out the types of teaching and learning that occur and stressed the importance of independent learning, indicating the places to go and people to meet in order for you to get the most out of your time at university. We have emphasised Careers and employability as key things for you to think about as soon as possible.

Don't forget to quickly review what you have read and done, why you did it, and what you feel that you have learned. Make a few notes so that you do not forget. Make those appointments, so you get started on making the most of your university experience.

Review points

When reflecting on this chapter, you might notice that:
- you now better understand academic communities and the nature of studying
- you now know the sorts of activities that go on in universities and are ready to be an independent learner
- you are now ready to make the most of your time at university
- you are ready to engage with support systems at your university, including Careers
- you have engaged with various activities, which have reinforced your understanding of the different parts of the chapter.

Checklist

Complete the following checklist, noting what you have done, why you did it, what you got from it and what your next activity will be.

Teaching and Learning

I have been to my first:

☐ *Lecture*

    It was about:

    It linked to this bit of the assignment question:

    I learned:

    I will now read:

☐ *Seminar*

    It was about:

    It linked to this bit of the assignment question:

    I learned:

    I will now read:

☐ *Tutorial*

    It was about:

    It linked to this bit of the assignment question:

    I learned:

    I will now read:

☐ *Independent learning and interdependent learning*

    I have explored the following:

    ☐   library

    ☐   counter loans (KTA)

    ☐   books

    ☐   journals

    ☐   quality press

    ☐   electronic information systems

    I was looking for:

    In connection with this bit of the assignment question:

    I learned:

    I will now read:

☐ *People to see and places to go*

I have now met with:

☐ *Personal tutor*

It was about:

I learned:

I will now:

☐ *Academic tutor*

It was about:

I learned:

I will now:

☐ *Subject librarians*

It was about:

I learned:

I will now:

☐ *Learning development and support*

It was about:

I learned:

I will now:

Student support services

☐ *Careers*

It was about:

I learned:

I will now:

☐ *Work placement/volunteering*

It was about:

I learned:

I will now:

☐ *Counselling*

It was about:

I learned:

I will now:

☐ *Student Union*

It was about:

I learned:

I will now:

3

How to understand your course

AIMS

To introduce you to the importance of gaining an overview and understanding of any course that you join. (In Chapters 4, 19 and 20, we will link this to an exploration of learning style, revision and exam techniques. Chapter 11 discusses how a course overview assists with academic reading.)

LEARNING OUTCOMES

After reading this chapter and engaging with the activities, you will have:
- considered the importance of the course overview
- an understanding of how to gain an overview of a course
- considered how having an overview of a course will assist your active learning
- put overview theory into practice with respect to this book.

'I never enjoyed school, not at all. I never understood what we were doing or why. It was all so frustrating and I felt so powerless. Now I'm at university because I want to be, studying what I want to study, and everything is so different. It's great!'

Activity 1: Goal setting

As always, before you progress through the chapter, pause and reflect quickly on the chapter topics, asking yourself:

- What do I already know about the course I'm on?
- What do I need to know in order to develop my understanding of my course?

Once you have brainstormed and set your own goals, you are ready to move on as an active learner.

The big picture: the importance of the overview

Having the overview or the big picture of your course can really make a difference to your understanding of what is going on and why. This chapter looks at how university courses are constructed and the importance of learning outcomes for you as an active student. We close this section by considering how a detailed understanding of the overview can directly help with an assessment.

Don't be a passenger

Every university programme has been designed and planned by other people, not by the students. Unconsciously, this can have an unhelpful effect on us as learners. We can get the sense that the course 'belongs' to other people, not to us.

A negative consequence of this is that it can make us passive receivers, rather than active negotiators, of that course. The passive receiver might just drift through the course in a bit of a daze, moving from week to week maybe accepting what is going on, maybe not; but not actively engaging with the course.

Obviously, you cannot get the most from a course, or from yourself as a student, if you approach your studies in this way. In this book, we continually stress the importance of active, interactive learning and of you, the student, becoming an active learner – an active student in control of your own learning. So how can you make this happen?

Owning your own learning

A simple way of starting the process of taking control of your learning is to gain an overview of your course. Then you can use the overview to help you understand the shape, direction and make-up of the course, and to then take control of your own learning of the information in that course. This process is sometimes called 'owning your own learning'.

A very simple analogy is that a course can be compared to a jigsaw puzzle that is being put together week by week. It is much easier to put the puzzle together if we have the big picture in front of us as we go along. And it is much easier to actively engage with study if you have the big picture of the course (the overview), before you start to try to piece all the different bits of information together in a way that makes sense of the whole course.

How courses are designed

University tutors often design their own courses; a university committee including external examiners then validates these. Planning a course includes deciding on the 'learning outcomes' for that course. These describe what the student has to learn as they work through the taught sessions – lectures, tutorials, and seminars – and other activities, such as reading and assignments.

The achievement of the set learning outcomes is tested when the student is assessed. Hence, the assessments, whatever they are, are designed to test whether or not the learning outcomes have been met.

Typically, once the assessments are collected in, a course tutor marks all student work. A sample will be double-marked. A selection will be sent to an external examiner who will be checking that marks are awarded appropriately and against learning outcomes.

> **Tip:** Know the learning outcomes for a course and you know what you will be tested on.

How to gain an overview of a course

The easiest way to gain an overview of a course is to understand its learning outcomes. They give the big picture; once you have that, you can work out the small steps that you would have to take to get to the end of the course, and to pass it.

Many university course tutors produce course booklets or module handbooks that reveal the learning outcomes quite explicitly. If they do not do so, there may be online materials that might help. Failing that, students might have to use past exam papers as a source of information as to where the course is going, what is to be assessed and how it is to be assessed.

Exploring course/module handbooks

Once you join a particular course of study, there are several really useful things to do immediately to gain an overview of the course:

Course booklet/module handbook: If your tutor has prepared a booklet or handbook to support the course that you are on, make sure that you have a copy. Once you have a copy, read it!

Aims and outcomes: Many course booklets or handbooks spell out the overall aims of the programme, as well as the specific learning outcomes. (You might have noticed by now that we also do this at the beginning of each chapter of this book.) Your first task as a student would be to explore the course booklet or handbook to see what the aims and outcomes tell you about the course.

> **Tip:** Highlight key words and make notes or a list. Pin this list up in your study space to help keep you focused on the goals of the course. Look at the learning outcome key words when preparing for a class, for your reading and for an assignment.

Assessment: Once you have analysed the aims and outcomes, move on to examine the way the course is going to be assessed. The course may be 100 per cent course work, 100 per cent exam-based or a mixture of the two. Course work tends to involve the production of one or more of the following: essay, report, write-up of a practical, presentation, etc. Exams can be just as varied: seen or unseen paper (with the former, you receive the exam paper in advance of the exam itself; with the latter, you receive the paper at the beginning of the exam proper). Exams can be one, two or three hours in length. They might involve you writing essay answers, short answers or responding to multiple-choice questions. Exams may be 'open book', where you can take certain books into the examination room, or closed book, where you can't.

> **Tip:** In assessments, you must answer the questions but you must also meet the learning outcomes!

Read the question(s): Often, course work questions (assignments) are given at the beginning of the course, in the handbook. Read the question! You are not expected to know the answer yet, but if you read the question, you will know what the course is designed to get you to be able to answer.

> **Tip:** Write out the question. Underline the key words. Pin the question on your wall. Read up around one word at a time (using your active reading strategy – see Chapter 11); and listen for information on the key words in lectures and classes.

Look at the Reading List: Note essential reading – you should attempt to read some of all of these sources. Note the recommended reading – you should read the sources here that will help you with the question you have chosen.

> **Tip:** When reading, have a word or phrase from the question in your mind as you read. Make notes that would help you write about that part of the question. See also Chapter 11.

Look at past papers: If there is an exam component to your course, find past exam papers and read them. As with the course work assignment, these tell you what you should be able to answer by the end of the course. They help you to set your learning goals for the course.

> **Tip:** Don't forget to add any relevant information to the whole batch of timetables that you are advised to draw up in Chapter 5.

Examine the syllabus: Sometimes we are lucky and we are given a week-by-week programme for the course that we are on – this is sometimes called the timetable, syllabus or scheme of work. Read it. Have a look at how the course has been put together. Notice which weeks are designed to cover which learning outcomes.

> **Tip:** Colour-code your learning outcomes – you can then also colour-code your syllabus. When attending lectures or seminars, have a word or phrase from the question in your mind; this should help you make relevant notes.

Now let us go through the various processes recommended above, with respect to this very book.

Activity 2: Putting 'overview' theory into practice with *ESS2*

Aims

The aims of this study skills book are to introduce you to a range of skills, techniques and strategies that are designed to facilitate effective study.

Learning outcomes

By the end of engaging with this book, it is hoped that you will:
1 have considered the study and academic skills and practices necessary for effective study
2 have practised the various study and academic skills and practices covered in this book
3 have reflected on your use of the various study and academic skills and practices, so that you can select relevant skills and practices at appropriate times in your study (for example, notemaking skills, research and reading strategies, effective communication practices)
4 have reflected on the overall practices of successful study, so that you have started the process of becoming a more effective student.

▶

Query: What do you think about these aims and outcomes?

Discussion: Hopefully, the above aims and outcomes are clear and logical, but more than that, they should tell you what the book is designed to do, and hence what you could get out of the book. This allows you to set your own goals as you work through the book.

Tip: If you have not already done so, now might be the time to fill in a learning contract for this book. Try answering the following questions:
1 What do I want from this book?
2 What am I prepared to do to achieve my goals?
3 What might stop me?
4 What's in it for me?

Discussion: There's more – learning outcomes help with assignments. The learning outcomes should also inform you that any assessment activity based on this book would have to be designed to test that you had met all of the above learning outcomes.

So, in any particular assignment attached to this book, you would have to demonstrate that you had:
- considered the skills and practices – that is, read and thought about them
- practised the skills – that is, done something with them. Ideally, you should have used one or more of the skills and practices covered in this book
- reflected on your use of those skills and practices – that is, once you had used the skill, you would be expected to think about your use of that skill. As this is a practical book designed to help you develop those skills, your use of the skill might tell you how much more practice you think you would have to put in to become more confident with the skill. You might also reflect on how you would continue to use the skill, and how valuable it is to you as a student
- started the process of becoming a more effective student – that is, have some sort of overall comment to make about yourself as an effective student. And that conclusion would be based on the above – that is, your knowledge of, use of and reflection on particular skills and practices.

▶

Query: Can you now see that once you know the learning outcomes, it should be very difficult to get a course 'wrong'?

Tip: See Chapter 15 on the reflective essay that has a suggested essay plan on this area.

Do all learning outcomes help?

Maybe not all learning outcomes will be as easy to translate into specific assignment requirements as others. But the overall principle is always the same. Further, the more practice you get at reading learning outcomes and comparing them with assessment questions and criteria, the better you will get at making and using the links between the two.

Tips: If you are ever in doubt with your learning outcomes, there are several things you can do:
– Work through the learning outcomes and assessment criteria with another student or study partner.
– Ask the course tutor to help you make sense of the outcomes and criteria.
– Ask the learning development people for help with this technique.

Conclusion

In this section, we have looked at the importance of understanding the shape and requirements of any course that we study. We have called this the gaining of the overview or the 'big picture'. Further, we argued that gaining the big picture allows you to make sense of and understand a course, and hence helps you to become an active learner on that course.

Once you have a sense of what a course is trying to do, you can take control of your own learning and navigate your way through, rather than being a mere passenger on that course.

We moved on to explore how university courses are put together, and noted that learning outcomes work to define the assessments. We emphasised that knowing the learning outcomes of a course helps you to prepare for the assessment, for you should then know exactly what you have to show that you know.

Checklist:

Photocopy Activity 4: 'Get ready for your exams' checklist on pages 296–7 and complete for every module or course that you undertake.

Review points

When reviewing this chapter, you might realise that you now have:

- an understanding of the role of the overview with respect to active learning
- a sense of what the overview (especially aims and outcomes) tells you about the direction of a course
- an understanding of how the overview will tell you what you need to do and learn to pass a particular course
- an understanding of how the overview can directly assist with assessment preparation.

SECTION 2

Learning Effectively

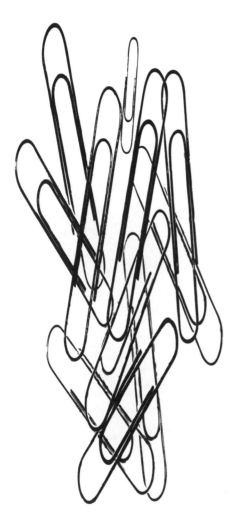

4

How to learn effectively

AIMS

To prepare you for academic study by examining learning, studying, critical thinking and learning styles.

LEARNING OUTCOMES

That after reading this section and engaging with the activities you will have:
- considered the processes of learning
- realised the active nature of learning
- explored aspects of academic study
- gained an understanding of analytical and critical thinking
- gained an understanding of learning styles, and how to make them work for you.

Introduction: What is learning?

> "Education" involves the integration of knowledge with the self, where knowledge is defined by and helps to define the self (after Noble, 2002 in 'Digital Diploma Mills').

There are many definitions of education and learning; the model that we follow suggests that learning is a social, interactive and constructionist activity. That is, that in order to learn, we must engage with other people and with knowledge claims in an active and interactive way; we must be in a position to question and challenge the arguments and evidence that are put before us in lectures and other classes and in our reading. That ultimately we must decide for ourselves, utilising valid evidence, rational, critical and analytical thinking, what knowledge we believe and act upon; that we integrate with ourselves. This, thus, is a very active vision of learning and the learner, where the successful student is one who reaches out for what they want and need from a course, and who then actively builds that into their mental picture of the world and of themselves.

For the purposes of this book, we are going to connect this vision of learning with some skills, strategies and styles that will enable you to make your learning more conscious and more effective. Firstly, we will refer, as a shorthand for learning, to Devine (1987) who argues that learning is not one thing but a series of activities:

- gathering new ideas and information
- recording them
- organising them
- making sense of them
- remembering them
- using them.

Following on from that, we will explore learning styles, offering some practical activities to allow you to explore your learning style and discover what supports or impedes learning for you. Finally, we will suggest the use of the learning contract to make your own motivation and commitment conscious. Before moving on, please complete the Personal Skills Review.

Activity 1: Personal skills review – focusing questionnaire

In Chapter 1, we discussed the six steps to success and we argued that no one is born just knowing how to learn and how to study. In Chapter 2, we looked at how universities 'work', giving very specific advice on places to go, people to meet and things to do in your university. In Chapter 3, we examined how university courses are put together and explored how understanding this (gaining the overview of a course) can help you to succeed in any course that you are on. In this chapter, we are looking at effective learning strategies, including the use of your learning style, in order to get you to think about your own approach to study.

To get you started, please complete the following questionnaire:

1. How do you feel about yourself as a learner at the moment?
2. How positive do you feel about being a student? How committed are you to developing your skills? What are you prepared to do to improve? How much time and energy are you prepared to put in?

▶

3. How organised are you? (If you have brought up a family or juggled work with a hobby or family, then you are used to organising your life. This is a useful, transferable skill.)

4. If you have studied before, did you have set times to work? Do you have a place to study? Have you got an overall approach to studying? Do you feel you have successful strategies overall? What do you need here to enable effective study?

5. What reading do you do at the moment? Are you happy with your reading skills? What do you need here?

6. How confident do you feel about using the library? Can you do successful online searches? Have you used journals or e-journals yet? What do you think you need here?

7. Do you make notes when you study? Are you happy with your notes? What do you do with your notes? What do you need here?

8. What sorts of writing do you do at the moment (e.g. letters to friends, business correspondence, etc.)? Have you written essays before? What sort of marks did you get? Are you happy with that? What do you want here?

9. Have you ever had to make a presentation to a group of people? (A presentation is a talk of a set length to a specific audience, usually on a specific topic.) How did it go? What do you feel about the idea of having to do presentations on your course? What do you want to know about presentations?

10. Have you revised for and sat exams? How did it go? How do you feel about your memory? How do you feel about exams? What do you need to know about revision and exam techniques?

Discussion: The list breaks down academic practices into some necessary constituent elements – you cannot write an essay, for example, if you cannot organise your time, make useful notes or read academic texts successfully. The rest of this book will take you through these constituent activities, so that you not only understand their significance but you also get the opportunity to practise and reflect upon them. Thus, while there are no right or wrong answers here – only your answers and what you are prepared to do about them – this preliminary brainstorming activity should have set you up to get the most from this chapter, and from the book as a whole.

Tip: Your answers to these questions will tell you what you want to get from each section of this book. Use them!

Devine learning

First, let us examine Devine's six aspects of successful learning in more detail. One thing that you might notice immediately about Devine's list is that it consists of many verbs: gathering, recording, organising, making sense of (understanding), remembering and using. Learning is doing – it is active – it is not just storing bits of information in the brain, ready to spill out onto an exam paper and then forget. Everything covered in this book is designed to build your active learning skills: we will encourage you to engage with, question and understand your course work, and to express yourself successfully within the academic conventions of your subjects. Let us now look at Devine's list in some detail.

Gather

Learning is about gathering new ideas and information. We call this research, and it can involve actively acquiring information from classes, lectures, seminars, tutorials, discussions, practicals, reading (texts, journals, newspapers and more) and watching documentaries, films, videos and television programmes.

Record

You have to record, organise and make sense of information for yourself. Recording involves some form of notemaking activity. That is, recording points that you have heard, read or seen, in some form or other, so that you have a record of them. You will go back to your notes at some point, in order to use the information that you have recorded, in your assignments. (See especially Chapters 11 and 12 on reading and notemaking.)

Organise

When we research, we encounter information in many forms, in many places and at different times. What we are doing here is encountering the various accepted and contested knowledge claims for our subject (hence the brief section on analytical and critical thinking, below). What we have to do is rearrange the information to make sense of it for ourselves. In the process, we have to notice that one argument might contradict something else that we have already encountered, and that other things that we discover agree with or 'back up' each other. We have to navigate this difficult terrain for ourselves.

Make sense of – analytical and critical thinking

So we have to look for information in a variety of places, and then we have to rearrange and record it for ourselves. During this process, we have to notice that certain ideas agree with, while others contradict, each other. Basically, we have to think about all the different things that we have heard, read or seen and make sense of them for ourselves. We have to criticise it (break it down into its constituents parts: arguments – evidence – points made), and we have to analyse it (is it true or false? Is sufficient evidence offered to back up the statements made? Is that evidence valid or invalid? How do I know?). Ultimately, we have to understand it for ourselves.

When looking at this aspect of studying, people sometimes talk about surface and deep learning. 'Surface' describes where you might record key bits of information – names and dates of battles, for example. 'Deep' describes where you understand the significance of the events that occurred – this battle was actually the turning point in the war and brought about. . . . Or that bit of evidence contradicts what I read in. . . .

That is why we encourage an active learning approach, an approach that gets you continually asking questions of, and doing things with, the information that you acquire. An active learning style is designed to ensure that both surface and deep learning occur; it helps you both to remember those important names, dates and events and to understand their significance.

> **Tip:** Good notemaking skills can help you to organise and understand information as you gather and record it – see Chapter 12.

Remember it

So we have looked at acquiring information as actively as possible, but this information is not yours unless you remember it. Thus, as you listen to or read material in your subject area, you have to select important information and then make a conscious decision to remember it. In terms of being a successful student, we can call this ability revision and exam technique, and it is covered in Chapters 19 and 20.

But a quick word on this now. Do not try to learn everything you need to know just before your exams. This does not work, and it does not help you remember information 'for keeps', for life.

> **Tip:** Learning or remembering information starts at the beginning of a course. Our successful exam strategy (SQP4) in Chapter 20 outlines a system for understanding and learning course material – use that information *now* – do not wait until your exams are upon you!

Use it

Finally, you have to be able to use the information yourself for it to be really your own: you have to be able to explain it and write about it; you have to be able to discuss it with other people and use it in your assignments.

> **Tip:** See Chapters 13–18: write to learn.

It's all active learning

The problem perhaps with using what we know is that we often don't notice that this is what we are doing when we read and think, when we discuss ideas with other students, when we participate in seminars. This means that we do not necessarily make the most of these powerful learning activities.

Another potential problem is that when we use information in our assignments, we tend not to feel that we are using information and that we are in control. We feel that we are being tested (perhaps that we are being used). Typically, no one likes to be tested – it means that we can fail or we might show ourselves up. These thoughts bring negative feelings and these negative feelings interfere with our progress.

When we prepare assignments, we do not pour out ready-formed ideas and already polished words – what we actually do is struggle to understand and use infor-mation; we struggle to form our ideas. This struggle, in speaking or writing, is the learning process.

The beauty of using information when preparing and writing assignments is that it helps you to understand and learn the material.

> **Tips:** Get a study partner or form a study group. Convince a member of your family to be interested in your studies. Discuss your lectures and seminars. Discuss your reading. Discuss your writing. This is all active learning. Read Chapter 9 and practise positive thinking.

Learning style

In the section on memory, Chapter 19, we ask you to think back to your experiences at primary school in order to recall how you used to learn and remember. If you went to a Montessori primary school, you would perhaps have noticed that you were actually encouraged to see, hear, say and do in order to learn effectively. This is because we learn a proportion of what we see or hear or say or do, but the argument is that we learn 90 per cent of what we see, hear, say and do.

NLP (neuro-linguistic programming) practitioners developed this into an exploration of primary, secondary and tertiary learning pathways, and they then linked learning pathway to learning style. They argue that we all favour either visual (sight-based), auditory (sound-based) or kinaesthetic (touch-feel-or movement-based) learning styles. To make our learning effective, we should favour our personal learning style, but to guarantee complete learning, we should utilise all the learning pathways, hence the success of see, hear, say and do techniques.

Using your learning style

To really succeed as a student, you not only need to be as organised as we suggest in Chapters 5 and 20, or to communicate as effectively as we cover in Chapters 13–18, but you also have to be aware of and develop your own learning styles, and to build them consciously into your learning strategies. We do re-visit learning style in relation to developing your memory in Chapter 19, but we are also going to look here at learning style in connection to becoming an effective learner.

Activity 2: What's my learning style?

For online tests to discover your learning style, access one of the online sites flagged up below. For a quick check on what your learning style might be, consider the following:

One way to check your primary learning pathway is to examine the language that you use. For example, are you the sort of person who says:

– I see what you mean, or
– I hear what you're saying, or
– It feels good to me?

'I see what you mean' indicates that you use sight-based language, and you might favour the visual learning pathway.

'I hear what you're saying' indicates that you could favour an auditory pathway (hear and say).

'It feels good to me' possibly indicates that you are a kinaesthetic type person (touch, feel, movement).

Still not sure? Well, if remembering a spelling, would you:

– see the word in your mind, possibly write it down, and see if it looks right? (visual)
– sound out the letters and hear if it sounds right? (auditory)
– look at or say the word, but check if it feels right? (kinaesthetic)

Tips:

Sight: If you remember mainly by sight, you may enjoy learning by reading and watching television, film or video. You could use pictures in your learning and revision activities: draw pattern notes, put in colour, and put in memory-jogging cartoon images or visuals.

Sound: If you remember sounds best, you may enjoy learning through listening and joining in discussions or explaining things to other people. You could benefit from using audio-tapes to support your learning, and you could use songs, rhymes and jingles that you write yourself as learning and revision aids. Tape yourself and sing along.

Feel: If you remember the feel of things, you may enjoy practical learning activities from making something, to performing a science experiment, to role-playing. Making charts and patterns of the things you want to remember will help your learning and revision, as will acting out in some way.

So, are you auditory, visual or kinaesthetic in your approach to learning? Still not sure? Check out the Learning Styles websites listed below.

Learning Styles websites

For useful websites with information and activities to do to further explore how to discover and utilise your learning styles, go to:

http://www.i-learnt.com/Thinking_home.html

Learning styles, with reference to Kolb and Gardiner:

http://www.i-learnt.com/Thinking_Learning_Styles.html

Learning styles test:
http://www.ldpride.net/learning-style-test.html

Learning styles and multiple intelligences explained:
http://www.ldpride.net/learningstyles.MI.htm#Learning%20Styles%20Explained

Another learning styles site, with a longer test:
http://www.learning-styles-online.com/

Research articles on learning styles:
http://www.accelerated-learning-online.com/research/default.asp

See http://www.sagepub.co.uk/burnsandsinfield/

Learning styles for students

When studying, you should build on all the learning styles – see, hear, say and do – to make sure that you perform at your best.

Visual learners may prefer:

- to see the lecturer – their body language and facial expressions
- to sit near the front with nothing blocking their view
- learning through visual media, film, television and video and the visual aids that a lecturer will use in their teaching
- to take detailed notes, but will learn best by adding colour, pictures and cartoons to make notes funny, bizarre or unusual
- to learn how to make key-word, pattern notes that are visually stimulating and memorable (Chapter 12).

Auditory learners may prefer:

- verbal lectures, listening carefully
- tuning in to the nuances of voice: tone, pitch, speed, passion

- taping lectures (and making shorter versions to revise from)
- rather than reading, finding audio versions of books (really useful in English Literature)
- learning by discussion and explanation, talking and listening
- making their own audio-tapes of things that they want to remember, utilising silly voices, tunes, rhythm and rhyme.

Kinaesthetic (touch-or feeling-based) learners may prefer:

- hands-on learning – engaging with the real world – typically preferring practical courses
- experiments, activity and role-playing in their learning
- to care about or 'feel' something for the subject
- to move about as they study, or move from room to room for different parts of assignments. **Tip:** As you cannot roam around in a lecture or class, have an object to squeeze (e.g. a rubber ball) to allow some movement
- make diagrams and charts of the key things that they need to remember.

All learners should try to see, hear, say and do!

Some things to do about your learning right now

Hopefully, we have encouraged you to think of learning slightly differently from how you might have thought about it before. We have tried to encourage you to see that learning is an activity, or series of activities, facilitated by your active use of visual, auditory and kinaesthetic techniques. We have further stressed that you have to be an active, analytical and critical student in order to learn. There now follow some activities that will help you reflect more upon your learning.

Activity 3: Good and bad learning

Before we finish this section, we'd now like you to think back to your own past learning experiences. In particular, think about the conditions that help you to learn, and the things that might get in the way of your learning. Make brief notes to answer the questions below:

1. Think back to a previous successful learning experience. It does not have to have been at school – it could be learning to drive or sky dive. Now try to work out why it was successful – why did you learn?
2. Now think back to an unsuccessful learning experience. What was it? Why did little or no learning take place?
3. Looking over these good and bad experiences of yours, can you sum up 'things that help learning to happen' and 'things that prevent learning'? Make a list.

▶

4. If you wish, use your list to write two paragraphs: one on 'Things that help me learn' and one on 'Things that stop me learning'.

5. Once you have completed your own thoughts, compare your paragraphs with those given by another student, below:

– Things that helped me to learn were an interesting course with a good teacher – you know, one that had enthusiasm for the subject and lots of energy. It also helped that I knew why I wanted to do that course, I had chosen it for myself and I actually wanted to learn. I was committed – I'd turn up and do the work, because I wanted to. Not only that, but there was a really supportive atmosphere – I felt challenged and stretched, but it was also safe to make mistakes. . . Nobody laughed at you or made you feel a fool.

– The worst thing I ever did was at school. I had to do the course – it was compulsory, but I never really saw the point of it. Not only that, the teacher was a bit of a bully and humiliated people when they got things wrong. Also, I just felt so powerless all the time – we never knew what we were doing or why or when or how. It was a nightmare, and one of the reasons that I left school the minute I could!

Discussion: Were these points like your own? What does this tell you? One thing could be that if we are going to be successful when learning, then we must want to learn – we must be interested and motivated, and we should have our own clear goals. On the other hand, what seems to stop people from learning is feeling unmotivated, confused, unhappy, fearful and powerless.

Now, look at your points again – how can you make use of this information to help you be a better learner and a better student? Things to ask yourself:

• How do I learn best?
• What subjects do I enjoy?
• What job do I want later on?
• What sorts of courses will help me get where I want to go?

Things that other students have said are their reasons for studying:

• I want to know more about this subject
• I want a better career
• I want to earn more money
• I want to make new friends.

These reasons may or may not be like your own – again, we are not trying to say there is only one successful way of approaching this, but the trick is to really understand your own reasons for doing something, and then to use those as motivation, especially when your energy is low.

Tip: Whenever you start to study anything – from a long course (like a three- or four-year degree programme) to a short unit of a course (a 15-week module) – sit down and set your own personal goals for that course. Write your goals on stickers and put them over your desk. Cut out pictures that represent your success to you and stick these up also. Use these to keep you motivated and interested.

The 'learning contract'

Another motivation tip that we offer here is the use of a 'learning contract' that you write for yourself for every course that you study. (Note: Currently some institutions are bringing in formal agreements or contracts of their own that they expect students to sign. These contracts will typically focus on the student's attendance at lectures, seminars and tutorials, and is a quasi-legal document. Your contract with yourself is not like that, it is your own motivating tool.)

For us, a learning contract is where you make clear to yourself:

- your reason for doing something: 'What I want from this course (or job or whatever)'
- what you are prepared to do to achieve your goals: 'What I'm prepared to do to make this happen'
- what might interfere with your progress or prevent you from achieving your goals: 'What might stop me'
- what you will actually get from the activity (course or job) in the long term: 'What's in it for me'.

Now that we have looked at the elements of the learning contract, please complete a contract for reading this book.

Activity 4: *ESS2* – The learning contract

Why not write a learning contract for this book? Think about the following questions and try to come up with some answers:

1. Why am I reading this book?
2. What am I prepared to do to get the most from this book?
3. What might stop me?
4. What's in it for me?

Tips: When you have drawn up your *ESS2* learning contract, stick it on the wall. When you settle down to read another bit of this book, look at the contract and remind yourself of your own goals. (For an example of a learning contract, see Figure 4.1). Always do your own learning contract for any course that you do – use it whenever you need to push yourself a bit to get the work done!

▶

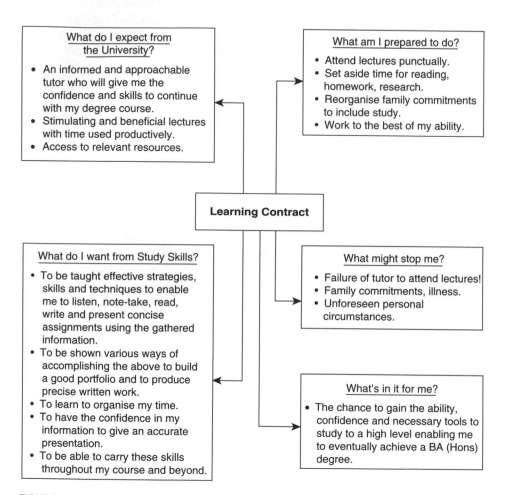

FIGURE 4.1   A sample learning contract

Discussion: Your learning contract for this book could help you when you don't feel like doing anything, let alone reading a study skills book. When you feel like you should be reading, but don't actually *want* to read, look at your contract and see if that gives you the motivation to proceed.

Tip: Now look back at your personal skills review (from the chapter opening). Can you add things to your learning contract in the light of your answers to the questionnaire?

Don't worry if you did not get your contract 'right' first go. Learning is not about being right all the time. In fact, feeling that you always have to get things right is the biggest barrier to learning that we know. This feeling prevents you from taking risks, making mistakes and learning from your mistakes.

Now that you have completed the personal skills review and amended your learning contract, you should be in a position to get the most from your reading of this book.

Conclusion

So, we have looked at learning and thought about it as an active process – gathering, recording, organising, understanding, remembering and using information. We used this to look briefly at active learning, analytical and critical thinking, surface and deep learning.

We also started you on your exploration of your learning style, with tips about how to build learning styles into your study habits.

We moved on to the good and bad learning exercise, enabling you to explore your own learning preferences, and as a spur to drawing up a personal learning contract for this book. Obviously, if the contract works for you, you might try it on the course that you are doing at the moment.

Finally, we'd like you to reflect on what you have read and done, why you did it, and what you feel that you have learned. Make a few notes so that you do not forget.

Further reading

Tutors reading this book might like to have a look at:
Devine, T.G. (1987) *Teaching Study Skills*. London: Allyn and Bacon.

Review points

When reflecting on this chapter, you might notice that:

- you are more aware of the processes of learning
- you have thought about your own learning and study skills
- you have thought about active learning and analytical and critical thinking
- you have completed a learning contract for this book
- you have completed a learning contract for the course that you are currently on, and will do so for other courses
- you have started the process of using your learning styles in your actual study practices.

5

How to organise yourself for independent study

AIMS

This chapter is designed to prepare you for successful independent learning and academic study with a focus on organisation and time management.

LEARNING OUTCOMES

That after reading this chapter, and engaging with the activities, you will have:
- realised that university study in the UK requires you to be an effective independent learner
- considered the impact of personal motivation with respect to study success
- realised the time required to be an effective independent learner at university
- explored organisation and time management issues with a special focus on when, where and how to study
- started the process of organising yourself for effective study
- engaged with various activities that have reinforced your understanding of the different parts of the chapter.

Organisation and time management

In a UK university, you are considered to be an independent learner. Rather than someone who is being taught, you are supposed to be organising your own learning. Elsewhere in this text, we stress that if you are a full-time student, then, even if you have a family, are working 20 hours a week and want to keep a full social life, you are supposed to be dedicating between 35–40 hours a week to your studies.

This means that as well as attending lectures, seminars and other classes, you are supposed to be motivating yourself to 'read around the subject', to understand new ideas, to discuss your learning with other students, both in class and over coffee, and to practise your academic writing.

This is why we explore how universities work and how to understand your course in Chapters 2 and 3, and why we focus on the nature of learning in Chapter 4; it is really important that you understand very quickly what *you* will have to do to succeed at university.

Unlike when you were at school or college, where you might be described as a 'dependent' learner (relying on the tutors to structure your time and your reading through lessons and a heavy homework regiment), when you are at university, you are deemed to be an *independent* learner. This means that you have to be organised, you have to work out your own independent study programme, and you have to find the motivation, discipline and time to study and learn.

So, a very basic good study technique is being able to organise ourselves for study – to get mentally and physically prepared for study. Organisation is widely thought to be the key to success in business, even in life itself, let alone in studying. Now this is fine if you already see yourself as an organised person, but a bit of a blow if you feel that you are chaotic and disorganised.

Tips: We offer two really useful checklists to help you get organised:
2: Going to university, on pages 36–7
20: How to understand and pass exams, on pages 296–7.

Activity 1: Have you completed your skills review?

In Chapter 4, we asked you to complete a personal study skills review. This review was to get you thinking about the sort of student that you believe you are now. It also gets you thinking about the sorts of skills that you already have, and those that you might like to develop or improve. If you have not already completed the skills review, why not do it now?

Discussion: In the skills review, we asked you two sets of questions, designed to get you thinking about some of the issues related to organisation and time management. The first asked:
   How positive and committed are you to developing your skills?
   What are you prepared to do to improve?
   How much time and energy are you prepared to put in?

▶

This question is designed to get you thinking about the very real impact of time. It does take time to develop your skills, just as it takes time to study your subject. One danger is thinking about all that time and saying to yourself, 'I don't have the time to learn how to study – I've got too much to do!'

While this is a perfectly natural panic thought, it leads to a false economy of time. Without developing good skills, everything else takes more time, too much time. So this is a repeat of the encouragement we offered in the Introduction – with good study strategies, everything else gets easier, quicker and more effective. So, try to think about your skills development positively:

– I am enjoying this.
– I can really see the point of this.
– This is working for me right now!

This might not be your normal thinking habit (maybe you are more used to thinking, what am I doing this for? This is all taking too long! This will never work for me!). But try the positive thoughts above for a change and see if it makes a difference.

The organisation skills you bring with you

We raised the issue of organisation and time management in Chapter 4. In particular, we asked:

How organised are you? (If you have already brought up a family or juggled work with a hobby, you are most probably already used to organising your life to make the most of your time. These are really useful transferable skills.) If you have studied before, did you have set times to work? Do you have a place to study? What do you need here?

This question was trying to do at least two things – first, to remind you that you bring many skills with you when you come to university. It is all too easy to focus only on the things that we do not have – on our weaknesses and our failings. Not only is this very demoralising, it's not the complete picture. If you want to improve, you have to notice your strengths as well as your weaknesses. As well as noticing what you lack, try to realise just how good you already are. This will give you a better picture of the task before you, and it will give you some confidence.

Secondly, it is trying to encourage you to think about how to adapt the skills that you already have, so that they are really helpful to you in your studies. In particular, this question is asking what organisation and time-management skills you already have. And that is what we are going to focus on here, in terms of exploring when, where and how to study.

When to study

Studying is often really hard work – there is reading to do, notes to make and learn, essays and other assignments to plan, prepare and produce. Far from feeling fun and exciting, sometimes this can feel really overwhelming, and sometimes it even feels quite frightening. We can work to overcome this by doing a little bit of work each day. We can read, make notes, plan an assignment, draft a sample paragraph. This can all happen over time, and having study timetables can help. However, several things can hinder working in this way.

I can only work under pressure of a deadline

'We know we are supposed to start work weeks before the deadline, but usually we start two or three days before.'

There are many students who do not start work until a deadline really frightens them. In our workshops at our university, students will rush up asking us to look at their essay draft quickly because it has to be submitted in half an hour.

No matter what useful comments we might make, these students have not left any time to act on that advice. Further, because they have not paced themselves properly throughout their course, they have not given themselves the time to understand new material, to extend their learning with additional research, and to plan, prepare and refine their assignment.

These students never give themselves the time to do themselves justice. Their work never reflects what they are capable of and never receives the grades they might get. They never get to feel good about themselves as students.

> **Tip:** Get used to doing a little bit of work: reading, writing a paragraph, talking new material over with other students, every day. This may seem impossible at first, but working consistently in this way ensures that you make the most of your time and produce really good work.

It all seems too much, I just can't start!

'I know what I should do, I really know . . . but I just can't face it.'

Studying can feel like climbing a mountain. But there is more than one way to face a mountain! For some, a mountain is so large and dangerous that they are afraid of it. For others, a mountain is an exciting challenge. For still others, a mountain is just a thing to be tackled sensibly one step at a time.

How do you view the mountain? Whatever your normal attitude, try to approach the mountain – and your assignments – one step at a time.

> **Tip:** If you feel that it is all so overwhelming that you cannot even begin your work, read Chapter 8 on creativity – this will give you ideas on how to start assignments.

But I have no time and never seem to feel like studying

'I have my job or I'm looking for a job. I have my family. I have no time.'

Nobody leaps out of bed in the morning, going 'Wheee – this is the day that I tackle that huge assignment!' So do not rely on 'finding' time or on 'feeling' like studying. You have to put a study system in place and you have to make the time.

While schools do set homework, and colleges and universities give reading lists and set assignment deadlines, every university student has to work out for themselves just how much time they are prepared to give to their studies (35 hours or more per week). They have to decide how much work they are prepared to put in, to get the results – in crude terms, the grades – that they want.

Checklist: So when should I study?

When studying, a good rule of thumb is to build up to one-hour study periods and to then take a break. The second rule is to plan a timetable. When planning out your time, think about:

☐ Whether you are a morning, afternoon or evening person – try to fit your study times around your maximum performance times. Work with your strengths. Consider how much time you spend travelling: reading on the bus or train is a really effective use of time.

☐ How much time you would like to give to friends and family – your studies are important, but most of us would like to have friends and family still talking to us when our studies are over!

☐ How much time you have to give to chores – we need to keep our homes at least sanitary. Watch out though – housework and all chores can become excellent excuses for not working. They become displacement activities – sometimes it feels as though it is easier to completely re-build the house, rather than write an essay!

☐ How much time you have to give to work – these days, we need to earn money while we study, and sometimes universities help by fitting lectures and other classes into one or two days a week. Beware, this does not mean that all your studying can fit into two days. Remember, you have to give 35–40 hours a week to your studies – if you cannot do this, you will be in trouble.

☐ Whether you will be able to keep all your hobbies and interests going – do you fight to keep your hobbies now, or do you plan to take them up again after your studies?

☐ Do you acknowledge time limits and decide that, in the short term, your studies become your hobbies? Or, can you juggle time effectively and so fit more in?

☐ Time for rest and relaxation – as we have said, studying is hard work – it can also be very stressful. It is important to get sufficient rest while you study, and it is useful to build stress-relief activities – dancing, exercise, meditation, massage, yoga – into your timetables right at the beginning of your studies.

☐ Timetables – timetables give you a strong guide to your work, if you keep to them. But more than that: without timetables, you may feel that every time you are not working or spending quality time with friends and family, you ought to be studying.

You may not do that studying, but you worry, and this is exhausting in itself. Eventually, it may feel that your whole life is work, work, work. Something will have to go, and it could be your studies!

Things to think about

- **Study timetable**: This is a 24/7 timetable (twenty-four hours a day, seven days a week) that covers how many hours per day go to non-study, and how many go to your studies. It is where you can plan which subjects to study and for how long. It takes some trial-and-error and experiment to get this right, so do give it that time.
- **Assignment timetable**: This is a record of all the assignment deadlines that are coming up either in a term, a semester or across a whole year. Fill in deadlines and pin up on your wall, and place in your folder and diary. Never let a deadline take you by surprise.
- **Exam timetable**: Similar to the assignment timetable, this is a record of all the exams you will be taking. Note dates, times and locations. It is all too easy to turn up at the wrong time, on the wrong day and in the wrong place!
- **Revision timetable**: At the appropriate time, each student should devise their own revision timetable, where they work out when they are going to test their knowledge and practise for the exams that they are going to sit (more on this in Chapter 20. Tip: follow the checklist there now!).
- **Make lists and prioritise tasks**.
- **Keep a diary** and note when you plan to read or write.

> **Tip:** Photocopy the timetables below, and play around with using them to help you focus on your work and get the most from your time.

Where to study

Everyone deserves a nice place to study, but real life is not always as convenient as that, and sometimes we just have to adapt what we have and make it work. And, just as it is important that you decide when to study – and work at it until you get it right for you – it is important that you work out where you are going to study and you make that place work for you. With most of these things, there is no right or wrong, there is only what works for you. So take the time to find out what does work for you. There are some things that you may need to think about though.

Your study space

Negotiate a space with family or flatmates: your studies are part of your life now, and they must fit in. Creating a study space helps everyone in your life – including you – realise just how important your studies are.

A good place to study needs light and air – you need to see and breathe – but does not necessarily mean a completely quiet place; some people really do work best with a little bit of background noise going on.

You will need space to lay out your work, pin up your timetables, deadlines and notes. Have your textbooks out and visible. Have subject files neatly labelled and ready to hand. Write up all the new words that you are learning, so that you are immersed in your learning. All this is practical and also helps you to feel like a student.

Leave out work; do not tidy it all away. Having your work visible keeps it alive in your mind; putting it all away can give the false impression that you're finished.

You need pens and pencils to hand, and also highlighters, a stapler and staples, paper clips, correction fluid, Post-its, coloured pens, and all sorts of different sizes of paper. All these resources make it easier to write notes, annotate source material, mark important pages in books, and so forth. The different-sized paper gives you paper to make notes on, paper to make plans on, paper to print work on. Further, if you play around with materials and colour, you feel an injection of energy and enthusiasm, and this just makes the job easier.

You should also have access to a computer. A computer allows you to word-process work so that it looks neat and tidy, and makes it possible for the tutor to read and mark. More than that, it makes it easier to draft and re-draft work till you get it right.

Once you have a study space sorted out, you should practise using it positively. Say to yourself as you sit down: 'Now I am working', 'I enjoy being a student'. Try to avoid those old negative thoughts: I don't want to be here. This is too hard. I'd rather be. . . . Negative thoughts have a negative effect, while positive thoughts have a positive effect.

Remember to make that study space work for you. Get into the habit of giving 100 per cent whenever you sit down to study. Act as if you and your studies are important – they are, and so are you.

> **Tip:** Experiment with working at home, in the library and when you travel (being a commuter adds hours of study time to your week, if you take your books with you). But whether you want to work in a library or on a bus, you will also need a study space at home.

Activity 2: Sorting out a study space

1. If you have not already done so, sort out a place to study. Make sure that you can use this space at the times that you have planned to study in your timetable.
2. Over time, collect the resources that we have mentioned above.
3. In the meantime, make a list of all the resources that you need. What materials do you have already? Which ones are you going to buy? Which books can you get easily from the library? Which ones are so important that you ought to buy them? How many can you afford? etc.

Having that study space: some comments from other students

- It felt really good having my own study space. It made me feel like a real student.
- I felt that at last I could settle down to some real work.
- I felt a bit frightened at first, you know? Like, now I couldn't put it off any longer! I'd have to take it seriously.
- Sometimes I use my space to sort of trick myself into working. I think, I'll just sit there for a minute. . . . Next thing I know, I've been working away for an hour and I feel really good.
- I felt guilty at having to cut myself off from the kids. It just felt so selfish. I have to work really hard at still giving them some time.
- I used to get so frustrated; it was like every time I sat down to work, they would start demanding things from me. Now, we all sit down to work at the same time, even if they are just crayoning or reading a storybook. This has helped us all feel better.
- I still like going to the library to work, but it's great having a proper place for my stuff at home. It really does help.

Discussion: As you can see from the student comments, there is no right or wrong response to having your own study space. For each of us, there is only our reaction, and what we choose to do about it.

If having your own space makes you feel like a 'proper' student (and there is no one model of what a 'proper' student is), then you will only have to sit at your table or desk to put yourself in the right mood to study. You can always do what one of the other students (above) does and sometimes 'trick' yourself into getting some work done.

If it makes you feel a bit lonely or frightened, console yourself. New experiences are often frightening, at first. It might help to say to yourself several times, 'I am a proper student', each time that you sit down to study.

If your family always chooses that moment to want you – again, do what the other student did, and try to get them to 'study' at the same time as you. Depending on their age, this might mean real study, in which case the tips in the book will also help them! Or it could be 'nearly study' if they are very young. If that will not work with your lot, you may have to wait until they are in bed to study. Whatever works for you.

How to study

This is the longest section and it will cross–reference with information that you will be getting in other parts of this book. The whole book is also designed to get you studying in more successful ways. However, here are some practical tips on how to study.

Want it: Everyone should know what they are studying and why. Make sure that you do know what you want from each course that you are studying, and how your life will be changed when you reach your goals.

> **Tip:** Remember to write your goals on Post-its and stick them up in your study space. Fill in your learning contract (Chapter 4) for each course, module or unit that you do.

Get the overview (see Chapter 3): When on a course, do not drift from week to week wondering what's going on. Work out how the course has been put together. Know how the course is being assessed. Read the assignment question at the beginning of the course, not the end. If there are to be exams, check out past papers at the beginning of your studies, not the end. All this gives you a sense of how the course has been put together and where you are going each week.

> **Tip:** Use the 'Get Ready for Your Exams' checklist, in Chapter 20. The advice there will help you to plan and use your time throughout your course.

Epistemology: We mentioned this in Chapter 2. Remember, every course has its own theory of knowledge – what counts as argument and evidence for your subject. Make sure you know the what, why and how of all your subjects.

> **Tip:** Read the journals to get a model of how to argue and write in your subject. Use a dictionary and a subject dictionary.

Be positive: Just as an athlete will perform better if they feel like a success and think positive thoughts, so a student will learn more if they can adopt positive attitudes and develop self-confidence.

> **Tips:** When your motivation runs low, role-play, or act like, a successful student. Remind yourself that you can be a successful student. Read Chapter 9 on dealing with your emotions.

Timing: Set those study timetables in motion. Remember, work for an hour then take a break. A short break will recharge your batteries and make your work profitable. Long study periods are not the most effective way to work, yet one study myth is that this is what we must do. We might sit there for hours, but not much work is getting done. This belief can make you very frustrated, angry and tired, but it rarely produces good work.

Time tips: We concentrate best in 15-minute bursts. When we study, we have to get into the habit of regularly recharging our mental batteries to wake up our brains. We can do this by:

- taking a short rest
- changing what we do
- making the task very important
- making the task interesting, stimulating or more difficult.

Prioritise time: When working, we need to be strategic, note which assignments carry the most marks, and note which deadlines are coming first. When you make lists of what needs to be done and when, do first that with the nearest deadline; give more time to the assignment which carries the most marks.

Tip: Have a diary and note when you are going to do what. If you don't do something, re-schedule.

Use the time: We know students who sit down to study – out come the pens and paper – they get rearranged. Out come the books and the highlighters – they get rearranged. They go for a coffee. They go for a glass of water. They put one lot of books away and get out another set. They look at the clock – oh good! An hour has passed, so they put their materials away. But they have done no work! Watch out for this.

Tip: Goal-setting will help you benefit from independent study time.

One worry at a time

One thing that can stop people achieving enough when they sit down to work is too much worry. They sit down to write an essay, and worry about the two other essays that they also have to write. They worry about the weather or the bills. They worry about anything and everything.

If we worry about everything, we do nothing. One of the hardest tricks to being a successful student is to learn how to worry about one thing at a time.

It is as if we need to set up a set of shelves in our brain. We then need to put all our different worries on the shelves. Learn to take down one thing at a time and

▶

give it our total concentration. When we have finished with that, put it back on the shelf and take down something else.

Like everything else recommended in this book, this is a skill that has to be learned and developed through practice.

Goal-set: Before you sit down to study, set yourself some goals. Know what you are doing and why. Do not just start reading a book because it is on the reading list. Know why you are reading a section of that book. If you are not sure, have a look at the assignment question and find a bit of the book that will help you with a bit of the assignment. Then you will know what you are doing and why. This makes all the difference.

> **Tip:** Read Chapter 11 on reading. Each time you read, brainstorm first: what do I know? What do I need? Which bit of the assignment will this help me with?

Be active: When studying independently, be just as active as when you are in a lecture or joining in a class discussion. Read actively, asking questions as you go. Think about the information that you are receiving: what does it mean? Do you understand it? If not, what are you going to do about that? How does it connect with what you already know (things that you have heard in class or read in other places)? Connecting up information in this way is a really important part of active learning. Make active notes – typically, key word notes – in patterns (more on this in Chapter 12). Revise those notes actively.

> **Tip:** Before reading, re-read the assignment question – make notes that would help you answer that question.

Review actively: At the end of each study session – independent study or a lecture or class – take some time to reflect on what you have read or heard. Check what you have done. Recall what you have learned. Make brief notes to make the learning conscious.

> Tip: Complete a learning log at the end of every day or week (see Chapter 10).

Study partners and groups: Study is best when undertaken actively and interactively; this is where a study partner or a study group can be invaluable. Talking over new information with other people is the easiest way to understand and learn it, to make it your own. Further, if you encounter a problem you can talk to (or phone) your partner. Probably, they will not know the solution either. Oh, the relief! You are not alone and you are not stupid. Then the situation changes as you work on the problem and sort it out together.

Tips: If you have not got a study partner, persuade a friend or family member that they are interested in your course and talk to them. If your course has an online chat space or discussion board, use that to air your views and ask your questions.

Don't end on a sour note: Try not to end a study session on a problem – it is de-motivating and it can make it that little bit harder to start studying again. As suggested, use a study partner, friend or online discussion space to talk it over.

Tip: Make a note of the problem and sleep on it – sometimes the solution comes to you when you wake up. But don't lie awake fretting all night – this does not solve the problem, and you have made everything worse by losing sleep and gaining stress.

Relaxation and dealing with stress: Remember to make time to rest, relax and let go of stress. This is important. You need rest to carry on. Stress relief allows you to let go of tension, and this helps you to perform better. When we are stressed, our body releases cortisol, a hormone that has a direct impact on the brain causing the cortex to shrink. Further, stress releases adrenalin, the flight or fight hormone. The combination of these hormones eliminates short-term memory and produces the narrow, tunnel vision necessary for fight or flight. This might save our lives when escaping from a burning building, but works against us when studying, where we need breadth and depth of vision.

Tips: Read Chapter 9 on dealing with your emotions. Practise positive thinking. Take up yoga.

Do it! Review it!

As always, the advice given above will only work if put into practice. But much of it is there to be played with and adapted to suit you. So note the useful points and try them out. After a while, review how they are working for you and adapt them, so that they become more tailored to the sort of student that you are, and thus you do become a more effective student.

Conclusion

In this section, we have considered some basic organisation and time-management techniques via a discussion of when, where and how to study. Remember, though, that none of this will mean anything unless and until you put the ideas into practice. If it seems too difficult to put them all into practice at once, sort out one thing at a time. As you do this, take the time to reflect on how the things that you are doing are working for you. If something is not working – or stops working – change it. These tips work best once you adapt them to suit yourself.

Review points

When you reflect on this chapter, you might notice that you have:
- considered the impact of personal motivation on study success
- realised the time commitment necessary for developing effective study skills and academic practices, and for being an effective student
- explored organisation and time-management issues
- started the process of organising yourself for effective study
- engaged with various activities that have reinforced your understanding of the different parts of the chapter.

Activity 3: Filling in your timetables

Below, there are several timetables, including a blank 24/7 timetable. Complete all your timetables, but first follow the guidelines for your 24/7 timetables.
Filling in the 24/7:

1. Fill in the first one, indicating when you expect to work, sleep, do chores and so forth. Think about the time that you have left. Put in times for study and relaxation. Think about it – are you being realistic? Make sure that you are not underworking or overworking yourself. Run that programme for a few weeks.
2. After a couple of weeks, review your success in keeping to the study times that you set and in achieving the goals that you had in mind.
3. Change your timetable to fit in with reality! Use the second blank timetable for this.
4. Remember to do this every term, semester, year.

Keeping a timetable

Mark in the following details:

Tip: Use a colour code

- time in paid work
- time which must be spent in college or university
- time spent travelling
- personal/family commitments (children, shopping, etc.)
- any important, regular social commitments
- hours of sleep required
- time for independent study.

Table 5.1   Blank 24-hour timetables

TIME	MONDAY	TUESDAY	WEDNESDAY	THURSDAY	FRIDAY	SATURDAY	SUNDAY
1.00							
2.00							
3.00							
4.00							
5.00							
6.00							
7.00							
8.00							
9.00							
10.00							
11.00							
12.00							
13.00							
14.00							
15.00							
16.00							
17.00							
18.00							
19.00							
20.00							
21.00							
22.00							
23.00							
24.00							

Table 5.2 Events and deadlines calendar

EVENTS AND DEADLINES				
Write down the dates of the following events each term:				
	Course 1	Course 2	Course 3	Course 4
Course title				
Exam(s)				
Essay deadlines(s)				
Laboratory report Deadline(s)				
Seminar presentations				
Field trips/visits				
Project report or Exhibition deadlines				
Bank holidays or other 'days off'				
Other events (specify)				

Table 5.3   Term plan

Term Plan – what is happening over your terms/semester?							
	Mon	Tue	Wed	Thurs	Fri	Sat	Sun
Week 1							
Week 2							
Week 3							
Week 4							
Week 5							
Week 6							
Week 7							
Week 8							
Week 9							
Week 10							
Week 11							
Week 12							
Longer term deadlines:							

Table 5.4   Weekly plan

Keep a WEEKLY PLAN – key events and activities each week							
Week Number:	Mon	Tue	Wed	Thurs	Fri	Sat	Sun
8am							
9am							
10am							
11am							
12 noon							
1pm							
2pm							
3pm							
4pm							
5pm							
6pm							
7pm							
8pm							
9pm							
10pm							
11pm							
12 midnight							
1am							

6

How to use computers and e-learning to support your learning – Debbie Holley

AIMS

To introduce you to the broader concepts of using Information and Communications Technology (ICT) for your learning.

LEARNING OUTCOMES

By the end of this chapter, you will:
- understand that ICT skills will be important both for study and for employment
- understand the difference between Web 1 and Web 2 technologies
- have been introduced to Virtual Learning Environments (VLEs)
- have some of the techniques at your fingertips to be an effective Web researcher
- know how to find Reusable Learning Objects for your subject
- have an appreciation of the importance of personal development planning (PDP, with further information in Chapter 21)
- have no fears about trying out new technologies.

And so it begins ...

During welcome week, you join a group of students all talking excitedly. When you hear them mentioning 'delicious', do you:

- think they are discussing last night's meal at the Student Union, or
- know they are talking about social bookmarking software, where you can easily create and maintain your bookmarks for studying (or managing your social life, key careers websites, your interests, etc.)

Still wondering? Read on ...

Super Study Tip

When you study for your degree in psychology, business, biology, or media, you will find that, over time, the same authors and themes keep re-emerging, and each time you locate a new source you can bookmark it.

Bookmarking tools work by marking or 'tagging' the websites, resources and even books you read and find useful. You can store all your electronic bookmarks in one place, and more importantly, categorise them into topics.

By the time you are writing your final year projects or extended essays, you will have a whole collection of bookmarks in one place, covering various aspects of your chosen subject. Even better, you can view the bookmarks of others on the same topics, which makes this a very effective tool to learn about.

Now go to http://del.icio.us to find out more ...

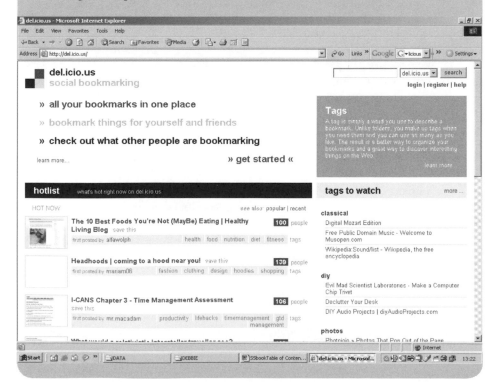

Activity 1: Test Your IT Knowledge Quiz

1. *Which is the largest unit?*
   a) megabyte
   b) terabyte
   c) gigabyte

2. *What does http stand for?*
   a) hypertext transfer protocol
   b) hyperspace translator protocol
   c) hypertext transfer technology product

3. *Who invented the World Wide Web?*
   a) Tim Berners-Lee
   b) Bebo White
   c) Bill Gates

4. *What do the initials DVD stand for?*
   a) Digital Version Disc
   b) Digital Versatile Disc
   c) Database Version Databank

5. *What is a digital signature?*
   a) This is the option you choose to add your name at the bottom of your email.
   b) Digital signatures are embedded into every page of a company website.
   c) Digital signatures are little bits of code that can be used to verify who wrote a document.

6. *When would 'tagging' be appropriate?*
   a) When you use a type of metadata involving the association of descriptors with objects.
   b) When you see your friends in a videoclip on YouTube, you can tag them and share the resource.
   c) It is never appropriate and the police monitor the Internet to check it doesn't happen.

7. *What is a 'mashup'?*
   a) a combination of two or more websites – see, for example, http://www.weatherbonk.com/
   b) a mixture of a company website with a communication package
   c) when you and your friends create a group together on a social network website like Bebo or Facebook

8. *Who first popularised the term 'surfing the Internet' in print?*
   a) Jean Armour Polly, a librarian in an article entitled 'Surfing the Internet' in 1992
   b) Bill Gates, when creating a new mission statement for his newly set-up company, Microsoft, on 4 April 1975
   c) Beach Boys singer/composer Brian Wilson originally had this as a soundtrack on their 1971 'Surf's up' album

▶

9. *What is a 'Linden Dollar'?*
   a) a unit to represent currency that Microsoft companies use to trade internationally
   b) an virtual currency that London Mayor, Ken Livingstone, is going to use to enable Londoners to pay for transport to the Olympic Games in 2012
   c) a unit of currency in the 3D world Second Life
10. *If a lecturer asked you to click on 'SquirrelMonkey', what would you expect to find?*
    a) a game involving squirrels and monkeys racing each other for peanuts
    b) an online survey
    c) an online assessment activity

The answers can be found on page 97.

> *Discussion:* The score is not really important; most of us can learn something new and useful about Information and Communications Technology (ICT). This chapter is designed for everyone, from those who want to extend their skills, to those who take one look at the banks of PCs in the university laboratories – and all the very confident students sitting there working – and panic.

Introduction

No matter what your existing computer and information skills are, one of your aims should be to leave university with excellent ICT skills. Not least because most employers expect graduates to be confident with seeking, handling and interpreting electronic information, as well as having their specialist subject knowledge. This chapter is designed to introduce you to the what, why and how of the key ICT skills you will need, both to be a successful student and to get and keep that great job.

> **Tip:** Large employers often have the first stage of their selection process online, so ICT skills will help you apply for the best jobs.

ICT and PDP

The government is currently encouraging all universities to offer their students the opportunity to undertake PDP activities as part of their Higher Education studies. Some universities offer paper-based PDPs, but others are starting to introduce electronic PDPs. These schemes are usually voluntary and are not assessed, but they offer you a fantastic chance to gather evidence to show prospective employers at a later date.

How to de-code a Web address

Here is a quote from a website:

PDP is defined as 'a structured and supported process undertaken by an individual to reflect upon their own learning, performance and/or achievement and to plan for their personal, educational and career development'.

Query: What can we tell about the status of the information, how reliable it is, etc. from the address itself?

http://www.heacademy.ac.uk/ourwork/learning/pdp

1   → 2   →3   → 4   → 5

1 Hypertext Transfer Protocol (http) is a communications protocol used to transfer or convey information on the World Wide Web (if the site starts with https:// this is commonly used on the World Wide Web for security-sensitive communication, such as payment transactions and corporate logons).
2 The World Wide Web (www) is a system of interlinked, hypertext documents accessed via the Internet. With a Web browser, a user views Web pages that may contain text, images, and other multimedia. In a Web address however, the www is the name of the computer that is connected to the Internet to provide the Web service – by convention, it is called www but obviously delicious decided to call theirs del!
3 The registered name of the company/organisation (or individual) domain names can be bought.
4 .ac means part of the academic network (other common ones are.org/.net/.co.uk/ – the latter being a company based in the UK).
5 UK is the country where this site is registered.
But always remember that a Web address can be manipulated – the fact that a link on an email looks like it goes to your bank does not mean that it does – it may not! Also, the website www.phoneycollege.ac is not part of the academic network, but is in fact just registered in the Acsension Islands.

A quick guide to Web 1

Web 1 is becoming the common term for traditional websites. These are usually used to deliver a large amount of content. They tend to be large sites and are often quite functional in design, concentrating on the technical processes.

A favourite quiz question is, who invented the Web? The answer is Tim Berners-Lee, and what is amazing is that he chose to share it with the world, and not develop it commercially for

Tip: Set yourself a new ICT target for each course/module you study. Keep a note in your PDP and then, at the end of the semester, review your learning and identify any 'learning gaps' you need to close.

For example:
- I want to learn to give a PowerPoint presentation
- I want to learn to give a PowerPoint presentation and use sound in it this time
- I want to learn to give a PowerPoint presentation and include the photographs I took on the subject
- I want to learn to give a PowerPoint presentation and, because it is on a crucial aspect of a topic I need to know more about, I want to upload onto my TikiWiki site to share with my study group.

profit. There is a tradition in computing for sharing knowledge and expertise, called the open-source software movement. Open-source software is free to use. An example is Open Office, which is a free alternative to Microsoft Office.

On 6 August 1991, Tim Berners-Lee posted a short summary of the World Wide Web project on the alt.hypertext newsgroup. This marked the debut of the Web as a publicly available service on the Internet.

'The WWW project was started to allow high energy physicists to share data, news, and documentation. We are very interested in spreading the Web to other areas, and having gateway servers for other data. Collaborators welcome! I'll post a short summary as a separate article.

Tim Berners-Lee	ti …@info.cern.ch
World Wide Web project	Tel: +41(22)767 3755
CERN	Fax: +41(22)767 7155
1211 Geneva 23, Switzerland	(usual disclaimer)'

http://groups.google.com/group/alt.hypertext/

Searching the Internet: getting started

To start searching on the Internet, you will need to use a Web browser, which is a software application that enables a user to display and interact with text, images and other information typically located on a Web page. Text and images on a Web page can contain hyperlinks to other Web pages at the same or a different website. Web browsers allow a user to quickly and easily access information provided on Web pages at many websites by traversing these links. Web browsers format HTML information for display, so the appearance of a Web page may differ between browsers. So if a page appears unformatted, or something will not work, try to open it using a different browser. Some of the Web browsers available for personal computers include Internet Explorer, Mozilla Firefox, Safari, Opera and Netscape (http://en.wikipedia.org/wiki/Web_browser).

About Web 2

Tim O'Reilly's Definition:
'Web 2.0 is the network as platform, spanning all connected devices; Web 2.0 applications are those that make the most of the intrinsic advantages of that platform: delivering software as a continually updated service that gets better the more people use it, consuming and remixing data from multiple sources, including individual users, while providing their own data and services in a form that allows remixing by others, creating network effects through an "architecture of participation", and going beyond the page metaphor of Web 1.0 to deliver rich user experiences. Tim O'Reilly, October 2005 http://www.oreillynet.com/pub/a/oreilly/tim/news/2005/09/30/what-is-web-20.html Who is Tim O'Reilly? Go to a search engine and type Tim O'Reilly into the search box.

Web 2: Taking advantage of the way the Web works now

Web 2 is about getting involved. It is about getting the Web to work for you for fun, for work or to support your learning. It can work for you personally as well as you 'the student'. There are lots of different packages out there that will make your life as a student (and a busy person) much easier. You can organise your social life and keep in touch with friends by using one of the social networking sites, such as My Space (http://www.myspace.com/), Facebook, (http://www.facebook.com/) or Bebo (http://www.bebo.com/). These packages allow you to keep track of friends back at home, your teammates, colleagues and anyone else you want to invite to join your network.

People are also now creating their own content on the Web – see, for example, the video clips on You Tube (http://www.youtube.com/). The Web is becoming far easier to use, navigate and take part in.

You can even join in a virtual world and create a profile for yourself. One of the best known is Second Life, a 3D online digital world that is imagined and created by its residents (http://secondlife.com/). The video tutorials really give you an idea about the kinds of things that are possible. See http://wiki.secondlife.com/wiki/Video_Tutorials to get started.

Some universities are starting to use Second Life for some aspects of teaching and learning. The University of Ohio has combined representations of their 'real buildings' that are familiar to students and a virtual welcome site that is completely different. Their graduate students, part of the University's Russ College of Engineering and Technology, are designing a series of Second Life science activities for middle-school children, as part of a $.7 million science project. See http://vital.cs.ohiou.edu/vitalwiki/index.php/Ohio_University_Second_Life_Campus_Places_To_See

You do not need to wait for a tutor to develop a Second Life course. If you are interested, go to the Second Life website, create an account and go and explore.

Web 2: What does it all mean? IM, Wiki and Blog

IM – Instant Messaging

With IM, you can interact with friends or colleagues who are online now. As long as the person is connected to the Internet, you can type messages to each other. These appear in a small window on both of your computer screens.

Most IM programs provide these features:

- **Instant messages** – send notes back and forth with a friend who is online
- **Chat** – create a chat room with friends or co-workers
- **Web links** – share links to your favourite websites
- **Video** – send and view videos, and chat face-to-face with friends
- **Images** – look at an image stored on your friend's computer
- **Sounds** – play sounds for your friends
- **Files** – share files by sending them directly to your friends
- **Talk** – use the Internet instead of a phone to actually talk with friends.

(http://communication.howstuffworks.com/instant-messaging.htm)
Some universities block access to Instant Messaging sites to prevent students overloading the network.

Can you blog it?

A 'blog' (from the term 'web log') is a website where entries are written in chronological order and show the most recent message first. 'Blog' can also be used as a verb, meaning 'to maintain or add content to a blog'. Blogs provide commentary or news on a particular subject, such as food, politics, or local news; some function as more personal online diaries. A typical blog combines text, images, and links to other blogs, Web pages, and other media related to its topic. The ability for readers to leave comments in an interactive format is an important part of many blogs. See http://en.wikipedia.org/wiki/List_of_search_engines# Blog_search_engines

Query: Why have I used Wikipedia for this information?
Answer: See the section on being an effective Internet researcher below.

Use blogs to start your research

There are numerous useful blogs for any academic subject. For example, the Guardian newspaper reporters also contribute to the blog: http://blogs.guardian.co.uk/news/ If you are interested in current affairs, – and keeping up-to-date with current affairs should be part of your life as a student – create your own blog and add this link, or the link from your preferred broadsheet newspaper to your delicious account. Then search for useful blogs to do with your subject area, and add these to the list.

Tip: Create your own blog, perhaps for your PDP entries? There are a number of ways of setting up a blog – see Wikipedia for a list: www.blogger.com is quick and easy to use.

Wiki

A wiki is a collaborative website which can be directly edited by anyone with access to it. It is very simple to use and the only computer skill you need is being able to type. This makes it a very useful tool for students. For example, if you are put together with two others to work on a group presentation, you could use a wiki.

Using a wiki for your group presentation

You are, of course, a model student, available at any time and on any day to meet the others, with your share of the work already completed. However, one of your team members is still living at home, which is a one-hour commute away, and has a job in the evening in the local pub. The other team member has a young family, and only seems to come to university for the classes, and can be unreliable for meetings because of family problems.

The wiki can provide a solution. You and your team members can set up your presentation wiki and add information and AVA as you find them. You can see each others' contributions. You can edit each others' work. You can leave messages and have a debate and you don't need to be in the same place at the same time.

How to do it

You set up a wiki by visiting one of the 'wiki farms', some of which are public, which means anyone can read them; some can make private, password-protected wikis. PeanutButterWiki, Socialtext, Wetpaint and Wikia are popular examples of such services. For more information, see the list of wiki farms on Wikipedia. Note that free wiki farms generally contain advertising on every page.

Go to http://pbwiki.com/ and create your own wiki in three easy steps. If you want to use a wiki as a way of organising your notes, a 'tiddly wiki' available from Tiddlyspot.com can be downloaded onto your computer or a USB memory stick.

There is a good example of wiki use at http://evolvingessay.pbwiki.com/. Here, a student is typing up her thoughts as she is writing an essay, and other students and staff are adding their comments as the essay develops. This is a useful resource for the process of writing essays.

Wikipedia?

It is a multilingual, Web-based, free content encyclopedia project. Wikipedia is written collaboratively by volunteers from all around the world. With rare exceptions, its articles can be edited by anyone with access to the Internet, simply by clicking the 'edit this page' link: http://en.wikipedia.org/wiki/Wikipedia:About

Researching with Wikipedia

Wikipedia can be a great tool for learning and researching information. However, like all sources, not everything in Wikipedia is accurate, comprehensive or unbiased. Many of the general rules of thumb for conducting research apply to Wikipedia, including:

- Always be wary of any one single source, or of multiple works that derive from a single source.
- Where articles have references to external sources (whether online or not), read the references and check whether they really do support what the article says.

- In all academic institutions, Wikipedia, along with most encyclopaedias, are unacceptable as a major source for a research paper. See http://en.wikipedia.org/wiki/WikipediaResearching_with_Wikipedia

> **Tip:** Start your research on a topic with Wikipedia, but use other sources to support your arguments. Be careful, as some teachers really don't like students using Wikipedia as a source of information and will mark you down for it.

RSS feeds

Have you noticed a small orange button on some of your favourite websites? One of the best sites for getting started with news feeds is the BBC. Here is their explanation of RSS feeds.

'News feeds allow you to see when websites have added new content. You can get the latest headlines and video in one place, as soon as it's published, without having to visit the websites you have taken the feed from.

Feeds are also known as RSS. There is some discussion as to what RSS stands for, but most people plump for "Really Simple Syndication". In essence, the feeds themselves are just Web pages, designed to be read by computers rather than people. In general, the first thing you need is something called a news reader. This is a piece of software that checks the feeds and lets you read any new articles that have been added. There are many different versions, some of which are accessed using a browser, and some of which are downloadable applications.'

Go to http://news.bbc.co.uk/1/hi/help/3223484.stm#mysite

Now scroll down the BBC site to the section called 'How do I get a news reader?' to check which news reader will work with your computer operating system. Then, follow the instructions and you will have your first RSS feed. An RSS aggregator is useful when you start to develop your skills. This will automatically update you when a new posting appears on one of the sites you have visited.

This will:

- help you keep up to date when information on a favourite website changes
- alert you to new information on a subject
- save you lots of time by managing the information sensibly.

E-learning and Virtual Learning Environments (VLEs)

E-learning, blended learning and virtual learning are all terms used to describe learning activities supported by or accessed through electronic channels – computers, CD-ROM, DVD, Internet, Intranet, and so forth. If you are a full-time, 'face-to-face' student, you may well be a little surprised to find sessions on electronic (e-) learning being discussed in your Welcome Week or induction activities. But, these are for you! As well as attending lectures and classes, you are expected to use any online materials or resources that your tutors provide.

E- or online resources for students are often gathered together in one place in a university virtual learning environment (VLE). In your university VLE, you may find some combination of lecture notes, seminar materials, course information, discussions, blogs, online assessment, a calendar, revision tasks, announcements, links to other resources, assessment information and lots more.

> **Tip:** What is offered in your VLE will vary – some universities have standardised information available for all the subjects; others are dependent on lecturing staff developing resources independently. Discover and use your VLE.

> A Higher Education Academy study (2006) found that students really appreciated the flexibility of being able to access materials from home or a cyber café, via their mobile phones or anywhere there is high-speed Internet access.
> *Query:* What makes a good e-learning student?
> *Answer:* The same as what makes a good student!
> The Learner Experience of E-learning (LEX) Project:
> Characteristics of effective learners in an 'e-' context include being:
>
> * effective at learning generally
> * confident
> * effective at time management
> * skilled at integrating learning into life
> * willing to learn IT skills
> * highly skilled networkers.
>
> http://www.jisc.ac.uk/whatwedo/programmes/elearning_pedagogy/elp_lex.aspx

What kinds of Virtual Learning Environment (VLE) are available?

VLEs can be divided into two types: open-source based, such as Moodle and Boddingtons, and commercial packages like Blackboard, WebCt or Lotus Notes. The open-source VLEs, http://moodle.org and http://www.bodington.org/, are available for use by anyone, which could be very useful if you are on the type of course where you are developing materials and need somewhere to place them, for example, if you are a student teacher, but, typically, the materials will not be used by students themselves.

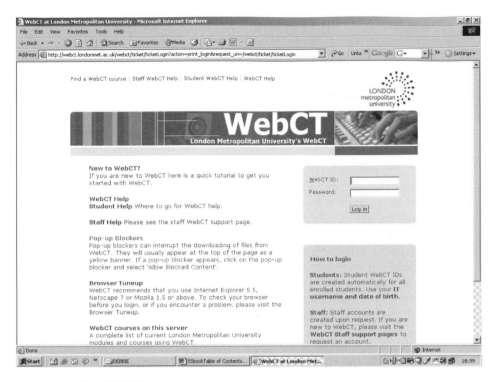

An example of a VLE login screen

Blackboard, WebCt or Lotus Notes

These are examples of commercial VLEs that universities purchase because they can be linked into other university IT systems. Universities can then offer their students a 'portal', which is one point of entry to personalised online information about your learning, your courses, administration, exam results, graduation, and so on.

The advantages of a VLE are that you can access these 24 hours a day, 365 days a year. They are easy to access via a high-speed Internet connection, and can be used even if you only have basic computer skills. To maximise this resource, plan regular visits to make sure you are up to date with any changes. Most students log in daily to check up on any changes.

Making the most of your VLE

Once you have access to your VLE, check you have access to the modules/courses specified, and also see if you can have access to any more general resources. Some librarians put information up on the VLE, and many learning development units or study skills units put material up for all students to use.

Then, for each module, check:

- Is my lecturer using the VLE for this module mainly to store lecture notes?
- Does this lecturer use a bulletin board to communicate changes?

- Is there a facility where I can add my questions?
- Is there a frequently asked questions (FAQ) section?
- Is there an area where I can get in touch with my fellow students?
- Is there any assessed work on the site?
- Do I use the site to submit my coursework?
- Are there any quizzes or other tools available to help me check my knowledge?
- Which areas will be useful when it comes to revision?

Tip: Virtual Learning Environments help lecturers track your progress, so if you forget to log in for a few days, you may well get an email asking if you are having any difficulties. So, make sure you are working through the online material regularly, and report any problems you have quickly, to maximise your learning from these supplementary resources.

VLEs should not be the only form of online information for your studies. They are a supplement to, and not a replacement of, your own efforts for developing your subject knowledge.

Find out about *all* the resources available on your VLE, not just the subject ones.

Make sure you attend the university IT training sessions to maximise the use of the VLE. At the start of each module, explore the resources available through the VLE – not all modules are the same, and different lecturers may use different tools.

E-learning

Many first time e-learning users think that learning online is going to be dull, one-dimensional, and that the classroom atmosphere will be completely lacking. That may well have been true years ago, but today's e-learners have a whole range of activities at their fingertips. Below is what one student thought about an online discussion.

Emotionality:
'I have learnt that online learning can be really inspiring and really frustrating. Discussions can be really involving and interesting, as you read and relate to others' comments, make your own contributions, etc. Then you hit a low (could be a technical problem – can't add the attachment or something more major, such as computer not working, or could be a personal issue – feel daunted by expertise of other participant or just don't relate to what they are saying) which throws you back. I did not expect to experience highs and lows in this way'.
   (Online tutoring course participant, in Sharpe et al., 2005: 6 at http://www.jisc.ac.uk/media/documents/programmes/elearning_pedagogy/guide1_evaluation.pdf)

The effective Web researcher

With so much information available on the World Wide Web, ignore this resource at your peril. The modern student needs to demonstrate their skill researching not just paper- based books, journals and newspapers, but to show they are equally skilled at extracting relevant information from online resources. Some resources, of course, are available both online and on paper – for example, government statistics. These can be found in your library, but by entering the website, there is so much more information at your fingertips. For example, there is a summary of the most recent statistics released, a search facility to customise your search, a key statistics explanation, as well as links to other useful sites. You will also spot the orange RSS feed icon, if you want to add this website to your list.

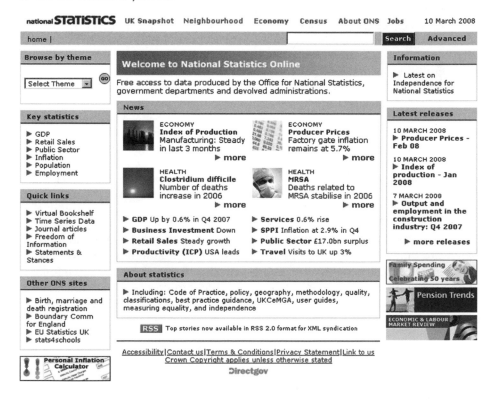

http://www.statistics.gov.uk/

How to get started: the Internet detective

Internet Detective is a free online tutorial that will help you develop your Internet research skills (http://www.vts.intute.ac.uk/detective). The tutorial looks at the critical thinking required when using the Internet for research, and offers practical advice on evaluating the quality of websites. It is really important to develop your critical skills, and learn how to judge how reliable a website is for your studies.

Using electronic library resources

Another way of demonstrating how good your search skills are online is to use the electronic databases available via your university library. Universities pay many thousands of pounds each year to subscribe to these, and the articles published have been through a rigorous peer-review process to ensure they are accurate and of the right quality. This makes these resources much more reliable to cite for your arguments than a website that could have been put up by anyone. A mix of traditional (paper-based) and e-learning resources are needed to show you have effectively researched your subject. Textbooks are an essential part of your reading, just as much as online resources. Your lecturer will expect you to show you are reading broadly across your subject, as well as deeply to gain expertise in particular areas.

Your subject librarian is *a really important person*. He or she will usually do a presentation at Welcome Week or in one of your first lectures. Find out his/her email address, because, like your lecturing staff, there will be specific days and times when they are available for consultation. Subject librarians can give you advice and assistance with all kinds of research, whether you are having difficulty locating a book, to explaining to you the best key words to enter for successful searching of a particular online database.

Check your library homepage, the Web page for your university library. See if you can find which electronic resources are available for your subject. Most libraries sort these by subject indexes, as well as having search tools to enable you to search by journal, by author and by topic. Newspapers and current periodicals like the *Economist* are also available online for free from your library. Check to see if your lecturer has placed a reading list online – this is often in with the library resources. Your librarian may also put useful subject information on the library Web page.

Tip: Open an ATHENS account. ATHENS is a personal username and password that verifies you as a student or member of staff at the University of Wherever, and, therefore, as eligible to access a range of online resources. These could be as databases, where you will find references to online journal articles' e-journals and e-books. These resources are available both on campus *and* to use from home (or wherever you access your high-speed Internet link).

Bookmarking

We talked about http://del.icio.us at the start of the chapter – this is one example of bookmarking software. As you expand your skills, why not form a study group and learn how to share your bookmarks? **Furl** (from **F**ile **U**niform **R**esource **L**ocators) is a free social bookmarking website (http://furl.net) that allows members to store searchable copies of Web-pages and share them with others. This is a really useful tool if you are working togther on a group project or coursework. Every member receives five gigabytes of storage space.

Create folders for your different bookmarks, and also organise your 'favourites' on your Internet browser so you can easily find the Web-page again.

'**Google Scholar** provides a simple way to broadly search for scholarly literature. From one place, you can search across many disciplines and sources: peer-reviewed papers, theses, books, abstracts and articles, from academic publishers, professional societies, pre-print repositories, universities and other scholarly organisations. Google Scholar helps you identify the most relevant research across the world of scholarly research'.

http://scholar.google.com

'**Google Book** Search works just like a Web search: Try a search on *Google Book Search* or on Google.com. When we find a book whose content contains a match for your search terms, we'll link to it in your search results. Clicking on a book result, you'll be able to see everything from a few short excerpts to the entire book, depending on a few different factors'.

What can I view?

'Each book includes an "About this book" page with basic bibliographic data like title, author, publication date, length and subject. For some books, you may also see additional information like key terms and phrases, references to the book from scholarly publications or other books, chapter titles and a list of related books. For every book, you'll see links directing you to book-stores where you can buy the book and libraries where you can borrow it'.

http://books.google.com/

Tips: Lecturers will not appreciate lots of information from wikipedia. Use wikipedia to get you started, but follow up the links to more academic sources, and see the 'how to be an effective Web researcher' section above.

- Make your subject librarian your best friend. Do not leave getting to know them and the services they offer until you have a crisis.
- Work out which are the quiet times in your library, and make an effort to get there early and/or stay late when there is less pressure on the resources.
- Most lecturers are experts in their own area. Check whether they, or other colleagues, have written anything that you could read.

Reusable learning objects (see http://www.rlo-cetl.ac.uk/)

Reusable learning objects (RLOs) are Web-based interactive chunks of e-learning, designed to explain a stand-alone learning objective. RLO-CETL is being funded by the Higher Education Funding Council for England (HEFCE) to develop a range of multimedia learning objects that can be stored in repositories, accessed over the Web, and integrated into course delivery. London Metropolitan University is the lead institution in this CETL, in partnership with the Universities of Cambridge and Nottingham. See http://www.rlo-cetl.ac.uk/rlos.htm for the showcase, and join the mailing list to be kept up to date as new RLOs are added to the repository.

Your tutors will expect you to provide them with a list of the sources you have referred to when preparing your report, essay or other coursework. This is called a reference list. The three multimedia resources, below, take you through the creation of a reference (our examples show Harvard References, one of the most commonly used ones). By working through the examples and testing your knowledge as you go, you will end up with perfect references – a key part to achieving your goals of high marks!

Tips: Always make sure you list your references as you draft your work – trying to find out where you got some information from weeks later is onerous and time-consuming.

Use a range of references to show you are reading widely across the subject, and deeply within the subject.

All facts and figures, quotes and indirect quotes should have a corresponding reference.

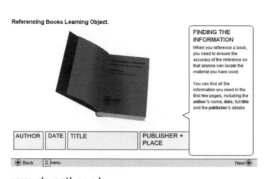

www.rlo-cetl.ac.uk

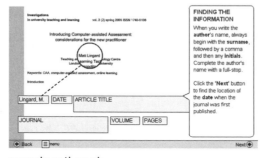

www.rlo-cetl.ac.uk

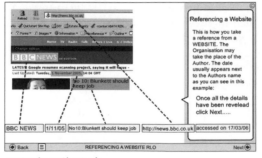

www.rlo-cetl.ac.uk

Finally: tools to personalise your learning

There are more tools emerging that enable you to merge and blend all your online and off-line activities. Below are *two free* examples, but by now, you will be ready and able to search for more, try them out and evaluate their usefulness. And you will soon be one of the confident students sitting in the IT studios, managing all your time and resources effectively and efficiently, and terrifying the new students looking through the window with how easily you move between your online resources.

Google toolbar and much more

Free Resource: Google toolbar. Customise your google page with maps, images, currency converters, jokes, quotes, a calculator, a thesaurus, free sudoku puzzles and lots more – see http://www.google.com/ig

Free Resource: Airset.com. *Airset:* http://www.airset.com/

For groups to coordinate, collaborate, communicate and share calendars, contacts, lists, files, blogs and links.

Community tools to get your community connected, be it your seminar group or your sports team.

Individual personal information management for syndicating with Outlook, Palm and mobile phones.

These tools will enable you to:

• manage your time more efficiently
• coordinate meetings with others
• combine resources online with your mobile phone
• have useful tools on your desktop, ready for when they are needed (e.g. calculator, currency exchange and thesaurus)
• communicate with friends, colleagues, students
• create and manage links from a variety of sources – ready for every time you start a new piece of work
• keep all your materials in one place
• also have fun and learn new skills as you learn.

Enjoy!

Answers to Test Your IT Knowledge Quiz

1 (b); 2 (a); 3 (a); 4(b); 5(c); 6(b); 7(a); 8(a); 9(c); 10 (b).

7

How to succeed in group work

AIMS

To consider the role of group work in the academic environment and to build your group-work skills.

LEARNING OUTCOMES

It is intended that after reading this chapter and engaging in the activities set, you will have:

- developed an awareness of the role and potential of group work in the academic environment
- engaged in activities designed to develop your group-work skills
- considered how to reflect on your group-work skills, for your CV and for assessment (see also Chapter 15).

Introduction

Group work can be one of the most emotionally charged areas of a student's life. Many students see only the problems associated with working in a group. Perhaps because they never get heard in a group, perhaps because they usually do all the work – whatever the problem, group work makes them unhappy. If you have doubts about group work, or if you just want to get the most out of all the group work opportunities with which you will be presented while a student, then this section is for you.

Colleges and universities are increasingly building group activities into their programmes. Some, because they have an ideological commitment to collaborative learning; they believe that we are interdependent beings and should recognise and build on that. Others feel that group work offers support to their students; tasks are easier when they are shared. Still others feel that they are pragmatically preparing students for the world of work – for, if you cannot work with other people, you are unlikely to be able to keep a job.

Whatever your university's reasons for asking you to engage in group work, we recommend that you try to get the most from it – and to help you, we are going to explore the what, why and how of group work. In order to do this, we have drawn very heavily on the group-work theories of business – for, it is in business that group work is particularly valued.

What is group work?

A group has to have a membership of two or more people. There should be a sense of shared identity, that is, you should all have a sense that you are a group and that you have shared or common goals. Further, within the group, there should be a feeling of interaction and interdependence, a sense that you can achieve something together.

Perhaps it is in these initial definitions of a group that we have hit upon some of the problems with academic groups. How many people in an academic group do feel that sense of identity and interdependence? How many embrace the task and the sense of shared goals? How many resent and resist the whole group-work process?

If this sounds like groups that you have been in – or that you are in now – what are you going to do to make your group feel and operate like a group?

Group work made simple: the pyramid discussion

A simple initial group activity is the pyramid discussion. When asked to start a group project:
- think about the topic on your own
- discuss ideas in pairs
- build arguments in fours
- feed back your thinking in a whole group plenary.

Students in groups

At university, there can be many forms of group work. For one thing, and as we keep reminding you, you can sort out a study partner, or work with an interested friend, to make study more collaborative and supportive. You can build your own study group to share the reading for assignments, to discuss assignment questions and to proofread your work (as the tutors did in Chapter 9).

There can also be group activities organised by the tutor: from class discussions, presentations and seminars to the formal, assessed group project. Typically, the best thing you can do is participate in these as positively as possible.

Academic groups

There are many different forms of group that you might engage in at university – here are some of them.

- Class discussion or activity – This is a simple collective activity that you are asked to do in class, with other people.
- Tutorials – Typically this involves two or more students meeting with a tutor and discussing, or working together on, a topic or task.
- Seminars – This is a group of students – around 15–20 – working together, usually with a tutor. This may involve whole-class discussion, activities or reading being undertaken, or working on an issue together; these are often related to a lecture programme.
- Group assignments – this is where students are asked to produce something collectively. For example, you may have to prepare a presentation or a seminar, or write and produce a report, magazine or a video. Perhaps you will be awarded a collective grade.

Tips:
- Group work is typically designed to reduce the workload, while increasing the amount of active and interactive learning that takes place – take advantage of this.
- Sometimes the process, as well as the product, is assessed. Here, students will be asked to reflect on the whole group- work process. That is, how you worked as a group, roles that were adopted, problems that occurred and how they were solved. Make notes as you go along. Read Chapter 15.

'They keep making us work in groups, but this is a competition – why should I help other people?'

'I love group work. I enjoy working with other people – I like the camaraderie and I like the fact that I'm not on my own as usual.'

Why groups?

Group work offers many advantages to students of all ages – yes, really. Group work can foster supportive, active learning, giving the opportunity to develop your personal and interpersonal skills.

For one thing, working with others offers an opportunity to share the workload. It really is easier to do all the reading if you share it out and discuss it. When embarking on a group project, you can develop assertiveness rather than aggression; tact and diplomacy rather than bullying and hectoring; flexibility and compromise rather than intractability and stubbornness. You can learn to listen as well as to speak, to encourage others as well as to establish yourself, and to work cooperatively and collegially with others. Another advantage of group work is that a good group offers social support that can break down the isolation often associated with being a student.

Disadvantages to group work

Of course, there can be disadvantages to group work. One disadvantage is linked to the fact that many group activities are now assessed. Students have become increasingly aware of the importance of good grades and do not want *their* grade based on the effort, or otherwise, of other people. Thus, they are incredibly resentful of those in the group who do not pull their weight, who do not turn up, who do not stay on track, who dominate or bully or distract. There can also be groups where members stay silent, where no one is interested or committed, or groups where the same people always speak. None of this feels satisfactory and it causes much resentment.

Resolving conflict – and developing your CV

But every disadvantage can become an advantage if you work out how to resolve the problems that you encounter. So notice what is happening in your groups. Notice how difficult situations are resolved. For example, if there are people who do not speak or don't turn up for meetings or do not contribute to the group task, instead of being angry and frustrated, try to discover the real problem, and see if you can find a solution. (See also Chapter 6 – can you use virtual meetings or blogs to take your projects forward?) Your attempts at finding solutions may not work. Don't worry. Noting that you recognised and attempted to address a problem is what will make you employable.

Put notes on these problem-solving activities in your curriculum vitae file. When you apply for a job, you will be able to prove that you are good at group work by giving examples from your time at university. It is the examples that you give – and the way that you resolved these problems – that will make all the difference in that vital job interview. And this does refer to another 'why' of group work – it can and does prepare you for your future employment.

> **Tip:** If you have to write a reflective account of your group work, make notes of your group sessions, your conflicts and resolutions, your strengths and weaknesses, the plusses and minuses of the experience. These will help when you write your reflective account.

Activity 1: SWOT your group work

SWOT stands for Strengths, Weaknesses, Opportunities and Threats.
- What are your group-work strengths? What do you already like about group work and the way that you perform in a group?

▶

- What are your weaknesses? What do you really dislike about group work and/or your own performance in groups?
- What opportunities are there for you in group work?
- What threats?

Once you have answered these questions, think about your answers and discuss them with your study partner.

Query: What do your answers tell you about yourself?

- What do they tell you about how you should approach group work?
- What are you going to do differently next time?
- What are you going to do now?

How to 'do' group work

The best way to get the most from group work is to approach it positively, determined to get the most from it. If you really dislike group work, but have to engage in it, fake it to make it. Role-play being an active, positive student.

Another simple and very effective strategy is to choose your groups with care. Do not just team up with those people sitting next to you, or those nice chatty people from the canteen. Group tasks normally involve hard work: choose people who are as motivated, positive and industrious as you.

Activity 2: Belbin's group roles

There are eight key roles that management experts like Belbin (1981) have identified in group activities. We have listed these below, indicating the possible strengths and weaknesses involved.

Note: While eight roles are indicated here, research suggests that academic groups work best if they only contain four or five people – any more and you start to get passengers.

- Company worker – a dutiful, organised person, who may tend to inflexibility
- Chair – a calm, open-minded person, who may not shine creatively
- Shaper – a dynamic person who may be impatient
- Creative thinker – one who may come up with brilliant ideas, though these may be unrealistic

▶

- Resource investigator – an extrovert character who may respond well to the challenge but who may lose interest
- Monitor – a sober, hard-headed individual who keeps everything on track, but who may lack inspiration
- Team worker – a mild social person with plenty of team spirit but who may be indecisive
- Completer/finisher – a conscientious perfectionist, who may be a worrier.

Query: When looking at that list:
- do you recognise these roles?
- which description most fits you?
- are you happy with this?
- what are you going to do about it?

Tips:
- In a small group, allocate roles wisely, but make sure that you have a chairperson, and that everyone does know what the task is, what they are doing, and when it all has to be completed.
- Experiment with group work. Adopt different roles in different academic groups. Each time you vary your role in a group, you will develop different aspects of your personality; this is a good thing.
- Decide to use your group-work experiences to develop your CV, and get you that job. So, as you move through team worker, leader, information gatherer, creative thinker, completer, etc., make notes on your experiences for your CV folder.

A business-like approach to group work

Management theorists like Belbin and Adair (see boxed information and tips) have worked to de-mystify group-work forms and processes, so that businesses can run more effectively. Have a look at the information in the boxes and see what they tell you about how to make groups work. As always, ask yourself, 'How will knowing this make me a more successful student?' For, in the end you must work out how knowing those things will help you to succeed in the group activities that you will be expected to undertake at college or university.

Tip: If you are expected to reflect on your group-work experiences, using the boxed information will definitely improve your grade.

Remember the ten steps There are many things that good groups have to do to work well, that is, for everyone involved to have a good time and for the task to be accomplished: we refer to these here. Remember also the ten steps to successful assessment (see Chapter 13).

Activity 3: Adair's processes

As there is theory as to the roles adopted in group situations, so there are arguments as to the processes that groups go through. Adair argues that groups have distinct forms, or pass through distinct transformations, as they encounter the task, settle down to it and finally pull it off. These are known as forming, storming, norming and performing; some people also speak of a fifth stage, mourning.

Forming is where the group comes together and takes shape. This forming period is a time of high anxiety as people work out:

- who is in the group and what they are like
- what the assignment is and what it involves
- what the 'rules' are about behaviour, about the task, about assessment
- what they will have to do to get the job done and who will be doing 'all the work'.

> **Tip:** In group tasks, keep in contact. Set times and tasks for meetings. Work out who is doing what by when.

Storming is where conflict arises as people sort out all the confusions highlighted above. This is where people seek to assert their authorities, and get challenged. Typically, this is a 'black and white' phase – everything seems all good or all bad; compromise is not seen. At this stage, people are reacting emotionally against everything as they challenge:

- each other
- the value of the task
- the feasibility of the task (you cannot be serious!).

> **Tip:** If you do not like group work, ask yourself, is it because you do not like conflict? Perhaps you just find this phase uncomfortable? If this is so, remind yourself that this phase passes.

Norming, as the name suggests, is where the group begins to settle down. Here, that sense of interdependence develops as:

- plans are made
- standards are laid down
- cooperation begins
- people are able to communicate their feelings more positively.

▶

Tip: If you cannot attend meetings, apologise and keep communicating with other people in the group.

Performing is where the group gets on and does what it was asked to do. It is now that the task can be undertaken and completed, and success can be experienced. Here, it is useful if:

- roles are accepted and understood
- deadlines are set and kept to
- communication is facilitated by good interpersonal skills.

Tip: Share your phone numbers and your email addresses. Do have a group leader who will take responsibility for chivvying people along. Do set people tasks that they *can* do.

Mourning: The fifth stage, mourning, is supposed to follow a successful and intense group experience. As you work hard to complete an assignment with people, you develop links and bonds. Typically, you enjoy the sense of mutual support and commitment. The feeling of interdependence is very satisfying. When all this ends as the task ends, there can be a real sense of loss.

Tips:
- Be prepared for the sense of loss.
- Work to keep in contact with good team players – you may be able to work with them again.

Queries:
- Do you recognise any of these stages?
- Now that you know about them, think how you might use this knowledge to your advantage.
- How will you draw on this information in your next group activity?
- Make notes so that you do not forget.

Discussion: There is debate about these group-work stages and whether or not they are helpful to students in groups. For a useful resource that looks at students going through group-work struggles, go to the group-work section of www.learnhigher.ac.uk below.

How to succeed in group work

When undertaking a group task, it still helps to use the ten-step approach to success:

1. Prepare to research:
   - understand the task – know what you have been asked to produce
   - analyse the question – all of it – and know what you have to cover
   - have the overview and fit the task to the module learning outcomes
   - use creative brainstorming and notemaking strategies
   - action plan – work out who is doing what, why, where and when.
2. Follow the action plan.
3. Review your findings.
4. Plan the product.
5. Prepare a first draft.
6. Leave a time lag.
7. Review, revise and edit, and agree on a final draft.
8. Proofread, or rehearse if it involves a group presentation.
9. Hand work in on or before a deadline.
10. Review your progress (see 'A reflective account of group work' below).

Tips: Useful things to say and do in your group
For progress
Initiating: What about trying . . . What if we did . . .
Questioning: Could you explain that? Could you elaborate a bit?
Giving: This has worked for me before... What would happen if we...?
Clarifying: Do you mean...? Is this like...?
Summarising: Do you think this is what we have agreed so far...?
For a good atmosphere
Supporting: I see what you mean... I understand...
Observing: We are making good progress or We seem to be stuck...
Mediating/reconciling: You two seem to be seeing this differently, but what about...?
Is there anything that you can find to agree on?
Compromise: What about if I gave ground on this... Would that work?
Humour: Well, obviously the UN lost a diplomat in me...
For more tips, go to:
http://www.learnhigher.ac.uk/learningareas/Group_Work.html
http://isites.harvard.edu/fs/html/icb.topic58474/wigstudents5.html

A reflective account of group work

If a reflective account of your group work forms part of the formal assessment of your course or module:

- ask your tutor exactly what it is that they are assessing before you even start the group activity. In this way, you can note the relevant information as it arises, and have it there ready for when you perform your formal review of your group project.

- do not just write things like, 'We all argued and did not agree on anything'. *or* 'I really like group work'. You need to comment on how you made your group function effectively. It helps if you note problems and how you overcame them.
- do mention Belbin and Adair and how their theories helped you do better in your group task.
- do use theory and practical examples from your weeks working as a group to make your reflective account sufficiently academically rigorous.
- do read Chapter 15 on the reflective essay to see a model of how to write a good reflective account of your group work practice.

Activity 4: Group-building exercises

There are management team-building games that you might like to experiment with to develop your group-work skills, and for the fun of it. We have included one below with suggested variations; you can search out others if you wish.

The Paper Tower
For this activity, you will need to gather together some students who want to develop their group-work skills and some simple resources. The goal will be for groups to construct a paper tower with a given supply of resources.

The non-breakable egg container: Variations on this exercise include designing, producing and testing a non-breakable egg container, or balancing a spoon on a paper tower. The egg container is the more dramatic.

Aim
To develop group-work skills through practical activity, observation and feedback.

Learning outcomes
By the end of this activity, participants will have developed:
- a sense of the social support offered by group work
- an idea of their own approach to group work
- a sense of the fun of group work
- an idea of the positive benefits of undertaking tasks in a team rather than alone
- some strategies for successful group participation.

Resources
Large quantities of newspaper, cellotape, paper clips and rubber bands – sufficient for all participants.

The Paper Tower Exercise
1 Divide participants into groups of 5–6 people. Each group has to choose an observer who will not participate but who will note how the other people do so. The participants have to build a tower with the resources to hand. Each group will 'present' their tower to the other groups. Each observer will feed back how his or her group performed. (Allow 20–30 minutes' tower-building time.)

▶

2 While the students build their towers, the observer makes notes as to the roles adopted by individual members or the processes engaged in by the group. The observer notes how people engage in the group task.

3 Groups report back on the criteria they had chosen for their tower, the tower itself, and how they felt the group performed. The observer feeds back (in constructive terms) on the roles and/or processes of the group.

4 Plenary: hold a plenary to discuss what the participants have learned from the activity, and how they will draw on this in the future.

Review points

When reviewing this activity, participants might note that they:

- enjoyed it – it was fun
- benefited from being part of a team
- have some idea of how they performed in a group activity
- have learned something useful about group work that they will build on in the future.

Conclusion

We have used this section of the book to explore group work in the academic setting. We have stressed that group work can be a positive, supportive and interactive learning experience, especially if you tackle group activities with enthusiasm and commitment and with the cooperation of similarly committed group members. We stressed how an awareness of group roles and processes can help you understand and succeed in your group activities. At the same time, we stressed that you can benefit even from problem groups by noting how your problems were overcome, and that you use such reflections in a formal group review and in your job applications. We compared success in group assignments with success in any assignment, making links with the ten-step plan, prepare and review strategy introduced in Chapter 13. Finally, we suggested that where group activities require a formal reflective account, you will complete a really successful one if you draw on the information in Chapter 15, on the reflective essay. Good luck with your group activities. Enjoy your group work – groups really can be supportive, exciting and productive.

If you are interested in this topic, you may wish to have a look at the following:

Adair, J. (1983) *Effective Leadership*. London: Pan Books.

Adair, J. (1987) *Effective Teambuilding: How to Make a Winning Team*. London: Pan Books.

Adair, J. (1987) *Not Bosses but Leaders: How to Lead the Way to Success*. London: Kogan Page.

Belbin, R.H. (1981) *Management Teams: Why they Succeed or Fail*. London: Heinemann.

http://www.learnhigher.ac.uk/learningareas/Group_Work.html

Review points

When thinking about what you have read and the activities that you have engaged in, you might feel that you have:

- developed an awareness of the forms and processes of group work, so that you are in a position to make the most of group activities in the future
- developed an awareness of the potential of group work in the academic environment
- developed an awareness of how to use your group-work experiences at college or university to improve your job applications. You now put group-work notes into your CV folder and your reflective essay folder.

8

How to be creative in your learning

AIMS

To introduce you to creative aspects to learning, with a special emphasis on brainstorming and question matrixing (see also Chapter 12, How to make the best notes).

LEARNING OUTCOMES

It is hoped that by the end of working through this chapter, you will have:
• realised the importance of creative learning strategies
• been introduced to creative assignment preparation techniques – the brainstorm and the question matrix.

Introduction

Much of the advice given in this book with respect to active learning strategies, skills, techniques and practices is logical, rational and straightforward. Such techniques can turn learning and studying around for you, so that your learning becomes effective, satisfying and successful. In this chapter, we are taking this a step further. Logical strategies are fantastic, they will make all the difference in themselves, but to really shine, to go that one step further, everyone also needs to build creativity into their learning.

Why be creative?

Some people do not see the need to be creative in their studies. Perhaps it just seems like more hard work, perhaps they think that their subject does not need creativity, or maybe they feel that this is a whole new area that they wish would just go away and leave them alone! However, we have found that students really do benefit from creative thinking. For one thing, it can make things feel lighter and more fun, for another it stretches and develops another part of you – and this is a good thing in itself. However, we would like you to feel really positive about being creative when you study, so we have gathered a few arguments here – read them through and see what you think.

Use all your brain

Buzan's work on the psychology of learning tells us that there are two parts to the brain: the logical left and the creative right. Learning strategies that are rational and logical work well with the left part of the brain, but this has its limitations. Buzan, for example, calls this monotonous learning, as in monotone, one-colour learning. He criticises this learning as being ineffectual because it only utilises one half of the brain, and this means it is both limiting and boring. To exploit the way that our brains actually work, we have to involve the right side of the brain by being creative. Buzan follows his argument with advice on a notemaking technique that he calls 'mind mapping'. We will follow the argument through by exploring a creative, pattern notemaking system in Chapter 12 and brainstorming and question-matrixing techniques, below.

Play with it

Graham Gibbs, in his work on teaching students how to learn, has another argument that connects to creative learning strategies. Gibbs tells us that the word 'knowledge', which has Greek and Norse roots, actually means to 'have sport with ideas', that is, to play with ideas. If we cannot play with the ideas with which we are engaging as students, we will never be able to use them with confidence, hence we will not make them our own.

Typically, when we approach new subjects, we might be over-awed by them – and a natural response, as we mention elsewhere, is to think something along the lines of 'Who am I to challenge all this?' And yet if we do challenge and question and generally play with ideas, we will learn them; if we don't, we won't.

This is why we encourage you to adopt a creative (pattern) notemaking system for recording your ideas, for making notes during research and in the process of brainstorming your assignments. These things are all designed to allow you to open up ideas and to introduce elements of colour and the bizarre. They are in their very nature playful, and encourage you to play with the ideas you are learning.

Active and significant learning

All the way through this text we place an emphasis on you becoming an active learner in control of your own learning. However, it can be very easy to feel trapped by the very nature of academic practice. How can you say what you want when you have to say it a certain way, or you have to read so many things before you can even give an opinion of your own?

Carl Rogers, humanist, psychologist and teacher, addressed this by emphasising that significant learning takes place when students reach out for what they want and need when learning. We argue that creative approaches can help you to identify what it is that you want and need from your course. Yes, you will still have to read those set texts, and you will still have to frame your answers in certain ways. You will have to get to grips with academic practice. But getting an original angle on a question (brainstorming and question matrixing); seeking out original things to research and read; and then recording information in your own original and creative way – these things may help you to make the course your own.

Common sense

One last justification that we would like to offer for creative learning also touches on the notion of active learning, or the lack of it. Without a creative approach, the student is in danger of becoming (or remaining) a passive learner, only using information in the way that other people have used it. Because they have not used a creative notemaking system, but have passively recorded what others have said, and the way that they have said it, these students get trapped into other people's thought processes.

If you become trapped into using information in the way that other people have used it, you are in danger of producing assignments that only give back to the tutor what s/he has said and what s/he has recommended that you read. Obviously, this is neither active nor significant learning. But it gets worse.

Something that just passively parrots-back information to the tutor will at best only gain you an average grade. It is also really boring for the tutor. Imagine the tutor with 150 assignments to mark, all of them only giving back what s/he has said? Only using the examples that were used in the lecture? Only citing the books that the tutor recommended?

It is the assignment that has gone somewhere different, that has found an original example or illustration, that has put ideas together in an original way that will catch the tutor's eye, that will make them smile. And, oh what a relief from reading those 149 other essays that all say the same thing! Thus, at this very practical, common-sense level, it is good to be creative.

How can I be creative?

Some people believe that you are either born creative or you are not – in the same way that much of education is predicated upon the belief that you are either born a good student or you are not. But just as we argued that everyone can rehearse successful study techniques and thus learn how to be a successful student, so we argue that everyone can learn creative learning styles and with practice become more creative.

In Chapter 12, we go on to explore this with respect to notemaking, but here we look at creative ways of approaching assignment questions – the brainstorm and the matrix.

If you have not tried these techniques before, we will be asking you to change or adapt your learning style. And, as always, you might find that change uncomfortable. No one likes to be uncomfortable, even more so perhaps in the educational context, where, for so many of us, everything already feels so strange and uncomfortable. Try to reassure yourself that the discomfort will pass, and that the benefits of these strategies, in terms of improvements in your ability to study and learn – and in the grades that you will get for your work – will more than compensate you for the discomfort that you are experiencing.

Creative approaches to assignments

We have already advised brainstorming as a preparatory focusing exercise, designed to help you notice what you do and do not know on a topic, about which you are to read or on which you have a lecture. Indeed, we have practised these brainstorms with you several times already – from your original skills questionnaire to all the little brainstorms inserted just before a new topic in this book. Now we are going to explore how you can use this creative technique when approaching your assignments – specifically, we will look again at brainstorming and move on to consider question matrixing.

The brainstorm

The idea behind the brainstorm is to open up the creative side of your mind. It involves the use of a word-association process that operates without censorship and preconceptions. We have already used the brainstorming device as a focusing activity: the 'What do I already know on this topic? What do I need to know?' questions. Therefore, you should have started to familiarise your brain with this technique. When using brainstorming on an assignment topic, the strategy is to brainstorm all the key words in the question, allowing as many ideas as possible to float into your mind.

The trick is to respond immediately and not to censor your thoughts. Sometimes a thought might appear silly, irrelevant or frivolous. It may be that the thought seems odd, with no place in an academic context. Yet, it may be just that silly or odd thought that leads you on to a really bright or original idea.

Following up that idea is what will make your assignment clever, even unique. When our work has that spark of originality, when it is that bit different from all the other assignments that are dropping on to a tutor's desk, then we may gain the attention of the tutor – we may even gain a higher mark. Below, we have a diagram of a brainstorm (Figure 8.1) and an information box: Beginner's guide to brainstorming the question.

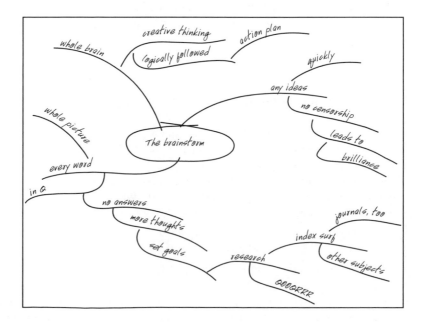

FIGURE 8.1   The brainstorm

Beginner's guide to brainstorming the question

Try this brainstorming strategy with one of your assignments and see how well it works for you.

The trick with an assignment question is to brainstorm every single word in the question.

1 Write the whole question in the middle of a really large sheet of paper – A1 is best.
2 Do not abbreviate the question. Any word that you do not write is a research avenue that you do not explore – this could well mean marks that you have thrown away.
3 Look at all the words in the question. Circle or underline the key words. Draw a line from each word.
4 Write anything and everything that comes to mind when you look at a word.
5 When you have finished, move on and do the same to another word. Keep this up until you have tackled all the words in the question.
6 Then go round again – even more ideas might pop out.v

Tips:
- Do this with another student (a study partner, if you have one).
- It gets easier with practice.
- Practise ten-minute brainstorms with every question in your module/course handbook. Choose to actually answer the question that gave you the most interesting brainstorm.

Query: Is this how you would usually approach your assignments? If so, you are already using useful creative learning strategies. If not, why not move on to the brainstorming activity below?

Activity 1: Practice brainstorm

We have given you a very small study–skills question to practise on:
Write the question out for yourself in the middle of a large sheet of paper.
Underline the key words.
Then brainstorm (jot down all those ideas) for about ten minutes.
When you have finished, compare your brainstorm with ours.
Remember two things:

1 There is no right or wrong when it comes to the brainstorm.
2 Brainstorming, like most other skills, gets easier with practice.

The question: Evaluate the usefulness of pattern notes to a student.

▶

Tip: Spend ten minutes on this initial brainstorm and then move on.

Query:
- How do you feel it went for a first attempt?
- What will you do next?

Discussion: Was your brainstorm similar to or different from ours? Did looking at our one give you more ideas for your own? It would be great if that were so, for we do argue that working with someone else, and here you would have been working with us, gives you more ideas overall. If you were actually going to write an essay on this question, you should now have ideas from both brainstorms, and be in a very strong position to decide just what you would read in order to get your answer ready. Now have a look at the section on the question matrix, below.

Now have a look at our example, in Figure 8.2.

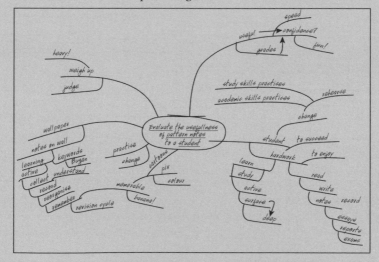

FIGURE 8.2   Brainstorm of activity question

The question matrix

Like the brainstorm, the question matrix (QM) is designed to open up a question, and hopefully let some creativity in. Some people see the QM as a more structured form of brainstorm.

As with the brainstorm, when using a QM, you should write the whole question out, preferably on a really large sheet of paper, underline all the key words, then generate a question matrix off each word. This involves turning all the key words in a question into a series of smaller questions – not answers!

One problem with assignment questions is that they push us to start looking for answers too soon. The point of the question matrix is to generate more questions before we even begin to think of answers. You can then investigate, research or read around all the smaller questions you have generated to get your brain working on the whole assignment. This research will lead you to gather the information that will result in your answering of the whole question. See Figure 8.3 for a QM on 'the question matrix'.

Tip: When generating our smaller questions, it is quite useful to use the journalism questions (five Ws and an H):

Who   Why   When   Where   What   How

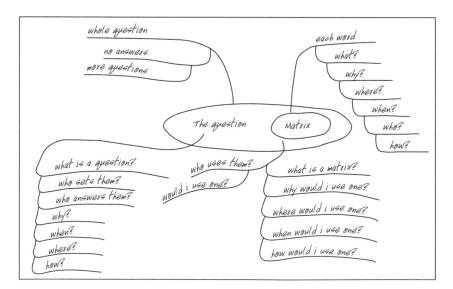

FIGURE 8.3   The question matrix

Discussion: Obviously, there are not very many words in 'the question matrix', however, you can see that even these few words could generate an awful lot of questions to follow up; this is very useful when you look at a topic and your mind just goes blank. Now have a go at performing a matrix on a sample question below

Activity 2: Draw up a question matrix

You have already performed a brainstorm – now use the who, what, when, where, why and how questions to unpack the following question. Then compare your results with the example below. Note, the QM technique gets easier with practice.

   We have given a very small study-skills question to practise on:

☐ Write the whole question out in the middle of a very large sheet of paper.
☐ Underline the key words.
☐ QM all the key words.
☐ When you have finished, compare your QM to ours (Figure 8.4).
☐ Remember – it will get easier with practice.

The question: Evaluate the usefulness of positive thinking to a student.

Again, we suggest that you spend ten minutes on this before moving on to compare your effort with ours, below.

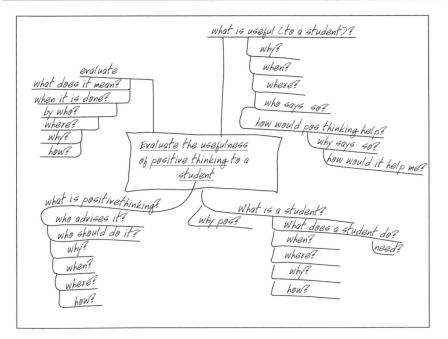

FIGURE 8.4   Question matrix on the sample question

Query:

- How do you feel after a first attempt?
- Is your matrix similar to or different from ours?
- Has this given you more ideas to follow up?
- What will you do next?

How did it go?

Once you have completed your first attempts at brainstorming and question matrixing here, move on to use these creative techniques on your assignment questions. Once you have tried the process for a while, remember to reflect on how the strategies worked for you.

Reflection questions:

- What has brainstorming/question matrixing been like?
- What do you like about these techniques?
- What do you dislike about these techniques?
- What will you do next?
- When will you do it?

Activity 3: Keep practising!

We have argued that both brainstorming and question-matrixing techniques do get easier with practice. The best thing that you can now do is to use these techniques a lot.

1 Go to one of your module/course handbooks, preferably one that offers a range of questions from which you have to choose an assignment to do.
2 Choose between three and six questions to work on.
3 Allow yourself ten minutes per question for either a brainstorm or a question matrix. Remember the journalism questions: who, when, what, why, where and how.
4 When you have finished, reflect again – how do you now feel about these techniques?

> **Tip:** These activities work much better with other people (a study partner or a study group). If you have not got a group, why not take your ideas to your university's Learning Development or Writing Support Unit, and see if someone there will compare notes with you?

Conclusion

This chapter has dealt with the notion of bringing creativity into your learning process. We looked at the importance of playing with ideas when learning, and stressed that creative techniques will help you be active in your own learning. We further argued that creativity can promote significant learning and also, because it helps you be original with assignments, it facilitates a sense of ownership. We referred you to a pattern notemaking system in Chapter 12, and you should have practised that at least once by now, and here we looked at brainstorming and question-matrixing techniques. As creative processes, these can really open up an assignment, so that you will cover the whole question in a creative way.

▶

This section of the book is deceptively short! Do not be fooled by that! Many students have told us that creative notemaking has changed their lives – and their grades – and that brainstorming meant that they actually saw the question for the first time. It is now up to you to try these things for yourself and see.

Further reading

If you are interested in taking the ideas in this chapter further, you might try the following:

Buzan, T. (1989) *Use Your Head*. London: BBC publications.
Buzan, B. and Buzan, T. (1999) *The Mind Map Book*. London: BBC publications.
Gibbs, G. and Makeshaw, T. (1992) *53 Interesting Things to Do in Your Lectures*. Bristol: Technical and Educational Services.
Palmer, R. and Pope, C. (1984) *Brain Train: Studying for Success*. Bristol: Arrowsmith.
Rogers, C. (1992) *Freedom to Learn*. Upper Saddle River, NJ: Merrill.
Rose, C. and Goll, L. (1992) *Accelerate Your Learning*. Aylesbury: Accelerated Learning Systems.

Review points

When reflecting on this chapter, you might notice that:
- you do realise the potential of creative learning strategies
- you have been reminded of creative notemaking, and made links between creative learning and active learning
- you have practised creative assignment preparation techniques – the brainstorm and the question matrix – and you will now use them on your assignments.

9

How to deal with your emotions

AIMS

To consider the emotional aspect of studying, with a particular focus on building self-confidence.

LEARNING OUTCOMES

It is intended that after reading this chapter and engaging in the activities set, you will have:
- reviewed the nature of the academic environment
- discussed from where fear and a lack of self-confidence might stem
- considered the importance of self-confidence and assertiveness for you as a student
- explored some steps that you might take to reduce your stress and improve your own self-confidence and assertiveness in the academic environment.

First-day experiences

'Panicky! Suddenly it hits you, because you feel that everyone is looking at you, which is stupid because no one is looking at you. But I remember coming up the steps and all these people are sitting down, and I felt everybody was staring at me and saying, why is that old woman coming here?'

'I felt very self-conscious, and terrified that I couldn't find the room. I saw this enormous building and it really scared me' ... It's frightening.'

'So I get half-way through and I say, why, why, why can't I just be happy going to work and going home? Why did I start this? I can't bear it!'

'I was desperate – I was very nervous. And, the more nervous you are, the less you pick up things. You can't listen and you want everything to go in and nothing's going in. So the first module was awful. . .'

'I was quite frightened and I think most of the students were as well! And after I spoke to and got to know a few students we realised that, even though some of the students were sounding confident, they were quite anxious and worried and frightened themselves.'

'It was really nerve-racking sitting in this room . . . I did feel nervous, but I thought you're here now, they can't kill you and you can run away if you don't like it.'

Fear, positive thinking and the student

In this chapter, we are going to explore the all-too-human dimension of studying: the emotional elements of being a student. In particular, we will be looking at the roles that fear and positive thinking can play in student success.

As someone who has chosen to be a student, you have entered an academic environment that may or may not seem strange to you. You have committed yourself to a programme of study – as such, you will be expected to understand the nature of your subject and what is involved for you as a student of that subject.

You have to establish and manipulate the key knowledge claims of your subject; you have to discover, and recognise the contribution made, by the key 'people' in your discipline; and you have to master the epistemological practices (the argument and evidence modes) of your subject.

You will be expected to attend lectures and seminars; you will be expected to undertake independent research, and to read around your subject. As part of making material your own, you will be expected to make useable notes of what you see, hear and do. From time to time, you will be expected to demonstrate your learning in assignments – written and oral – and in exams.

While the overall goal of all this activity is that you become a confident initiate into your subject – a graduate – many of the stages and processes involved in becoming this new, confident person can actually feel quite intimidating. Some are so intimidated that they give up on study altogether.

How does being a student make you feel?

We know that actively developing study and academic skills and practices will promote success and thus increase student self-confidence, and this is the goal of much of this book. But our work with students has shown us that directly focusing on and building self-confidence and self-esteem in students can immediately and dramatically affect their achievement, and that is the goal of this chapter.

It is our intention to reduce stress and anxiety by introducing you to strategies for increasing your self-confidence and self-esteem in the academic environment. In particular, we will explore the relationship between self-confidence and student success. We will move on to examine what causes fear and why we experience fear. Finally, we will cover some very practical things to do to overcome fear and build self-confidence and self-esteem.

'After we did that session on positive thinking, I went back to work and was able to speak up in a meeting for the very first time.'

'Not only did that session help me with my presentation, I was able to pass my driving test, first go.'

Confidence and study skills make a difference

A late 1990s research project at Oxford University investigated why, given the universal high A Level qualifications of the student intake, some students went on to get first-class degrees while others did not.

They found that different students had very different attitudes to studying. More importantly, it was the students with self-confidence who achieved the higher grades.

Students speak up

Here are the students quoted above (first day experiences) after a few weeks on their courses, and having had an opportunity to learn and rehearse their study and academic skills:

'It is part of my life now. In fact, I think I'm quite a sad person, because when the essay's done and handed in, I have to go and put the computer on and stroke it.'

'I had some anxieties . . . that were partly about my writing skills and structuring essays and a few other things . . . . I had a lot of anxiety over that . . . . So I came to study skills. And it all started making sense, and when it made sense, it all fell into place. And it sort of opened up a new world of knowledge for me as well . . .'

'In the beginning, you are all so shy and you're all very self-conscious, but as I said, we all feel the same, but because we don't talk to each other, we don't know that the other person feels exactly the same . . . . Now, it's a great feeling, you belong now; you are part of the university. The whole thing belongs to me. It's my university now.'

> **Tip:** No matter how anxious you may be feeling, you can turn that around and build your self-confidence. Read on.

Does it affect our work?

Do you think that a runner will achieve more by running along, thinking, 'I am a failure, I cannot possibly win!' or 'I am a success, I see myself winning this race!'? I think that most of us would agree that the runner who thinks and feels like a success has more chance of winning a race than the one who thinks and feels like a failure. Of course, the physical conditions have to be there, the training, the diet, etc., but basically, for the runner to do well, they must want to do well and must believe that it is possible to do well: they must have self-belief and self-confidence.

Tip: For more information on the role of self-belief in learning, see information on the research of Albert Bandura on self-efficacy: http://www.des.emory.edu/mfp/self-efficacy.html.

Activity 1: Reactions to studying

Take a few moments to read and respond to the following statement, and then write down your reactions to the statement.

'It is in order to return at this point to Jameson's "loss of the referent" theme, because it is precisely this phenomenology of the everyday that Jameson's work both lacks and consciously relegates to the ethnographic sidelines.' (Feather, H, 2000, *Intersubjectivity and Contemporary Social Theory*, p. 135)

Now compare your reactions with those gathered from some other students:

- I got really really angry! Why on earth do they have to write like that? It's stupid.
- This is strange and scary; but it's where I've got to get to.
- I read it several times trying to make sense of it.
- I used my dictionary of literary terms and tried to make sense of it piece by piece.
- It made me feel like giving up; it's obvious that I'm not welcome here.
- Well, I just laughed and laughed. They've got to be joking, haven't they?

Query:
- Were any of these reactions like your own?
- What do you notice about these reactions?
- Perhaps you noticed that there was a whole range of reactions to the statement?

Discussion: We are not arguing that there are right or wrong reactions, just different ones. However, when we are in a particular situation, we often feel that our feelings about that situation – and our reactions to it – are the only possible feelings and the only possible reactions. We do not know that there is any choice involved at all. Surely, if such and such happens, the only possible response is . . . ?

And, yet, you can see from the students we spoke to that what moves one student to fury makes another laugh. What makes one student resolved to progress makes another feel as though they ought to give up.

Once we realise that reactions to situations can vary, then we can begin to realise that there might be some choice involved in how we react. When we realise this, then we can start to build on our positive reactions and overcome our negative ones.

What is true for the runner is also true for students. You must want to do well and believe that it is possible for you to do well. You, too, must have self-belief and self-confidence. Yes, the study and academic skills and practices have to be learned and rehearsed, but a positive mental attitude will mean that you can become successful.

What, emotions count, even at university?

Human beings are rounded – they are made up of many facets: cognition, intellect, effect and emotion, feelings and affect. Our intellect and our emotions can both play a part in every aspect of our lives, including that of being a student. There is a danger in thinking that because studying is an academic, intellectual activity, there is no room for the emotional dimension. But you cannot abolish part of yourself as a human being, just because it does not seem to fit. In fact, it can be the very ignoring of our emotional side that causes the problem; for what we ignore or deny, we cannot deal with.

Activity 2: Thinking about positive thinking – SWOT analysis

Take a few moments to think about positive thinking and your reaction to the proposition that you might be able to affect how you feel about being a student. Now answer the following questions:

- Strengths: as a student, what are you confident about? What are you looking forward to? What are you enjoying right now?
- Weaknesses: what are you unconfident about? What causes you stress? What do you fear?
- Opportunities: what do you feel about developing your self-confidence? What opportunities are there in this for you as a student?
- Threats: do you feel threatened by the thought of changing your reactions? What are the dangers in this to you as a student?

When you have completed this activity, discuss your responses with your study partner or a friend.

> *Discussion:* Perhaps you noticed that there are opportunities for you in developing your positive thinking? You might have realised that a positive attitude will help you face academic tasks as challenges rich with opportunity.
>
> On the other hand, you might be a bit frightened of this choice. You know who you are at the moment and you do not want to change. Change is uncomfortable. Maybe you are doing OK in your work, but the thought of success terrifies you, for you do not know all the implications of this for you.
>
> These are all normal feelings. Change will mean entering the unknown – and success may well be a new experience for you – but you can learn to face this positively as well!

▶

> Tip: If this exercise has really unsettled you, or if you have identified areas that look as though they might give you problems or cause for concern, go to see someone at your college or university: for example, your personal or academic tutor, the study support people or the counselling service.

There are many things in the educational environment that will affect you emotionally as a student and as a human being. We hope that some of them will excite, stimulate and even thrill you. Others may frighten, intimidate or horrify you. It is important to notice what is happening to your feelings when you are studying. Where possible, try to do something about your feelings as a student. Ideally, it is advisable to harness your positive feelings and work to overcome your negative ones.

The feeling student

The above activities are designed to illustrate that, as human beings, our feelings will play a role in our lives as students. Negative feelings can actually prevent us from working to our best ability. At the same time, changing our feelings may not be entirely problem-free, but that does not mean that you should not do it. Let us now move on to explore the role of fear in our lives; in particular, we will look at what we are frightened of, where fear comes from and things to do to build self-confidence.

What are you frightened of?

What are we actually frightened of? We're not talking about phobias here (like a crippling fear of spiders or heights), but the sorts of things that make you feel uncomfortable or that you tend to avoid; things that make you sweat or cause you the odd sleepless night, and so forth.

All human beings are frightened of many things. Generally, we are all frightened of the new; we are frightened of change. We may be frightened of ageing, disease and death. More mundanely, we may be frightened of picking up the telephone . . . of entering a library . . . of writing our first essay . . . of giving a presentation . . . of anything and everything. All these fears are completely normal, and yet they can be very inconvenient for us as human beings, and especially awkward for us as students.

Let's face it, to undertake to become a student is to undertake to change. But this change does involve risk – we do not know all the implications of these changes for us as human beings. Risk is frightening. Yet, the only way to avoid risk is to do nothing at all, and this really is not an option for you, either as a student or as a human being.

It's just me!

It could be argued that there is another dimension to this fear, and that is that whenever we are frightened at school, college or university, we tend to feel that we are the only ones that are frightened. We feel alone in our fear, and that just makes it feel worse. We look at other people and they look fine – they don't feel what we feel. This is especially true for new students. When we ask new students how they are feeling, they all say that they are scared. And every scared one thinks that they are the only one carrying this burden.

Tutors as students

'I had been teaching for many years when I took a higher degree programme. All the students on the programme were lecturers like myself, and I thought that they all knew what they were doing, but I did not.

When I sat down in my first seminar and the tutor asked us a question, I went red, my heart pounded so much I felt that everyone else must hear it, and I absolutely would not volunteer a comment – I was too frightened to look, sound or feel a fool. I found myself experiencing exactly the same fears as my students. The fact that I was also a tutor did not help at all.

Later in the course, another student asked, "What on earth does 'overarching syntagmatics' mean?" We all looked at each other and we all laughed. We realised that none of us knew, and that we had all been too scared to admit it. We then decided to do something about this.

It was most probably easier for us as tutors to do something about our fears. For once we knew we all had the same fears, we did know what to do. We had an idea of what might work for us as students.

This is what we did – we:

- formed study groups
- met to discuss our thoughts on the difficult texts we had to read
- read one another's draft essays to give critical feedback
- read one another's finished essays to get extra ideas for our exams.

Suddenly, the whole course was more enjoyable, and all our experiences were more positive.'

> *Discussion:* What worked for the lecturer above can work for you. This is why we continually urge you to work with a study partner, and why we explore group/team work in Chapter 7.

We are in all the same boat

From our experiences as students, as tutors and as tutors who are also students, we can assure you that everyone tends to feel fear when they start studying. It is normal to be scared of the challenge of becoming a student. It is natural to feel scared if you do not feel like an academic. It is not shameful – it does not mean that you are not cut out for studying – and you really, really are not alone. Everyone else is feeling just the same as you.

Activity 3: The fearful student

- Can you think of any situation where you have let your fears stop you?
- What do you think about that now?
- Are there any aspects of your studying that fill you with fear?

▶

- Why don't you – and your study partner – make a list of all the things that frighten you about studying; then score each item on your lists from 0–9 depending on how fearful they make you? Compare lists with each other.
- What do your lists tell you about yourselves?
- What do they tell you about your fears?

One of the most liberating things about this exercise is to realise that you are not alone in your fear. It can also be reassuring that people have different fears from you. Make some notes to yourself about what you gained from this exercise.

Self-help

You may like to follow up some of the ideas that you find here on positive thinking by reading some more on your own. There are many books on positive thinking in bookshops and libraries that are all dedicated to helping people overcome their fearsand, in the process, to learn how to face life's challenges more positively. Some of these may appeal to you, and we know that the one that our students particularly like is by Susan Jeffers (1987), *Feel the Fear and Do It Anyway*.

> **Tip:** When doing extra reading, you will find that you like some books more than others, that you like some authors' writing style, but you definitely do not like the way others write at all. That is OK – the trick is to experiment until you find something that does appeal to you.

However, we have written this section of the book to introduce you to the ideas of positive thinking, such that you can begin to change things for your-self right away. In particular, we are looking at the relationship between fear and self-confidence.

Activity 4: Think about it

Can you remember times when you have worried and worried over a particular thing, perhaps for months – even for years – and then the thing happened?

- What was it like?
- What about all the things that you worried about that did not happen?
- What was that like?

> *Discussion:* It is said that 90 per cent of what we worry about just does not happen at all. It is really silly to spend our lives worrying. Developing a positive outlook can improve your whole life, not just your life as a student. But, at the moment, we are looking at this with respect to being a student. Being a student can be scary, especially as many of the things that we worry about will actually happen to us. We will have to understand the subject and make those notes. We will have to write those essays and give those presentations. Becoming more positive about yourself will help you as a student.

Believe in yourself

The overarching theme of most positive-thinking books is that fear boils down to a lack of self-confidence and a lack of faith in ourselves. The argument is that we fear things because we believe that we will not be able to cope with them. We think life will defeat us. And yet, consider the things that we do achieve as human beings.

We managed to learn our language. If we are able-bodied, we learned how to walk. We learned the behaviour that was expected of us in different situations – in the family, with our friends, in school, at work. We managed to go to school and survive that. Many of us then went on to get jobs, and maybe even raise families. All of these activities, and many more, we did eventually take in our stride – no matter how much we feared them beforehand.

Overall, we tend to be much more resilient than we give ourselves credit for. In the end, whatever life chooses to throw at us, we cope with it. Sometimes, we even cope spectacularly well. All we tend to do by doubting ourselves is actually make it more difficult to cope, not easier. Surely, it is not life that we need to fear, but fear itself? All we do when we listen to – or, worse, give in to – our fears is to damage our own lives.

Students do it in the dark

But can all this worry make us better students? Well, in our experience, the typical answer is no.

We worry about exams so much that we are too scared to prepare for them. Surprise, surprise – we often do badly in our exams.

We worry about the final assessment on a course so much, we are too frightened to look at the question. Suddenly, instead of having 15 weeks to slowly work on the assignment and really get to grips with it, we only have two days to prepare the assignment. And, no, we do not achieve the best mark possible for that assignment.

We worry for six months about that presentation that we have to give – it spoils our days and nights – our whole lives. Suddenly, it is over. We did not go up in a puff of smoke, and we found that we survived after all.

What was the point of all that worry? All it does is blight your life. And it literally blights your life as a student, for it means that you do not give of your best and you do not work to your best advantage.

We have to learn to pass though our fear – not to live with it.

Why do we experience fear? But, you might argue, surely this fear is there for a purpose? If not, where does it come from? Why do we have it? Evolutionary, cognitive and popular (pop) psychology all have something to say in this debate.

The Psychological Dimensions of Fear

Evolutionary psychology

Simon Baron-Cohen (1997) argues that fear, anxiety and even depression are a legacy of our animal evolution. He points out that when an animal is on unfamiliar territory, it is in danger of its life. As human beings, we also have this fear; we, too, are frightened when on unfamiliar territory. But more than that, as humans, we have a consciousness. Consciousness means that we are aware of ourselves in ways that no animal is. Birds looking around nervously on a bird table are not aware that they are nervous. They just are.

However, as conscious human beings, we are aware of our own nervousness and fear. We can focus on and really be obsessive about our fears – this is what makes fear so dangerous for us.

Remember, to be human is to constantly move onto unfamiliar territory. This means that we are constantly moving into fearful situations. The more we focus on our fear response rather than the situation, the more we are in danger of avoiding the things that make us frightened. We need to be able to face our fears in order to deal with the unfamiliar, and to grow.

Cognitive psychology

Bandura's work on self-efficacy indicates that a complex interplay of personal, environmental and behavioural factors, including one's family background, class, gender and ethnic group, will influence how we will feel in any given situation.

Some of us will avoid risk, danger and failure; others will relish those things. Some of us are prepared to persevere and push through problems; others will easily feel defeated and give up.

In terms of being a student, if we are from a group that traditionally does well in education, it will be easier for us to see ourselves also doing well; while, if we are from a group that traditionally does not succeed in education, it will be more difficult for us to see ourselves as succeeding.

Popular psychology

In popular psychology, Susan Jeffers (1987), for example, argues that we are accidentally taught fear in the way that we are brought up. You might remember:

- 'Mind how you cross the road.'
- 'Don't go climbing that tree.'
- 'Don't talk to strangers.'
- 'Don't go too fast.'
- 'Are you sure you can manage that?'
- 'Let me do that for you.'

When people say these things to us, they are really just expressing their fear ('I don't want anything bad to happen to you'); but what we hear, and internalise, is that they think that we are inadequate. This can have far-reaching consequences. It can be terribly damaging to our self-confidence to feel that the person who loves us most in the world does not think much of us. They must think we are pretty useless if they believe that we cannot even cross the road without their advice.

The fear within

Here, notions of self-belief and pop psychology overlap. For, just as Bandura notes that we acquire or do not acquire self-belief from our environments, including our social and familial environments, so Jeffers argues that the external warning voice of our carers becomes our own internal negative voice. We no longer need anyone else to criticise and doubt us – we can do it for ourselves. Eventually, it can be that every time we are faced with something new, a little voice pipes up inside, saying: Watch out! Why are you doing that? You'll only fail! You'll only look silly ...

This can be especially so if you are a student, for there will be so many new things to face, and if we see them all only as opportunities to fail, we will never get the most from them. Further, consider the role of mistakes in our learning. We really do have to learn by a process of trial and error, by making mistakes and learning from them. But if the thought of making mistakes makes us feel so bad that we feel like giving up, we are not going to do well. We have to work to overcome this. Face studying as an adventure, and realise that you will live through your mistakes and learn from them.

But I'm not really an academic

An accent on fear and a lack of self-confidence can be particularly harmful if you are a student but you do not feel like a student; if you are in an academic environment and you do not feel like an academic. And, given that these days, more and more 'non-traditional' students are entering higher education, this could be an issue affecting a very high proportion of students indeed. If this does describe how you are feeling right now, you will have to work to overcome your own negative feelings. You are a student. You have been accepted onto a degree pro-gramme. If you are interested and motivated, and you do the work, you can succeed, and you will grow into the role of an academic.

Do these thoughts on fear make any sense to you? Can you now review the fears that you noted before in a different light? Make some notes to remind yourself and read on.

Can we do anything to overcome fear and build self-confidence?

Obviously, the whole tone of this section – as with the book as a whole – is leading you to believe that you can do something about this state of affairs. Here, we are going to take a leaf out of the self-help type book and look at re-framing fear; taking responsibility for our lives; adopting a positive vocabulary; making positive friends; and utilising positive statements.

Re-framing fear

We have argued above that fear, while often uncomfortable, is a perfectly natural and normal response to life, especially to new or unfamiliar situations. What we can do is change our response to that fear. Fear does not have to mean run and hide under the duvet; it can actually mean some-thing completely different. Here are some new ways to look at fear; see if they help you at all.

- **Fear is good:** fear is OK, it is part of growth and doing new things. Fear does not mean, 'This is not for me!'. Instead, fear means that you are doing something new, you are facing a new challenge, you are taking a risk – and that is OK too, because that is all part of growing and changing. Thus, when we feel fear, we should celebrate the fact that we are growing and changing. This is a good thing, not a bad one.
- **Fear affects everyone:** fear really does affect everyone and realising that we are not alone in our fears can actually help. If Baron-Cohen is to be believed, everyone feels fear when on unfamiliar territory. Everyone experiences fear when they do something new. Realising that we are not alone in our fears can take away the stigma of fear; it does not mean that we are cowards, just that we are human. Once we accept this, we can move on.

- **The only way to get rid of the fear of something is to do it** ... the quicker the better: fear can be overcome and the only way to get rid of the fear of doing something is to do it – quickly. You know that this is true. You can spend months worrying about something, and then it takes two minutes to do it. Let's get rid of those months of worry – do it now: you know it makes sense!
- **It is easier to face fear than to live with it:** it really is easier to do what we fear than to keep living with the fear. Again, you know this is true already. The more we give in to fear, the more fearful we become. So, every time you decide to face a fear, remind yourself that this is not a hardship – you are taking the easier option.
- **It takes practice:** re-framing fear in these ways may not come naturally to you. However, with practice you will find that you can face fear differently, and it will make a big difference, especially to the way that you face the challenge of being a successful student.

We can take responsibility for our own lives

As well as re-framing fear, we can re-frame our whole lives. One way of doing this is to really embrace responsibility for ourselves. What do you think this means? We argued above that we can begin to take responsibility for our emotional response to events. Just because something normally causes us to feel angry or scared, does not mean that it has to continue to do so. We can work on our responses to events, and try to change our instinctive (or learned) responses and do something else. One of the most powerful things that we can do is to take responsibility for our own lives.

I'm not a number

Taking responsibility means dropping forever a victim mentality: the 'It's not my fault, it's his or hers or theirs!' syndrome. Now we all know that neither society nor nature is necessarily fair. But if we keep blaming everyone else for what happens to us, we end up being trapped in circumstances, instead of being able to rise above them. And if we become trapped by life's events, we are the ones that suffer – no one else.

Remember, if it's their fault, there is nothing I can do to change things. If it's my responsibility, then there is something that I might be able to do to take control of events. I can look to see what I can do, what I can change, what effect I can have.

This is really important as a student. Look at your course, look at the work that you have to do, and do something about it. Discover how to learn and study more effectively; if you have not already done so, make use of the advice in the rest of this book. All that advice is designed to make you more effective and more successful as a student.

And start right now – try saying, I am responsible:

- for my decisions
- for my actions
- for getting my work in on time
- for getting good grades.

If these things matter to us, we can take steps to make them happen. It may take hard work and sweat, but we can do it.

If we don't do it, perhaps it is because these things do not really matter to us. We just say they do because it is expected of us, because it is what our parents, friends or partners want for us, or because it makes us look good. In the end, we will only do well in our studies if it is what we want. It is our work that has to make it happen, not anyone else's.

So, the next time you find yourself blaming someone, anyone, for something that you are not doing, stop and think again. What can you do to make it happen?

Develop a positive vocabulary

A really good way to develop a positive and responsible outlook is to develop a positive vocabulary. Just as we can re-frame fear so that it does not mean what it used to mean, so we can also change the way that we talk about the world. Here we are going to look at problems, disasters and choice.

'It's an opportunity'

A simple, unconscious negative framing of the world is when we always see new tasks or events as problems rather than opportunities. When we do this, we tend to always focus on the negative in any event, rather than on the possible good that will come out of it.

Most people do this much of the time, but it is a very unhelpful way of viewing the world, making everything we do seem that much harder. Imagine starting a new job – would you see that as a wonderful opportunity to meet new people and face new challenges? Or do you see it as more hard work? Do you just see how difficult it will all be?

The instant negative response can be especially damaging when we face all the things that we have to do as a student as problems rather than opportunities. Just think about all that reading and all those lectures – gulp! It is too easy just to think of this as an imposing mountain of hard work and struggle.

Why not try to re-frame your negative into a positive? Try to realise what a wonderful opportunity it is to have this time to devote to yourself and your studies. Being a student can be the best time of your life – a time when you can think and learn, when you can make new friends and try out new opportunities, a time to flourish.

Each positive thought will make your life easier; each negative thought that you have just makes your problems grow.

> *Query*: Was that instant negative thinker you? How does it make you feel? Will you try using the more positive language? When?

Start now!

Now is the time to try something different. Thus, if you normally say, 'That looks really hard!' when faced with a tough assignment, try to see it as an opportunity not a problem. Try saying, 'This is an excellent module, it is really challenging, and it takes me much nearer my overall goal'. This very simple and basic re-framing stops it feeling like a burden: once this stops, you can grow with the work rather than being crushed by it.

So, from this moment forward, instead of saying 'That's hard', try saying, 'That looks really interesting' or 'I'm really looking forward to this assignment'. And do not just try this once or twice and then give it up. Even though these positive statements may seem really strange at first, if you keep them up, you will find that they make a difference to how you feel about your work. This will then improve the work that you actually do. And, yes, this will mean that you have to start to accept a more positive you. You will have to accept a change in yourself.

> **Tip:** Give this positive re-framing a chance to work. Try not to fear the change in yourself. Try to like the new you – it is still you.

It's a learning experience

If problems can become opportunities, similarly, disasters can become fully blown learning experiences. This is a bit like the old adage, every cloud has a silver lining. Rarely is anything so bad that we cannot benefit from it in some way. Perhaps you lost your job? Surely that left you free to get a better one? Maybe you lost your home? Then there was the whole world of change and excitement open to you.

> *Query*: Has anything like this happened to you? How did you cope? What did you do? Hopefully, although it really felt like a disaster when it first happened, whatever it was, you did get something from it. Can you remember what that was?

So whatever happens to you as a student, see what you can learn from it:

- Did you get a lower grade than you expected for an assignment? Spend time trying to work out what went wrong.
- Were you unable to understand the question in your latest assignment? Well, ask for help and talk it over with a study partner.

For every 'disaster', there is a lesson to be learned. Indeed, we repeatedly urge you to learn from your mistakes. And an irritating but true fact is that we can actually learn much more from our mistakes than we ever can from what we just do well.

Imagine getting an excellent grade for your very first essay in a subject, but not knowing what you actually did right? This can be a very disorientating and disempowering experience. You can end up feeling more lost rather than less. But getting feedback on all the things that you did wrong in that assignment can tell you much that will help you in future assignments. Of course, this will only work if you do something about it – if you look for the learning experience and try to get something from it.

Being positive at university

And the choice really is yours – you can just choose to sit there and cry, and say 'If only . . .', or you can do something. So, instead of feeling sorry for yourself or blaming other people, or just giving up when things go wrong (and things will go wrong) make the effort to analyse the situation. Find out what went wrong, and notice exactly what you will have to do differently to make sure that next time it is a success.

For example, if you do get a really low grade, use all the relevant sections in this book that might help you do much better next time. In particular, you might look at:

- organisation and time management, so that you manage your time more effectively
- creative learning, so that you develop a brainstorming technique that will really open up an assignment question, and a pattern notemaking system so that your research is more active and useful
- reading academically, so that you develop targeted research and active reading skills and hence get much more from your reading
- the essay, report or presentation, so that you make sure you understand how to present your work most effectively.

I have a choice

Another really important re-framing of our vocabularies is to replace should (obligation) with could (choice). 'Should' is a big victim word: I should do my homework; I should visit the library . . .. Oh, and don't we feel sorry for ourselves and don't we make everyone suffer for it! Remember, you always have choice: you can do your homework, visit the library . . . or go to the cinema.

If you do your homework or go to the library, go with good grace and work really hard. If you go to the cinema, relax, have a good time and try not to worry about your work for one evening.

Remember that whatever we do or do not do, there is always a consequence, a price to pay. Accept that. It's just like when you choose whether or not to become a student. Choice has a price attached.

- If you do choose to become a student, there is a price to pay in terms of time, effort and commitment, and there are the rewards that you have decided for yourself.
- If you choose not to become a student, there is a different sort of price to pay – you may have more time, but maybe you will be stuck in a job that you do not like and which does not satisfy you.

Once you do choose to do something, accept that you have chosen to do it, accept the 'price', give 100 per cent and do it with good grace. If you do not do it, accept that, too.

Query: How does this sound to you? What implications does it have for you as a student? How will it change the way you behave as a student?

Changes, changes, changes

We are now moving on to consider how change for you might have an impact on those around you, and we will suggest that making positive friends can help you as a student. But first let us ask you: What is your family like? How do your friends view the world at the moment? Are all the people in your world full of energy and a zest for life? Or do they all sit around feeling unmotivated and basically sorry for themselves?

If it is the latter, then you will stick out like a sore thumb if you suddenly become all optimistic and positive. You will be treated rather strangely if suddenly you see opportunity everywhere instead of the problems that they all see. This can be a real challenge for the positive student of whatever age.

Younger students have peer pressure to deal with; for it is not really acceptable to be all positive and enthusiastic as a student. Everyone knows that students have to go around looking bored and suspicious all the time. Enjoying life is ridiculous and enjoying studying is just plain bonkers!

If everybody you know has a negative attitude to life and studying, it can be really difficult to be optimistic and positive. And it can take just too much energy to remain optimistic when all around you are miserable. Something has to give. It may be that in this company, you just slip back into being negative and uncommitted yourself, and this will cost you.

With the more mature students, while on the surface it may seem OK to be a committed and motivated student, they can find that their family and friends really resent them changing. For one thing, the new positive person just feels rather strange to them. They felt more comfortable with the old negative person – they knew who that was, they knew what to expect. They do not want this person to change. It is too uncomfortable.

Another thing is that the new person has new interests and commitments. Suddenly, they do not have as much time to give to their family and friends. Suddenly, the family members have to help with the shopping and the cooking. Friends discover that you do not always answer the phone, you cannot go out with them three nights a week, and you do not drop everything for a cup of tea whenever they feel like calling. This does not feel like a good change to them.

This student has to be very strong to keep to their commitments, and they will have to make a special effort to convince family and friends that it will all be worthwhile in the long run.

Gently does it

Now, we are not suggesting that the only way to deal with negative responses from family and friends is to be confrontational, or that you ought to give them all up. Rather, we want to alert you to the fact that you may encounter resentment as you do change, and you will need tact and diplomacy to help your family and friends to travel with you.

You will need to help your family and friends to accept and, hopefully, to get to like and appreciate the new you. If being the new positive student is important to you, it is important to bring your family and friends along with you. You may well encounter resistance at first – remember, they will not like change either – but if it is important to you, you have to work through this somehow.

Positive friends

Further, as we start to build ourselves up as positive people, it will help if we can make some positive friends. Positive friends can reinforce our new positive attitude; positive study partners can make the whole job of studying easier, more rewarding and much, much more enjoyable. And at a very simple level, positive people will not be using up your energy just to keep them afloat – you will be able to use your energy to progress.

Query: Change for you will have an impact on those around you – how do you propose to deal with this?

And finally . . . even more positive things to do

We have already argued that adopting a positive vocabulary can make a difference to how you view the world. In this last, long, section we are going to take that one step further by exploring some other positive things to do to build self-confidence.

Positive Vocabulary

If every time you face something new, that little voice in your mind seems to call out, 'Watch out! You'll be sorry! That's dangerous!', as Jeffers says, you will have to work to drown out that negative voice with a new positive one of your choosing. You have to learn to respond differently to the things that happen to you.

So, instead of immediately saying things like: 'I'll never be any good at that', start saying, 'I can do it'. Wake up in the morning and let your first thought be, 'It's a great day!' Say, 'I am beautiful . . . I am loved . . . I am strong . . . I am a great student.' When you sit down to study, do not say, 'I don't want to be here.' Or, 'I can't do this'. Say, 'This is great!' or 'I'm looking forward to this topic'. Develop your own statements, the ones that make you feel good, energised and strong.

> **Tip:** Put these statements in the positive and in the present tense. So it's not, 'I will not be afraid' but, 'I am brave'. The former only emphasises the thing that you do not want to be, afraid. Also, putting things in the future tense always seems to put them out of reach somehow. And you want the positive energy now – not in some unrealisable future.

Don't stop

Once you start using these positive statements, it is important to keep them going. You will have had the little negative voice for a long time, so when it begins to disappear – to be drowned out by the positive voice – you can get a real sense of euphoria and release. Suddenly, it feels as though you don't need your positive statements any more.

But if you stop, that old negative voice will come right back. So, start the positive statements and keep them up. Every time you have a spare moment, maybe as you travel or as you tidy up, repeat your positive statements to yourself. When fear pops out, repeat your positive statements – we promise you will feel the panic subside.

Stick 'em up

Some people write their positive statements on cards and stick them around the house – by the bed, on the bathroom mirror, etc. You can even put a positive statement on the screensaver on your computer! (We've got 'I am powerful' on one and 'Joy' on another. These give a quick boost when they appear, making it easier to get back to work.) Immerse yourself in positivity as you immerse yourself in your studies.

It's win/win

We have had students feed back that positive thinking does not just help them with their studies, although it definitely does that. They also say that it has given them new confidence at work – suddenly, they can speak up in meetings where ordinarily they would remain silent. They volunteer for things that they would never have dared do before. They look for more challenging and rewarding jobs, because now they realise they have much more ability than they had ever given themselves credit for. They take and pass their driving tests. These students intend to use this new energy to improve their whole lives.

Investigate it – do it

When you do decide on new goals for yourself, investigate what it will take to succeed – and then do it. For, you will not get that new job if you do not investigate what they are looking for, and make sure that your CV provides this information. Neither can you sit in a corner glowing positively and expect that essay to write itself, for that really will not happen. However, you can investigate what it takes to do a good essay, and then do it.

Conclusion: *A positive outcome*

In this chapter, we have explored the human, affective dimension of the academic environment and of being a student. We have paid particular attention to the role of fear and the benefits of positive thinking, self-belief and self-confidence.

Entering education – the unknown – can be fearful for everybody, and perhaps even more so for those who do not see themselves as typical students or as academics. If this is you, we recommend that you immediately take the time to actively work on developing your positive thinking.

We explored briefly where our fears originate; we considered that they might be a legacy from evolution, a product of our environment or background and a conse-quence of an overprotective upbringing. In either case, we argued that there were steps that you can take to do something about this.

Specifically, we looked in some detail at how to overcome your fears and become more positive, paying particular attention to losing the victim mentality and accepting responsi-bility for your own life. We argued that re-framing fear itself could help, as would adopting a positive vocabulary and making positive friends, especially a positive study partner.

And remember, all the things that we have mentioned here have worked for all the students that have tried them out with us. You will only know if they work for you by actually trying them. So, give them a go, and once you have started, keep them going.

Further reading

If you want to follow up on some of the ideas in this chapter, you might like to look at:
Bandura, A. http://www.des.emory.edu/mfp/self-efficacy.html (accessed 28.08.07).
Baron-Cohen, S. (1997) *The Maladapted Mind*. London: Psychology Press.
Jeffers, S. (1987) *Feel the Fear and Do it Anyway*. London: Century.

Query: Has this actually made you a little more fearful? Well, you know the answer to that – feel the fear and do it anyway! It is exciting and liberating to be in charge of your own life – enjoy your fear, as it means you are still alive.

Activity 5: Active review

As this can be an especially emotional topic, we have put this little active review here for you.

- As always, reflect back over this section and make your learning conscious.
- What have you read?
- Why did you read it?
- How did it make you feel?
- What have you learned?
- Can you use it in your studies? How? Where?
- What else will you need to find out?
- What else will you need to do?
- When will this happen?

Review points

When thinking about what you have read and the activities that you have engaged in, you might feel that you have:

- briefly reviewed the nature of the academic environment, and reminded yourself how active you must be in learning the practices of your academic subject
- thought about the impact of fear and a lack of self-belief and self-confidence on you as a student
- considered the origins of fear in humans, in terms of evolution, environment and upbringing
- explored some steps that you might take to improve your own self-confidence and assertiveness in the academic environment.

10

How to be a reflective learner

AIMS

It is the intention of this chapter to consider the importance of reflection in effective learning, with a special focus on the reflective learning log.

LEARNING OUTCOMES

By the end of reading this chapter and engaging in the activities set, you will:
- understand the importance of the reflective review as an essential part of the learning process
- have engaged in specific review activities designed to get you reflecting on your development of the study and academic skills and practices necessary for becoming a successful student
- have utilised the opportunity to practise several review activities.

Introduction

Welcome to this chapter on reflective learning. We would like to remind you that this chapter works alongside Chapter 15 on the reflective essay, 19 on memory and revision techniques, and 21 on PDP. While these chapters are separated across the text, their 'message' is uniform: in terms of successful academic practice, reflection (review) is something that you should be engaged in all the time, for without review there is no learning. In this section, we are going to suggest a significant review strategy – the reflective learning diary, which we will cover in some detail – making links with successful assignment writing. We will also offer some review activities to get you thinking about different sections of this text.

Reflective learning – beyond the revision cycle

In our notemaking chapter (Chapter 12), we encourage you to make active and creative notes, and to engage in a revision cycle after every learning activity – lecture, reading and discussion. We stress that Buzan's research on the memory indicates that without active revision, 98 per cent of what we are trying to learn will be forgotten three weeks after any particular study period or learning session.

This emphasis on instant and ongoing revision also informs our advice on an overall revision strategy (Chapter 19) and a successful exam strategy (Chapter 20). That is, revision is something that should start at the beginning of a course, and it should be ongoing throughout each course that you undertake. We point out that this is different from ad hoc revision strategies typically adopted where, at best, students might try to learn material covered in a whole programme of study in the few weeks immediately preceding an exam.

In this chapter, we suggest an active writing strategy to support your revision cycle. Specifically, we are going to consider the reflective learning diary: a form of reflective writing that will help you to understand, learn and write about your course material.

What is a reflective learning diary?

Put very simply, a reflective learning diary (or log or journal) is an analytical, detailed and concise record that you make of your studies. The process of completing this diary makes your learning active and conscious, which improves the quantity and quality of your learning. It is also an opportunity for you to undertake your first structured thinking/writing in relation to your learning.

There is no one model for a learning diary – it can take any form or shape that you like, although we do recommend a structure, outlined below, that does work with us and our students. The point with this reflective writing is to notice what you have done and why you did it (i.e. its purpose, for your learning should always be purposeful). You may wish to consider what you have gained from any particular learning activity, and what you intend to do next. Some people like to note which bit of an assignment or which learning outcomes have been met by engaging in a particular activity.

We recommend that writing your diary follows swiftly upon a study session, and that the writing itself is purposeful and concentrated.

Tips:
- Keep a diary for each module that you do.
- Spend a few minutes after each study period – a class, lecture or independent study – completing your journal.
- Why not choose to blog one of your modules and keep an online learning diary? (For details on how to blog, see Chapter 6.)
- When completing these learning diaries, we advise that you complete them using the headings below.

The reflective learning diary

The diary structure that we recommend has six parts: what, why, reaction, problems, learned and goal-setting. This does not have to be a rigid thing – experiment until you find a structure that best meets your needs and suits your learning style.

> **Tip:** Write your diaries on one side of a piece of paper, and use a pattern note format for your reviews. Use key words to make them manageable, and colour and cartoons to make them memorable.

- **What:** Make brief notes of what you did. Here you can note the lecture or seminar that you attended or the reading that you have done.
- **Why:** Make brief analytical notes – why was this activity useful? What learning outcomes did it cover? What part of the assignment question is it helping you with? Knowing why you are doing something helps you move from being a passive to an active learner.
- **Reaction:** Make brief notes on your emotional response to the activity in which you engaged or the information that you received. This part of the review allows you to notice the affective dimension to your learning. It allows you to build a picture of yourself as a learner and as a student. (See also Chapter 9, on how to deal with your emotions.)

    This reflection allows you to notice the subjects and topics that you enjoy, and the ones that you do not like so much. It will also start to tell you the activities that you prefer, that is, whether you like lectures or reading, whether you enjoy group work or independent study. This means that, in future, you can choose modules and teaching and learning strategies that suit your subject interests and your learning-style preferences.

Tips:
- Be honest. You will not get a true picture of your own likes, dislikes and preferences if you paint a rosy picture of yourself.
- Use the discoveries that you make here to inform your subject choices.
- Use the information to help you refine your own learning style.

▶

- **Problems:** It is useful to notice any problems that you encountered as you studied, and the solutions that you found. It is good practice for you to notice your successes (overcoming a problem), for, as we warn elsewhere, it is all too easy just to focus on our failings.

> **Tip:** If you are submitting a reflective account as part of an assessment, reflecting on how you overcame problems demonstrates that you are a successful, reflective student.

- **Learned:** Make brief notes on all that you think that you learned from the lecture, class or reading. These notes are where you make your learning conscious. Making our learning conscious in this way improves both the quantity and quality of your learning. When we do not do this, we are in danger of leaving the learning behind as we walk away from that lecture or close that book. You can make this section of your review as detailed or concise as you wish.

> **Tips:**
> - When making the learning conscious, make links with the assignment question.
> - Use this section of your review to practise your academic writing.
> - Diaries, as with all academic writing, get easier with practice.

- **Goal setting:** Make brief notes about what you could now do, following the information you gained from the lecture, class or reading. Remember, we continually stress that no one lecture or piece of reading will ever give you 'all you need to know' on a subject. Therefore, when you have engaged in one activity, you should note what you need to do next.

> **Tip:** When noting what you will do next, note when you will do it. If you do not make a date to do it, it will not get done.

Review and effective writing

- Reflective writing is the precursor to successful writing in assignments. For more information on this, and for examples of other students' reflective writing, please use the following web addresses.
- This is the reflective writing section of the Queen Mary's University of London 'Thinking/ Writing' site. Go here to find more information on the value of reflective writing for the assignment writing process: http://www.thinking writing.qmul.ac.uk/reflect.htm
- This URL takes you to examples of real students' reflective writing: http://www. thinkingwriting.qmul.ac.uk/reflect3.htm
- Remember also the evolving essay wiki and blog that demonstrates reflective writing as part of the assignment process: http://evolvingessay.pbwiki.com/

FIGURE 10.1 Example of a pattern review completed by student

Review and effective self-assessment

Ongoing review of your own study and study practices allows active self-assessment and puts you in control of your own development. This is always useful, but even more obviously so, if asked to complete such reviews for reflective essays (see also Chapter 15) and PDP (Chapter 21). If engaged in these, you may find that you are asked to reflect on your overall development as a student, as a learner. These reflective moments can focus on any aspect of your development that you wish – from how you organise your time to how well you feel you are mastering the epistemology (theory of knowledge) of your subject. But remember, while your university will most probably have a PDP system, the more you set your own goals, the more you take control of your own learning.

Reflecting on ESS2

We have included some reflection activities here that are designed to help you think about how you are developing as a student, and that will also help you to make the most of other sections of this text. Please use these positively and enjoy them.

Activity 1: Self-assessment – What have you done with *ESS2*?

1 When reading and working through *ESS2*, why don't you complete a reflective learning log for each chapter that you have read?
2 When you have finished reading and working through *ESS2*, why don't you reflect on what you have learned from the book as a whole? At the end of such a self-assessment, you should have a picture of yourself as a student that would also help you to write a reflective essay or PDP entry.

> *Query*: If you have undertaken either of these review activities, how do you feel now? What will you do next? If you do still have any remaining issues, why not:
> - go to see the Learning Development or Support Unit at your institution?
> - go and see the student support services people?
> - sort things out with your study partner?
> see Figure 10.3 on page 149.

'Without doing my review, I wouldn't even have understood the class, let alone remembered it!'

Activity 2: Review your reading and notemaking strategies

Task: After reading Chapters 11 and 12, read the email below and make pattern notes. Note: this email is a piece of academic writing that is not as formal as either a journal article or an essay.

Before reading, remember QOOQRRR:

- **Question** – Why would an activity like this be in the book? What do you hope to gain from it? Re-read your learning contract for the book.
- **Overview** – How does this activity fit into the book as a whole? Remind yourself of the aims and outcomes for the book.
- **Overview** – Read the beginning and end of the email. Scan the first sentences. Decide what the email is about.
- **Question** – What is interesting about the email? Ask yourself: Why should I read it? What can I get out of it?
- **Read** – Once you know why you are reading the email, choose which sections to read in depth. Read these through actively and interactively, marking up the text. Underline key words and points. Make margin notes. Make notes of any links, such as between points in the email and sections of this book.
- **Re-read** – Re-read your own marginalia. Construct your own key-word pattern notes. Put the key word for the central topic in the centre of an A4 sheet of paper. Draw out branches and make connections from the central topic, and put in subsidiary words. Use colour and highlighters. Draw pictures to illustrate key points.
- **Review your notes** – Are they useable? Are they sourced? Plug any gaps.

Email on academic practices versus study skills (26 February 2002)

What I am suggesting is that the identity-practice model of learning and skill, which I have been working on for some years, both for the PhD and for various conference papers and articles, provides a significant move on from the 'skills-as-possessions' (like tools) model. The emphasis should be, I would argue, on getting students to become familiar with, and practised or rehearsed in, those practices which are associated with (a) being an undergraduate and then (b) being a graduate. This is, of course, congenial with the Situated Learning Theory Approach of Lave and Wenger ('legitimate peripheral participation'), but I have taken the identity issue further in terms of what I dub the 'claim-affirmation model of emergent identity'.

Particular forms of writing (and reading and talking) may be seen as examples of the practices associated with the identity of an undergraduate, and also of a graduate. Academic writing encompasses a range of types, particularly papers written for an academic audience – for a conference (or seminar, symposium, colloquium, etc.), for an academic journal, book, etc. The purpose is (or should be) to present an argument in support of a knowledge claim. The criteria for judging such an argument would include its location wrt [with respect to] existing, broadly accepted (and also contested) knowledge claims (the existing literature), the logical reasoning and the empirical evidence adduced. The style should be that which is generally accepted, including conventions for citations, etc.

▶

So by the time they graduate, the students should be familiar with such a style through examination of e.g. journal articles – not focusing on the content as something-to-be-learnt but on how the author attempts to present their knowledge claim. To write such a paper would require the student to read with a purpose (contribution to the argument to be presented), to summarise key points from the materials read for the purpose of advancing the claim, to construct a cogent article, to keep a note of bibliographic details in order to cite as appropriate, and so on. Above all, it requires the student to have something to say that is worth saying; their own voice writes the issues at hand.

But to get there, as educators, we need to help students to become adept at the various elements – peripheral participation in the practices of the community of academic practice, as Lave and Wenger might put it.

There are other modes of writing that graduates should be able to undertake, orientated towards arenas of professional practice outside academia – reports, briefing papers, etc. These too can be considered in terms of the various practices that constitute the elements for producing such forms of writing. But we need to ensure students recognise that these are different, and are appropriate for different contexts and arenas of practice.

I don't think that this is particularly revolutionary, but I would emphasise the notion of practices associated with relevant identities. In mundane discourse, we might talk of 'skills', but we must see them as ways of acting, not possessions which cause, or are used in, forms of action. 'Skills development' work still has an important place – more so, as it provides the basis for enabling students to practise and rehearse, and continue to do so, rather than being seen as remedial and something which is at some point finished – been there, done that, got the T-shirt.

Hope this makes sense. If you can stand reading some of my writing on this, the relational skills and learning website is at www.re-skill.org.uk. Obviously, the later stuff is more fully developed.

Regards,
Len

Discussion: When you have finished this activity, review your progress with your study partner:

- What was your first response to the email? Did you get angry, frustrated, confused or happy? Remember, there are no correct reactions, but do note how you are reacting to academic language and argument at the moment (see Chapter 9).
- What has this activity told you about your QOOQRRR skills?
- What has it told you about your pattern notemaking skills?
- What has it told you about academic practices?
- What will you do now:
  - about your research and reading skills?
  - about your notemaking skills?
  - about your familiarity with academic practices?
  - when will you do these things?

Now look at Figure 10.2 below.

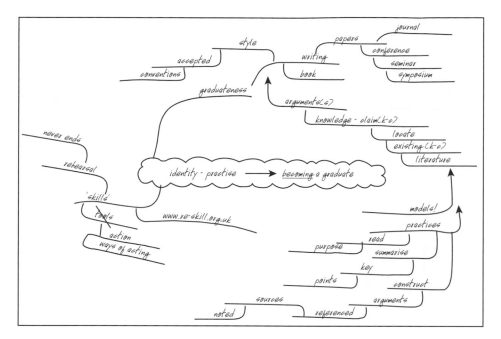

FIGURE 10.2 Pattern note of an email

Activity 3: Revising exam technique (Chapter 20)

The Study Skills Exam
Just for fun, we have included a possible exam paper for students of this book. If you want to see how well you would do under timed conditions, why not have a go at this exam. Afterwards, you can reflect on how well you did, and what that tells you about yourself as a student.

Study Skills Exam
Name:
Date

▶

Candidates must answer two questions: ONE question from Section A and ONE question from Section B. You have 90 minutes for the whole paper.

Section A

1 Evaluate the usefulness of a study skills book to you as a student.
2 Consider the value of building on your own learning style.
3 What aspects of study skills will you take with you, either into further study or into your work? Give reasons for your answer.

Section B

4 Consider the value of planning, preparing and writing an academic essay.
5 In what ways have you been able to use your whole study programme as a study skills laboratory? With this in mind, what advice would you give next year's students?
6 Evaluate the usefulness to you as a student of one of the following: active learning; trial and error; self-assessment. Give examples to justify your answer.

Exam ends

Query: How well did you do? If you are not sure, ask your study partner to mark your answers and to give you feedback. But here are some things for you to think about:

■ Did you follow instructions? Did you answer one question from each section? If not, you know that you will need to keep practising this.
■ Did you brainstorm/plan before you wrote your answer? Did this help? Do you need more practice at brainstorming? When will you do this? If you did not brainstorm, why not? If in doubt, go to Chapter 8 on creative learning. Remember that brainstorming, like everything else we do, does indeed get better with practice.
■ Did you manage your time well? What have you learned about your ability to manage time? What do you need to practise to get better at managing your time?
■ Overall, what have you learned about yourself as an exam taker? Make sure you do something with this information.

Tip: Why not brainstorm every question on this paper just to practise brainstorming? Do this with your study partner – allow yourselves ten minutes per question, and then compare brainstorms at the end.

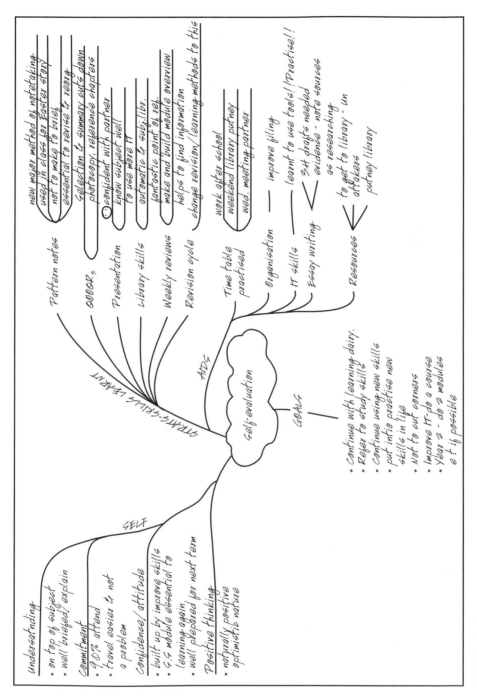

FIGURE 10.3 A self-assessment of a study skills programme

Conclusion

We have prompted you to reinforce your active learning by using the reflective learning diary – an ongoing and detailed review system that will allow you to make your learning conscious. This will improve both the quantity and quality of your learning and help you with the academic writing (or other assessments) associated with your studies. Further, we argued that this particular review structure will also enable you to notice the subjects and learning strategies that suit you best. This is information that can inform your module choices – and your learning strategies – and thus your development as a successful student.

We moved on to include a couple of activities designed to get you actively reviewing your engagement with this text – we do hope that you enjoy those activities. Good luck with the rest of the book.

Review points

When reviewing this section of the book, as well as noticing how revision reinforces your learning, you might notice how all the activities covered in this text will help you to succeed in your studies, and they will work to increase your enjoyment of and confidence in the academic environment. But will you engage in them? Remember our SOCCER mnemonic to ensure your study success:

- **S – Study techniques** and practices: organise yourself for study, use all the resources of your university, become familiar with academic practice, remember your QOOQRRR, your SQP4, and the 'how to . . .' of group work, assignments, etc.
- **O – Overview:** use your course handbooks – read the aims and learning outcomes and use these to direct your revision and exam strategies.
- **C – Creativity:** brainstorm and question-matrix ideas, and practise your pattern notes.
- **C – Communicate effectively:** using the academic conventions and practices of your subject. See Chapters 13–18 on how to prepare better assignments.
- **E – Emotions** – build your motivation: use the learning contract. Deal with your fear and build your self-confidence. See Chapter 9 on how to build your confidence.
- **R – Review,** review, review: use the revision cycle and the reflective learning diary. Write to learn.

Use it or lose it. Review your learning and your learning strategies.

11

How to research and read academically

To prepare you for successful academic study by examining targeted research and active reading skills.

LEARNING OUTCOMES

That after reading through this chapter, and engaging with the activities set, you will have:
- gained an understanding of the nature and purpose of academic reading
- made links between reading and writing (see also Chapters 13–18)
- gained an understanding of targeted research and active reading strategies
- thought about notemaking from reading (see also Chapter 12)
- engaged with various activities that have reinforced your understanding of the what, why and how of reading.

Brainstorm: Reading, especially at university, is another one of those skills or practices that we are not just born with; this chapter is designed to help you to organise and benefit from your reading. We will get you thinking about issues like: Why do we read? How much should I read? How can I read effectively? It is an important section and we hope that you find it useful. As always, before you start, think quickly:

■ What do I already know on this topic?
■ What do I need to find out?
■ How will knowing this make me a more successful student?

Reading for your degree

Even with the growth of the Internet, we are still a literate society. People who would not consider themselves to be readers will read newspapers, magazines, recipes, knitting patterns, the television pages and fiction. Obviously, once we talk about reading in the context of being a student, we are normally talking about another sort of reading material and another sort of reading strategy. As a student, you will be expected to undertake independent research, that is, to 'read around a subject' without being told or directed by your tutors. Indeed, students used to be described as reading for a degree, rather than studying one. However, we have found that, these days, many students:

• are not reading at all
• are not reading critically
• do not see the point of reading.

This chapter is designed to deconstruct academic reading for the uninitiated or sceptical learner, and to give very practical guidelines about how to manage your research and reading throughout your time as a student.

Reading is learning, it is developmental and necessary

As we stressed in Chapter 5: how to organise yourself for independent study, in the UK you are not taught your degree, rather you are supposed to research (read) it yourself. This means that, while you are given information in lectures, classes, seminars and tutorials, this will never be 'all you need to know' on a subject. You are supposed to develop your knowledge of the subject beyond that which the tutor has told you. This means reading! You are supposed to excavate the knowledge claims of your discipline; and read what the thinkers and experts have to say in the key textbooks, the latest journal articles, and the reputable parts of the Internet.

Tip: For a quick way in to your subject, see how it is covered in the broadsheet newspapers.

From novice to initiate – an emergent graduate identity

Reading is developmental, for example, if you are just beginning to study a topic, you may know very little about it at all. Thus, the first sort of reading that you do might be very general. With this reading, you are trying to understand the topic and may have many doubts, fears and questions:

- What is this subject about?
- What are the basic things that I ought to know and understand about the topic?
- Who are the people that I ought to read?

> **Tip:** Use your reading list – this tells you 'who' and what you should be reading

This is why the first reading that you do on your topic can be so difficult. It is not necessarily that it really is the most difficult – it is just that because you are new to the subject, it all feels new and uncertain to you. Fortunately, it does get much easier after this.

Extending your knowledge

If the initial reading that you do on your degree programme is to gain a general understanding of your subject, that is, an awareness of its knowledge base, key people and practices, the next stage is to extend your understanding: to engage with more difficult issues or more radical knowledge claims.

So, if your lecturer covers something in class, you might go to a textbook or journal to see what other people have said on that subject. And, once you understand the generally accepted wisdom, you move on to the more contested claims.

As you read more, the task becomes easier, because you are adding to or challenging what you already know. You are not starting from scratch but you are building on what you know about the subject. Yes, you are encountering new people and new ideas, but you are also revising the ideas that you have encountered before. Your graduate identity takes shape as your sense of familiarity with your subject develops.

For example, if this is the first study skills book that you have ever read, all this might be new to you. But if you now pick up another study skills book and go to their section on reading, you will be able to see what they write. If it is different to this, you might ask yourself why. This might prompt you to look at yet another study skills book to see what they say, and so on.

This is the basic principle of academic reading. You start reading to gain an understanding – you then challenge that understanding with contradictory or more up-to-date writing. You engage analytically and critically with all your reading, and you develop your knowledge and understanding as you bring the differing arguments together in your own mind – and this is where your writing comes in (see Chapters 13–18).

Now that we have made a case for reading, let us move on to our active reading system that gives advice on how to read as effectively and successfully as possible.

Tip: Remember that you are supposed to be studying for 35–40 hours per week – this allows a lot of time for reading!

Thoughts on reading from another student

'That week when you did that reading session, I hated that and I was really uncomfortable the whole lesson … because I was so unsure and not confident and, as I looked round, everyone seemed to be getting on with it and I thought I don't know what the hell she wants me to do.

And you know as soon as you're in that position, you can't learn anything, you can't take anything in. Things were being said, and I couldn't understand. And I was sitting with a couple of people who seemed to know what it was all about and I thought, oh crikey. You know? And it was awful. It was horrible. I didn't like that at all.'

Yet when the same student was asked later about a positive learning experience, she said:

'I was thinking about all those books on that booklist. I was thinking I had to read every single one of those books and I didn't know how I was going to manage that, so I thought I'd just bluff it a bit, you know.

But later on, I found from you that I didn't need to do that. When you did that bit about reading – about books. I mean, I wasn't aware that I didn't know anything about that first page bit, about this is the author and this is when it was published and this is where it was published. I didn't know any of that. I didn't have a clue because books have always been really alien to me, you know?

And when you showed us about looking in the index and looking in the contents, and then finding the bit that interests you and then going to your first paragraph and reading the first few lines and seeing if it's what you want. I found that really valuable.'

Query: What are your reactions to this student's feelings about learning how to read academically? Are her reactions similar to or different from your own? Did reading this help in any way?

Discussion: As tutors, we learned a lot from this student's reactions to learning how to read an academic text:
1 It was difficult.
2 The difficulty brought with it many negative feelings.
3 The negative feelings swamped everything else, so that nothing could happen at that time.
4 Later, the student did start to try the technique out.
5 Eventually, it became one of the most useful techniques that she felt she got from the study skills programme.

▶

Query: What does that tell you?

Discussion: Reading can be difficult – it can even be quite frightening. Worse, at first, even learning how to read academically can be frightening. As always, we offer the reassurance that these things do get easier with practice. Try to take comfort from this student's experiences. She managed to move from real fear and loathing to confidence and assurance comparatively quickly. You can, too.

What, why and how to read – the QOOQRRR approach

This section constitutes a very practical guide to academic reading. Successful academic reading is an active, interactive, analytical and critical process – it is about questioning and challenging a text as you read it. This may be a new technique for you, so we explain it in some detail.

Make a meal of your reading – use the QOOQRRR

We have called our active reading strategy QOOQRRR (pronounced cooker) and it is a system that promotes active reading, through:

- active selection of what to read
- active goal-setting before you read
- active questioning and cross-referencing as you read
- active notemaking of what you read
- active review of your notes from reading.

QOOQRRR stands for Question, Overview, Overview, Question, Read, Re-read and Review. We will look at each of these in turn.

Question: Reading with awareness

Reading with self-awareness involves identifying yourself as a reader and the reason for your reading. It is not about choosing the first book on the reading list and ploughing through it from beginning to end without any clear goals in mind. If you have already tried to do that, you will know that it is neither a happy nor a productive exercise. So, before you start to read, you should know exactly why you are reading.

Why do we read at university?

There are many possible goals for your reading – here are a few:
- You may read something to gain an overview of a topic that is new for you.
- You may read to discover the point of view of that person your lecturer keeps talking about.
- You may be reading to find someone or something that disagrees with that person the lecturer keeps talking about.
- You may be reading to find one quote that will finish off a paragraph that you have already written.
- You may be reading to find 'evidence' for every single part of your assignment.

> *Discussion*: There is no single reason to read, as we keep reminding you; there is only your reason to read, and making sure that you do know what that is. Knowing why you are reading can lead to successful reading, and it can help shape your notes.
>
> After all, there is no need for you to make key-word notes of a whole chapter, if you are only looking for one quote. On the other hand, just noting down a few quotes may not be helpful, if this is the first time you have studied something and you are really looking to gain an overview of a new topic.

> **Tip:** You will be expected to do and learn many things on each course that you take: don't try to read about them all at once – look for one thing at a time.

Why am I reading now?

So, what should you do? The first thing to do is to know why you are reading in the first place. You need specific goals each time you read (see box above), for example:

I am a novice:
- I must make really detailed notes to help me understand the whole topic
- I am making a subject dictionary to help me learn new words and phrases
- I am keeping a record of the key people and knowledge claims that will be useful throughout my time at university
- I have started to record all my reading on index cards to use throughout my whole degree.

I am an initiate:
- I already know much on this subject, so my notes will be brief
- I am just noting a couple of good quotes to use in my assignment

- I am looking for a counter opinion to the one I have just read
- I am looking for a really radical idea to surprise my tutor
- I am looking for an up-to-date article
- I am maintaining my index card record of all my reading
- I am able to use reading from one module in another.

Once you know why you are reading, on the novice to initiate continuum, you need to put your reading in the context of the course or module you are currently taking.

O is for Overview – of course

As we argue in Chapters 3 and 13 (How to understand your course and How to communicate effectively), you should have the overview of your course or module before you start to study, and especially before you start to read. So before you read anything, check your module:
- aims
- learning outcomes
- syllabus
- assignment question
- assessment criteria
- reading list.

Once you have read and understood these, you should know exactly what you have to do, learn and understand in order to pass the course – you know what the assignment question is and what it is asking you to do. Only now will you know why you are reading and what you are looking for.

Now, this may seem a very reductionist view of reading – maybe you have a deep and abiding passion for learning for its own sake. Maybe you love your subject so much that you are prepared to read anything and everything that you can on the topic. Well, this reading strategy will help you, too. Evidence shows that targeted, focused reading, with specific goals in mind, is highly productive.

O is for Overview – choosing what to read

Once you know why you are reading, and you have gained an overview of your course and selected something to research – a key word from your assignment question perhaps – then you can start the process of deciding *what* to read. There are some helpful hints in the checklists below.

Overview: Sources of information

Before you read, you need to choose what to read very carefully. Tick the activities you have undertaken.

- ■ Books:
  - ☐ I have found some of the books on the reading list and looked at them.
  - ☐ They are easy/difficult to read.

▶

□ I will read on my own/with a study partner.
□ I have booked time in my diary.
- Contents pages:
    □ I have looked for a word from the assignment question in the Contents pages.
    □ I have chosen which sections of the book to read and decided when to do my reading.
- Indexes:
    □ I have looked for the word in the index at the back of the book.
    □ I have looked at these pages and decided I will/will not read more of that book.
- Wider searches:
    □ I have used the electronic catalogue in my library – the key word, author or subject search facilities.
    □ I have found a couple of books and repeated the above with them.
- Help – I have asked the following people for assistance:
    □ my tutor
    □ other students
    □ the subject librarian
    □ I will now …
- The Internet: My subject librarian
    □ has directed me to these search engines...
    □ and these sites for my subject...
- Journals: My subject librarian
    □ has directed me to these journals...
    □ and these online journals...
- Dissertations and theses: My subject librarian
    □ has directed me to the dissertations and theses relevant to my subject.

Overview: Chapters and paragraphs

Complete the following checklist each time you approach a book chapter or a journal article.
I have:
□ read the introduction (first paragraph) and conclusion (last paragraph): I know what it is about.
□ decided which bits to skim and which bits to read in depth.
□ read the first sentence of every paragraph. I know what each paragraph is about.
□ chosen the paragraphs relevant to my topic.
□ a skeleton understanding of the whole chapter/article, and planned my reading of the article/chapter.

Question: Why am I reading this? Reading with a purpose

We are nearly ready to read in depth, and a good place to start is to focus on individual parts of your assignment question (the key words) and to read around one of those at a time. Thus, once you have chosen something to read, make sure you clarify your own goals. Ask yourself the following questions:
- Why am I reading this?
- What am I looking for?
- What do I need?
- Where will I use the information?
- How will I use the information?
- Which bit of my assignment will it help me with?
- Which of the learning outcomes will it help me with?
- How will I know when I have what I need?

Once you have your questions, you are ready to read.

> **Tips:**
> Choose a notemaking strategy that suits your reading purpose.
> Construct paragraph patterns as you read (Chapter 12).

R1 is for Read

Once you know what and why you are reading, you are ready to interact with a text mentally and physically – you are ready to read. This reading is the academic reading that can intimidate. No matter what your feelings are at the moment, we can assure you it does get easier with practice.

As with all active learning, academic reading requires the use of an active questioning approach. That is, when reading, you need to keep asking things like, what does this mean? Who else has said that? But didn't someone else say . . . ? And so forth. And each time you ask these questions, you should 'mark up' your text. That is, you should highlight, underline or annotate the thing that you are reading. Note: you must not get physical with other people's books, and you do have to get physical with a book to get the most from it. If you are using library books, always photocopy the relevant pages and mark up your photocopies.

Reading resources and tips

As reading requires physical as well as mental activity from you, we recommend that you gather resources around you when you start to read. Things that will help:

- Have paper, pencils, pens, highlighters, paper clips, etc. to hand.
- Write your assignment question out. Underline key words: each word is something to read up on. Have the question in front of you when you read.

▶

- Mark off the passage that you are actually reading. Place a piece of paper or a paper clip at the end of the section that you want to read. This gives you a physical goal and it helps the brain to relax a little bit (phew – I can manage that much!). Without the barrier or marker, it can feel like there is too much to read and this can swamp us.
- Use another piece of paper to guide your eye down the page. One of the problems with academic reading is working against the physiology of the eye. Typically, our eyes move around – as we read, they dart about over the page. Often, you find yourself reading the same sentence over and over again. By the time you have read it 50 times, an already difficult task has become that much harder. A piece of paper placed on the line that you are actually reading helps to bring your eye back to the correct place in the book. This alone can save you time.
- Now read one paragraph at a time in an active, interactive way. Typically, this will mean asking a series of questions of the text as we read, and marking up the chapter as we go.

Analytical and critical reading

Active and interactive questions promote analytical and critical reading, and they encourage you to cross-reference your reading with other things that you have heard or read. Remember to be physical with the text as you read.

Read one paragraph at a time, asking these questions as you go.

- What is the main idea here? The main topic of a paragraph is usually revealed in the first sentence. Highlight the word or write your own word in the margin.

> **Tip:** Reading the first sentences of all the paragraphs will give you a skeleton framework of the whole piece. This is very useful for getting the overview, and extremely useful for summary writing.

- What is the author's argument?

> **Tip:** Think! Analyse the argument. What is the author saying about the topic? Are they for it or against it? Again, highlight the text and/or write in the margin.

- Where is the author coming from? Are they on the left or the right? Are they Marxist or neo-con? Are they exploitative or green? Are they class-based? Do they have a feminist perspective?

> **Tip:** Find out whether or not these differences are important to your academic practice. For example, this might be extremely important information on a sociology or literature programme, but maybe not so important on a maths programme.

▶

- Have I encountered this argument before? Where? Make a note of who else would support this view.

> **Tip:** This gets you thinking about what you are reading – it is getting you to make connections and to make them conscious. Record your thoughts by underlining, highlighting or writing in the margin.

- Have I encountered a different argument somewhere? Where? Again, make connections, and notice consciously counter arguments.

> **Tip:** Here you are being analytical and critical. Make a note of the person or people who say something different to what you have just read.

- What evidence is being offered? Highlight it or make a note.

> **Tip:** Make sure you know what counts as a valid argument and evidence in your subject.

- Is the evidence valid? Why do I think it is or is not valid? Make notes.

> **Tip:** Put a question mark or an exclamation mark to show that you disagree with something, or jot down the name of the person who says something different.

- How does this change what I have already read/heard? Cross-referencing in this way is very active reading. Ask yourself, now what do I think?

> **Tip:** Sometimes what you read will reinforce what you know or believe already; sometimes it might make you question that Notice! Make a note.

- What is the author's final point? Usually the 'point' is in the final sentence of a paragraph. Notice what the author intended the paragraph to do.

> **Tips:**
> Ask all those questions of one paragraph, and then move on to the next.
> See this reading as an investment, not a problem – it is very productive.
> The only notes you should make at this stage are the notes that you scribble on the text itself – your annotations and marginalia.

Another strategy: Reading a research article

- Read concluding sections for summaries of hypothesis, method, results and significance of the study.
- Read introductory sections for hypothesis/research questions and agenda.
- Skim methods/results. You read these in depth later.
- Read opening paragraphs of the discussion/analysis for summary of results and methods.
- Read methods/results closely – imagine/visualise the study and its results.
- Read discussion/analysis very closely.

From 'how to read a research article':

http://cla.calpoly.edu/~jrubba/495/howtoread.html (accessed August 2007)

R2 is for Re-read

Once you have read your chosen section in this interactive and thoughtful way, you are ready to make your own 'to keep' notes. Make notes too soon, and they are too passive and too long. Construct your own key-word (pattern) notes of the text using your marginalia, highlighting and underlining to help you (see also Chapter 12).

Tips:
- Move to key-word notes in stages – see page 163.
- For a pattern note of this advice, see page 164.
- For an example of a student's notes on reading Tony Buzan, see page 166.

R3 is for Review

The final part of the QOOQRRR strategy is the review. This is where you review your own notes and judge for yourself whether or not they are useful, useable and suited to your purpose. As an active learner in control of your own learning, it is up to you to decide whether or not your notes are any good. But there are some things to look out for when you are judging your own notes.

Note review questions:

Are my notes sourced? That is, have I recorded author, date, title, publisher, town? Have I noted page numbers besides quotes?

- Have I copied quotes out accurately? **Tips:** When quoting, you must get it exactly right. You can abbreviate a quote, but then you must put in an ellipsis (dot, dot, dot: . . .) to show where you made the cut. You can change a word, but then you must put square brackets [] around the word that you have changed in the quote.
- Do my notes do what I wanted them to? (That is, if you needed a few quotes for a piece of writing, do you have them? Are they sourced? If you needed to gain the overview of a topic, have you?)
- Scan! If anything is missing from your notes, scan the piece again to find the missing bits of information. (This is the same as when you programme a telephone number into your brain, run a finger down the page of the directory and, lo and behold, the number just jumps out at you.)

- Is there anything else that I ought to read now? **Tips:** Many texts will mention other people (often as their own evidence), so you can read what these people have written. There will also be other books on your reading list and journal articles to read. Once you have read one thing, you have to decide what if anything you should now read, and when. Get out your calendar and see if you have time for it – make a date, because if you don't set a date, it won't get done.
- Do I stop reading now? At some point, your reading has to stop. Yes, you must read widely, but beware – do not use your reading as an excuse to put off writing – it is something that we are all tempted to do at one time or another. When you are happy with your notes, you are ready to move on to your next task.

When making notes from reading - consider taking notes in stages:
1. Underline key words in text
2. Summarise key points in sentences (first column)
3. Reduce sentences to key words (second column)
4. Construct pattern notes with the key words

SUMMARY	KEYWORD
Older people are an increasing proportion of our population, yet their presence is not equally reflected in adult education programmes. Participating in learning opportunities offers many benefits to older people. However, they often feel excluded because of their age and life circumstances.	Older people ↑ Educational opportunities ↓
Islington Age concern set up the Older Learners' Project to address these issues. Over the last year the group has been meeting weekly to look at the learning needs and ambitions of people over 55 years of age. It particularly wants to involve people who were not able to take up the learning they wanted when they were younger, or who feel they have not been able to make much use of their knowledge and skills.	55 Knowledge and personal skills
On the day, there were information stands providing up-to-date information on learning opportunities locally and nationally, which gave people the opportunity to speak to specialists, find out about training and most importantly, develop confidence in trying new things. The event also included a number of workshops on study skills, creative writing, access to funding and older people as tutors.	Opportunities New things Confidence

← Reduce to Keywords

Sum up in sentences or phrases

Use the words to construct a pattern

FIGURE 11.1 How to move to key word (pattern) notes from reading

---

Notes, sources and plagiarism

- Sources: When making notes from your reading, always put the source in your notes. You have to give this information in the bibliography that you must compile at the end of your essay. Record the information in the way that your tutor wants.
- Harvard System: Author (date of publication) Title (or 'title' if a journal article). Town of publication: publisher.
- British Standard System: Author, Title (Or 'Title'), publisher, date of publication.
- Quotes: If you copy sections of the text into your notes to use as quotes, put the page numbers in your notes. When you quote in your writing, you must give author, date and page number.

▶

- Building a permanent record: Start an index card collection of all your reading. Buy an index box and alphabet dividers. Each time you read, record author, date, title, and publisher on an index card. Write a brief description of the text – record a few key points. File alphabetically. In this way, you will build a huge record of all your reading: a fabulous resource to use across your time at university, and beyond.
- Plagiarism: Plagiarism means kidnapping, and if you do not give your sources when you write, you are in effect kidnapping someone else's work and passing it off as your own. Plagiarism is a major academic offence for which you can fail a module, be expelled from university, or even have your whole degree annulled.
- 'Well, I read it, I agreed with it and now I've put it in my own words – it's mine now. I don't have to give sources then, do I?' Yes, you do – the ideas still came from someone else. And anyway, you are supposed to be giving sources – you are not supposed to be making it all up. You are supposed to be using and acknowledging the knowledge claims of your subject.
- 'How many sources should I give then?' As a rule of thumb, a first-year degree essay should have between five and 15 items listed in the bibliography. It goes upwards from there.

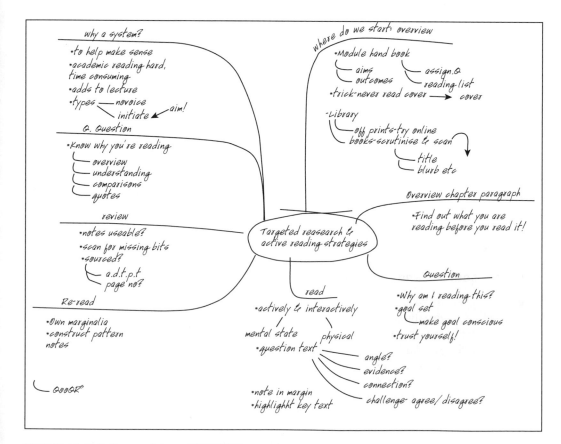

FIGURE 11.2 Pattern notes on QOOQRRR

Conclusion

We have covered academic reading with a special focus on becoming an active, analytical and critical reader of academic texts. We noted that the UK university system requires that students research their subjects through their own reading.

We have spent some considerable time on the QOOQRRR technique, a strategy that has proven the most useful with our students. We have emphasised the need for an active and interactive approach to reading, both physically and mentally. This will increase understanding as you read in critical and analytical ways.

We have mentioned that some people do find academic reading frightening, and that some also find even the notion of developing an effective reading strategy really intimidating. We did not do this to intimidate you, but rather to offer reassurance. If any of these fears are true for you, they will pass. As always, we recommend practice, practice, practice as the way of moving forward.

For research into the emergent graduate identity http://www.re-skill.org.uk/grads/grademp.htm

Further reading and resources

For research into the emergent graduate identity http://www.re-skill.org.uk/grads/grademp.htm

Active reading – from evolving essay:

http://anessayevolves.blogspot.com/2007/02/active-reading.html

How to read a research article:

http://cla.calpoly.edu/~jrubba/495/howtoread.html

Reading a psychology paper:

http://portal.psy.gla.ac.uk/index.php?option=com_content&task=view&id=13&Itemid=41&limit=1&limitstart=1

Internet detective – finding and evaluating information:

http://www.vts.intute.ac.uk/detective/

For summarising information:

http://learning.londonmet.ac.uk/busdev/hq1001nc/ecdl/summarizing.htm

Activity 3: Use QOOQRRR on this book

Continue through this book using these QOOQRRR techniques.

- Question: When reading, look back at your learning contract – what one thing are you looking for?
- Overview: Remember your overview of the book – what are you reading?
- Overview: With each chapter, get the overview by looking at the introduction and conclusion. Jot down what the chapter is about.
- Question: Set your own goals for a specific chapter: Why am I reading this? What do I want? What do I need? Where will I use the information? How will I know when I have what I want?
- Read actively and interactively, marking up useful sections as you go.
- Re-read your own notes – use those to construct your key-word notes.
- Review your own notes – judge whether or not they are helpful.
- Review again: Review the QOOQRRR system and see how it works for you.

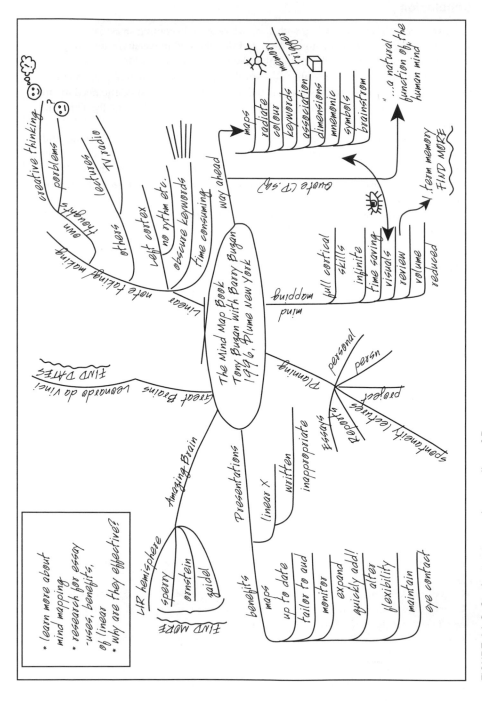

FIGURE 11.3 Student notes on her reading of Buzan

Make reading fun

Next time you struggle with a difficult reading activity, why don't you think, make or find:
- three words that describe how it made you feel
- a bare bones summary (25 words)
- a visual summary
- an object that represents something from the text
- one question that you would ask the author
- a one-minute presentation on the topic.

Review: Once you have finished, look at your representation:
What does it tell you about the text?
What does it tell you about yourself as a reader?
What will you do next?

Review points

When you reflect on this chapter, you might notice that you have:
- considered the nature of independent learning in the UK university – you are *reading* your subject
- realised the importance of active reading for the student
- started the process of reading effectively
- gained an understanding of targeted research and active reading strategies (QOOQRRR)
- considered how to make notes of your reading – from this chapter and with reference to Chapter 12
- engaged with various activities that have reinforced your understanding of the what, why and how of academic reading. (See the practice reading and notemaking activity in Chapter 10.)

Activity 4: Using your university library

Find your university library. If you find it an intimidating place, hopefully this worksheet will take you through the library in a useful way, so that you start using as much of the library as possible, as soon as possible, and it will not be intimidating any more.

For each activity, tick the box when you have completed it, and write in details where indicated.

Books

Find the part of the library that houses the books for your subject.

☐ My books are ....

☐ Write in the Dewey decimal number (the numbers on the spine of the book) for your subject ....

Journals

When studying, it is important to read the relevant journals for your subject.

☐ Where are your journals kept?...

☐ Write in the title of two journals that you could be reading:

Journal 1 ....

Journal 2 ....

Newspapers

☐ With most subjects, it is also important to read the 'quality' press. Where are the newspapers kept?...

Key text area (counter loans)

☐ The key text area holds the most important texts for each subject – find it.

My key text area is ....

Study areas

What facilities are there for independent study in your library?

☐ My library offers quiet study areas?...

☐ My library offers group study areas?...

Workshops

Some libraries contain student help workshops – does yours?

☐ My library does/does not have workshops.

☐ They are located ....

☐ Opening times are ....

Now that you have had a quick introduction to the library, list three things that you like about it:

1 ....

2 ....

3 ....

What would you tell someone else about the library?

1 ....

2 ....

12

How to make the best notes

AIMS

To introduce you to notemaking strategies, making connections with reading strategies (Chapter 11) and creative learning (Chapter 8).

LEARNING OUTCOMES

It is hoped that by the end of working through this chapter, you will have:
- been introduced to notemaking theory
- been introduced to notemaking practice, with the emphasis on creative, pattern notes
- realised the importance of active and creative learning strategies.

From notes to creative notes

In this section, we are going to explore notemaking per se; we will then go on to make a case for a creative notemaking system, specifically pattern notes. We will then ask you to put pattern notemaking theory into practice immediately, with an exercise on notemaking (see exercise in Chapter 10).

Activity 1: Structured brainstorm

Before you move on to the section on notemaking, spend a few minutes preparing yourself with a structured brainstorm around the following topics.

> **Tip:** When brainstorming, just look at the topic and write down anything that pops into your head – do not try to get things 'right'; just try to capture your immediate responses.

Spend five minutes jotting down your responses to:
- Why do we make notes?
- When and where do we make notes?
- How do we make notes?

Once you have jotted down some thoughts of your own, compare your responses with those of some other students:

Why do we make notes?
- To remember – I make shopping lists and lists of things to do
- To use the information, for example, in my essays and exams
- To recall key points
- To understand what I am learning.

When and where do we make notes?
- I take notes at work, especially in meetings
- In lectures, seminars and tutorials
- When I'm reading – I'm not going to remember it all, am I?
- In the middle of the night in bed – no, seriously. I often wake up and think of a really good point for my essay. So I keep a pad and pen by the bed, so that I don't lose the thought.

How do we make notes?
- Well, I write my notes down – I know other people who tape theirs
- I take down too much information – I really hate my notes
- I take down key words, but I sometimes forget what they mean
- I make rough notes and do a shorter version later.

▶

Query: Are any of these comments similar to your own? It really does not matter if they are or not. Remember, the point was to brainstorm and that is a creative activity – there is no right or wrong when brainstorming. What you may get are interesting ideas that you can follow up.

Discussion: As always with the preparatory activities that we set at the beginning of our chapters, the point of this brainstorm was to get you ready for the work that is to come. This happens in two ways: first, it quickly reminds you of what you do know on the subject (you are not empty). Second, it can indicate the gaps in your knowledge, thus it can tell you what you need to get from the chapter. We always learn more when we are reaching out for what we want and need.

Tip: Always brainstorm before a class, lecture, seminar, or any reading that you do. It acts as a goal-setting, focusing device and you will get more.

Notemaking – a dying art

Most people are aware that as students they are expected to make notes of some sort. They are aware that these notes would form some sort of record of their studies, and that they will need this record to help them remember key points. Maybe they intend to use the information in the notes in their assignments and exams. So far so good.

However, we have noticed a change in student behaviour over the last few years. When we started teaching, students tended to take down too much information. They would write page after page of notes that tried to capture everything a lecturer was saying, or everything that was in the book. But recently we have seen students who sit through lectures making no notes at all. We have also seen those who think that they can get a degree without doing any reading, let alone making notes of their reading. Now none of these strategies is going to prove particularly useful to you as a student:

Making too many notes is too passive: you do not need to take down pages and pages of information when in lectures or when reading. But you do need to take down new information, preferably just in key words or phrases, to seed further thought.

Making no notes – from lectures or reading – means that you are not really engaging with your learning at all. You might be there in body, but you have left your mind at the door.

A good notemaking system will help you to record, understand, remember and use key information. You need to excavate lectures, seminars and your reading for ideas to learn, follow up and use in your assignments. No notes means no engagement – no active learning. This is not a good thing.

There are many different notemaking systems that people use, but they tend to break down into two main formats: some sort of linear (line by line) system or some sort of non-linear or pattern system. We shall briefly discuss these below, but first we shall consider what every set of good notes should have.

Ideal notes

Successful notes should have the following:

Source – if lecture, title, lecturer's name, date. If text, author, date, title, town, publisher.

Headings – capturing key topics.

Key words – key points, examples, illustrations, names, new ideas.

Some structure – things that make the notes easy to navigate: patterns, numbering, arrows, highlighting, etc.; things that link the notes to the course aims, outcomes and assignment.

Mnemonic triggers – things that make the notes memorable: cartoons, colour, illustrations (the Von Rostorff effect – we remember that which is bizarre, funny or bawdy (in Palmer and Pope, 1984).

Further reading – people or articles to read – noted and highlighted.

> *Query*: Do your notes usually appear like this? If not, and you do want to get better at notemaking? Then read on.

> **Tip**: Even when your lecturer gives out handouts of a lecture, it is in your own interest to make your own notes to keep you active, developing and in control of your own learning.

What's my line? Linear notes

If you do make notes already, you might be writing down information in a linear fashion, that is, line-by-line writing – the way it is here on this page. And the 'old' student described above would feel that they had got 'really good' at notemaking, if they always ended up with pages and pages of information. There would be a very reassuring feel to having captured everything.

However, there are many problems with linear notes:

- You take so many notes you feel swamped by them.
- You take so many notes that you never use them again.
- If you cannot write really fast, you feel left out of studying.

- If you don't capture something in a lecture, you panic and miss even more.
- If you leave things out, you can feel like a failure.
- It is an exceedingly passive form of notemaking – you do not need to be able to think to make linear notes, but you do need to think to be able to learn.
- All the information looks the same, which makes it very difficult to recall specific points of information.
- It is a monotonous way of learning – Buzan's half-brain learning point. It is boring and it only engages a small part of the brain, which is not a good thing.

Of course, you do not have to make even linear notes in this really passive way. You can select key points and structure the notes with headings, sub-headings, numbers or bullets, adding highlighting and mnemonics to make these notes as memorable as possible. In fact, if you follow all the advice in the beginner's guide to pattern notes, below, you can choose to make linear or pattern note formations. See Figure 12.1 for an example of successful linear notes.

However, as our whole emphasis is on active learning, we are going to recommend a much more active notemaking system than the linear. Specifically, we advise you to consider – and then rehearse and develop – a pattern notemaking system that will improve your notemaking and your overall learning.

Creative notes – pattern notes

To build creativity and activity into your notemaking, we recommend that you develop a key-word, pattern notemaking system. As you might guess, the key-word aspect implies that instead of taking down every word that is said – or every word that you read – you devise your own key words that summarise or stand for the information that you have decided that you want to keep. It is important to reduce information to key words:
- they are easier to remember
- you have chosen them
- you should be using information for yourself, not rote-learning a particular lecture or chapter from a book.

The point of gathering information is that you understand it, then you practise using it for yourself in classes, in discussion, in presentations and in your written assignments. You want to strip back information to the basics, and learn them. They can then be the foundation to your own thinking, talking and writing, but you decide what you think and say with that information.

A beginner's guide to pattern notes

You can make key-word notes from lectures and from your reading. There are several stages that you can go through – the trick is to remember that you can draft and re-draft notes. You do not need to get them right first go.

▶

1 **Prepare:** Get an overview of the lecture or chapter before you start. With books, read the beginning and end of chapters. With lectures, you should get the sense of what the lecture is to be about from your syllabus or scheme of work.

2 **Brainstorm:** Once you know what the lecture or text is about, brainstorm – identify what you know on the topic and what you need to find out (your assignment question will help you here).

3 **Goal-set:** That is, work out the sort of information that you want to take away (an overview, key points, key names and dates, key quotes, etc.). Remember to look at your assignment question to help you here.

4 **Be active:** With your goals in mind, engage with the lecture or the text in an active way, searching for and identifying key words, points, etc.

5 **Draft:** Put the key points down in a 'rough' way first. With a book, we have suggested that you make notes on the text itself. With the lecture, you might put the title in the centre of a piece of paper and draw points away from the title. If things connect directly to the central topic, branch them off. If they connect with each other, draw them off from the sub-branches.

6 **Review your rough notes**. Decide what you need to keep and what you do not need. Think about how to connect ideas with each other.

7 **Construct** your own key-word pattern, adding colour, pictures and diagrams to illustrate points and to act as memory triggers.

8 **Revise:** Review your notes regularly to commit them to your long-term memory (see also Chapter 19).

> **Tips:**
> - The Von Rostorff effect – our minds are playful by nature, and the triggers that work best with our minds are funny, dramatic, obscene or colourful (in Palmer and Pope, 1984).
> - There are many, many different ways of arranging notes in patterns – from concept maps to mind maps and beyond. Go to: http://www.visual-literacy.org/periodic_table/periodic_table.html# to see a table demonstrating all the different forms of visual notemaking modes. Practise using different styles and select the mode that best suits your thinking style.

See Figures 12.1 and 12.2 for examples of notes on notes.

Patterns are best

This very active, interactive form of notemaking definitely requires some practice to get used to. But, when mastered, you will find that each time you make your notes, you create distinctive patterns that not only record key points but also help you to learn those points.

The advantages of pattern notes are:

- Instead of taking down masses of possibly useless information, you select only that information that will be of use to you.
- They are short notes and you are inclined to re-use notes that are manageable.
- You do not need to be able to write quickly, you just need to practise selecting useful information (working in stages from rough draft to revised key-word notes).
- Selecting and arranging useful information keeps you actively engaged with your information and hence you learn more.
- You can choose to make your notes interesting and memorable.
- Each set of notes looks unique – this also helps to make them memorable.
- Building colour, pictures, diagrams and unusual things (mnemonic triggers) into your notes engages the whole brain into your learning and therefore you learn more.

Notes:	When:
What:	*Listening:*
Bare bones	Lectures
Record	Seminars
Key words	Tutorials
For assignments/further research	Discussion
Names and dates	Radio and TV
Active	*Reading:*
	Books
Organised	Journals
Patterns – see Buzan	Websites
Linear – like this	
	Thinking:
	In bed
Why:	Travelling
Review and recall	
Future reference	*Planning:*
Research	Timetables
Assignments	Assignments
Exams	(shopping, etc.)
Active learning	*How:*
Understanding	Key points
	Emphasis and highlighting
	Structure and connections
Date	Linear or pattern

FIGURE 12.1 Example of linear notes: This is linear presentation of what is presented in a pattern in Figure 12.2

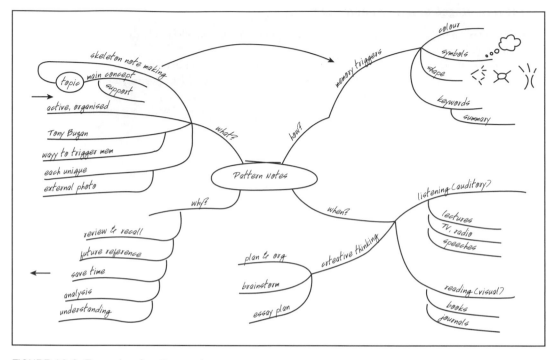

FIGURE 12.2 Example of pattern notes

But it feels so strange

As we have mentioned above, typically, this involves a dramatic change in your learning style, which will need considerable practice and will involve discomfort. The trick is to take your time, and don't try to get things right on the first go. To get better at pattern notemaking, you will need to make mistakes and get it wrong. You will need to do rough drafts of notes that you then shorten and rearrange. And, yes, it is difficult to make short notes when you do not feel that you understand a subject, and when you do not feel confident. But, it does get easier to make those short notes when you do know and understand more.

And, do remember, you will not be making your notes in 'the dark'. If you follow the advice on gaining the overview of a course (Chapter 3) you will know what you need to do and learn to pass the course, and this should tell you what notes you need to make.

Notemaking as learning

In Chapter 4, we discussed how learning could be said to be gathering new ideas and information, recording them, reorganising, understanding, remembering and using them. The creative, pattern notemaking system that we are describing here actually encourages you to *reorganise* the information you gather as you make sense of and record it. Thus we argue that a pattern notemaking system is beyond a mere recording system – it is a learning practice as well. But real learning will only happen with notemaking if you do something after you make notes, whichever system you eventually choose to adopt.

After you make notes, do something with them!

After every notemaking activity (lecture or reading), the active student should do something with their notes. The first task is to make time to do short, dynamic and memorable versions of the notes. Buzan argues that unless we do something with our notes, we will forget 98 per cent of the information in just three weeks. So, it is important to start a revision cycle as soon after completing a set of notes as possible.

So, once you have a first draft set of notes, spend ten minutes producing a shorter and more memorable set of notes (the first stage of your revision cycle). This may take more than ten minutes at first, but it will get easier with practice.

Another excellent, simple and really enjoyable revision strategy is to discuss the lecture or your reading with someone else (a study partner, if you have one). Talking really is the simplest way of improving understanding of a topic.

And don't stop at discussion; why not compare your notes with someone else? Not only is it reassuring to know that you will be doing this (thus, it doesn't matter so much if you miss a bit in a lecture), it is really interesting to see what someone else has taken away from the same lecture, or the same reading that you have done.

After the lecture – and the review and revision of notes – you should set new goals for yourself. That is, once you have made your notes, you should decide what to read or what to do next. It is always a good idea to book these activities on a calendar or in a diary. If it is not booked in, it tends not to get done.

Finally, take a moment every day to reflect on exactly what you have learned from the lecture/reading. Making learning conscious helps the learning process.

Tips:
- Buy an A1 pad and build up a pattern note of every module that you do. Add to your module pattern week by week.
- When preparing for an essay (or other assignment), put key words from the assignment question onto different sheets of A1 paper; then after every lecture or your reading, add new points to the different paragraph patterns.

Activity 2: Practising (pattern) notes

Here, we want you to practise your (pattern) notemaking techniques. Choose this or any chapter from this book. Prepare yourself for making pattern notes on the piece:
- Have a piece of paper that you turn sideways, landscape-fashion.
- Have plenty of coloured pens to hand.
- Remember your beginner's guide to pattern notes, above, or your active reading techniques (Chapter 11):
- Question: Remember why you are reading and what you want to get.

▶

- Overview: Remember your overview of your course – think about how your reading meets a particular assignment's goals
- Overview: Read the introduction and the conclusion of the piece first so that you understand what it is about.
- Question why you are reading it and what information you would like to take away from it.
- Read through once, marking up the text as you notice useful points.
- Re-read: Construct your key-word (pattern) notes.
- Review your notes and check that they are useable.

> *Query:* Have you made your pattern notes yet? If not, please attempt to do so before moving on. Do not be afraid of making mistakes. There are no mistakes, only rough drafts. The only way to avoid making mistakes is to do nothing at all, and that really is not an option if you want to be a successful student.

- Once you have made your own notes, compare them with the pattern supplied (see Figure 12.3). What do you think? Are you happy with your notes? I bet that they are not bad for a first attempt. What are you going to do now to improve? Mark some time in your diary for developing your notemaking.

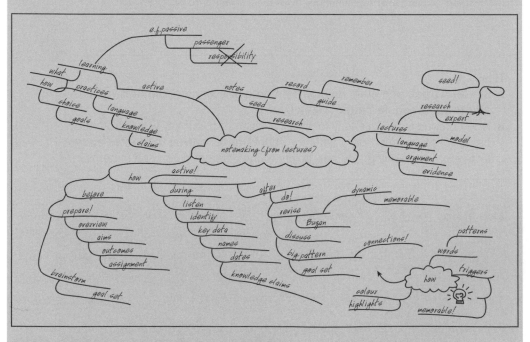

FIGURE 12.3 Example of a pattern on this chapter

Tips:
- Why not make pattern notes for each topic in this book? This will definitely give you the practice that you need to getstarted.
- Make pattern notes of television and radio programmes. This provides more practice, without the stress of it being vital for success in your own subject.
- Visit other people's lectures and make pattern notes in those. Again, there is no stress, just practice.

Conclusion

So we have examined notemaking as part of your active learning strategies, and argued that a good notemaking strategy helps you both record and learn information. We have explored linear and pattern notes, and given the Web address (http://www.visual-literacy.org/periodic_table/periodic_table.html#) of a website containing a periodic table of visual notemaking systems, so that you can eventually choose the system that best suits your learning style. We particularly wanted to make a good case for pattern notes, so that you felt persuaded to develop them for yourself. In order to start this process off, we included an exercise on notemaking and an example of a pattern on the topic of notemaking itself. So now it is up to you.

Further reading

If you are interested in taking the ideas in this chapter further, you might like to try the following:

Buzan, T. (1989) *Use Your Head*. London: BBC publications.
Buzan, B. and Buzan, T. (1999) *The Mind Map Book*. London: BBC publications.
Gibbs, G. and Makeshaw, T. (1992) *53 Interesting Things to Do in Your Lectures*. Bristol: Technical and Educational Services.
Palmer, R. and Pope, C. (1984) *Brain Train: Studying for Success*. Bristol: Arrowsmith.
Rogers, C. (1992) *Freedom to Learn*. Upper Saddle River, NJ: Merrill.
Rose, C. and Goll, L. (1992) *Accelerate Your Learning*. Aylesbury: Accelerated Learning Systems.

Review points

When reflecting on this chapter, you might notice that:

- you do realise the importance of notemaking and have decided to improve your note-making strategies
- you have practised pattern notes, and have found that it's a really useful strategy
- you have decided to construct module and/or paragraph patterns to improve your understanding of your studies and your preparation for assignments.

SECTION 3

Communicating Effectively

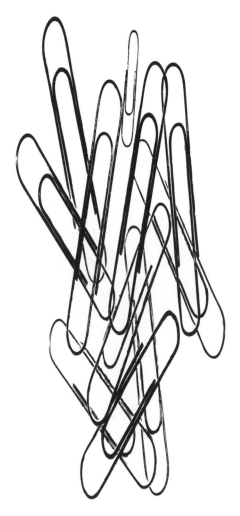

13

How to become a confident writer

AIMS

To promote confidence and success in academic writing, especially for assignments.

LEARNING OUTCOMES

That after reading through this chapter, and engaging with the activities set, you will have:
- considered the nature of assessment and issues surrounding assessment
- considered the nature of communication and issues surrounding communicating effectively in your assignments
- considered the value of writing to learn as opposed to learning to write
- started the process of organising yourself for successful assessment, with an emphasis on planning, preparation, practising and reviewing techniques
- made links between assessment activities and other activities covered in this text: organisation and time management, using the overview, being creative, notemaking, targeted research and active reading
- explored some free writing techniques to help with writing practice and development.

Introduction

Assessment is one of the most potentially fraught areas in a student's life. Nobody really enjoys being assessed: it smacks of being judged, evaluated, weighed up. This means that we can fail, we can make mistakes – mistakes that reveal us to be foolish or inadequate.

Funnily enough, that is not really the point of assessment. In this chapter, we are going to examine the nature of assessment – why do we have to be assessed? What is the point of it all? Succeeding chapters will move on to explore how to successfully plan, prepare and practise some of the major assessment modes: the essay, report, presentation and seminar. Examinations are covered in Chapter 20 – how to understand and pass exams. We will open with a consideration of the communication aspects of assessment, for if we can communicate our ideas effectively, we will do better in our assignments.

Communication

Many people might wonder why there is a section on communication in a chapter on assessment. Maybe that is the problem: when we are preparing an essay or getting that presentation ready, we are so aware of being assessed that we often forget that someone will have to read and understand the essay, that people will have to listen to, and follow, that presentation: that we will have to *communicate* with real people.

We have discovered that understanding what facilitates communication can help you to produce better assignments. We will be referring to that in the chapters below, particularly:

• on essay writing – look out for 'the paragraph questions'
• on report writing – look for the sections on 'the reader'
• on presentations – look for information on the audience, body language and the use of prompts rather than scripts.

The academic forms

In the following chapters, we are going to explore the major ways of communicating in terms of:

What: The formal conventions of assessment – essay, report, presentation, seminar. Knowing what these things actually are can remove the unnecessary worry – have I got this right? Is this what they are after? This allows you to be concerned about the real issues – what should go in my assignment? What will I have to do, what will I have to read, to construct a good assignment? When will I do these things?

Why: The particular purpose of each activity – that is, we will explore what you can get out of doing each particular assessment activity. If you can accept why you have to do something, you can often do it with better grace. This is a really simple way of getting better grades. See also Chapter 14, on 'a quick look at the most common assessment engines or forms'.

▶

How: Successful planning, researching and drafting techniques that will draw on the strategies and techniques introduced below (how to write better assignments), and help you to approach any assignment in the most successful way.

Before moving on to consider our advice for improving your communication strategies, we would like you to complete the questionnaire on your writing.

Activity 1: Writing questionnaire

Please take just five or ten minutes to answer the following five questions:

1. What writing do you do at the moment?
2. What do you like about your approach to writing at the moment?
3. What do you dislike about your current writing strategies?
4. Are there any aspects of academic writing that make you uneasy?
5. What do you think would help you to become a successful academic writer?

Once you have completed your own questionnaire, please compare your points with these from another student:

1. What writing do you do at the moment (letters, notes, memos, poetry, short stories, essays, articles, etc.)?
I actually do a lot of writing because I am working as a secretary to get me through university. It does not mean that I feel any good at it myself.

2. What do you like about your approach to writing at the moment?
I enjoy reading and always have done, so research tasks are manageable for me and I am interested in much of what I read.

3. What do you dislike about your current writing strategies?
Nearly everything! In fact, when I faced my first assignment, all I could think was, would it be good enough? What was being good enough? Would I have read enough and taken enough notes to write a well researched piece of work? Having been out of education for over 10 years, I felt very anxious about undertaking my first piece of assessed work – I didn't want to be judged negatively, because it might overwhelm me and make me want to give up the course. I had a very fragile student identity.

4. Are there any aspects of academic writing that make you uneasy?
Firstly, not knowing the level of learning required. By that, I mean that it would have been really helpful to get examples of an A-paper, B-paper, etc. to get an idea of the sorts of knowledge which is valued within HE.

I did not really know how to write in an academic tone. I picked up much of how to do this from reading the work of others and paying particular attention to

▶

the structure of the writing as well as the content. A lot of my writing skills were self-learned and self-developed, so inevitably I made a lot of mistakes. My early writing was not good quality and certainly not good enough for the high standards set by my university. It was very much a matter of personal perseverance and motivation that enabled me to go on and succeed with some of my later writing.

Also referencing, as I really struggled with the whole concept of this. I could have used some general pointers on the level and detail of work at degree level. My last studying had been 10 years earlier at GCSE level, and it was impossible to know how high I had to jump from that to succeed at degree level.

5. What do you think would help you to become a successful academic writer? More knowledge of what is expected of us and strategies of how we could reasonably achieve this. Small, manageable targets are better than masses of work with daunting deadlines. Some idea of the amount of time that should be spent on reading and making notes – this might have encouraged those with massive time pressures to get started, rather than leaving them to their own devices when they could easily become overwhelmed.

Try to build our confidence and make us take on a positive learner identity. Try to enable us to see that we can do it, we are good enough, but we just need to take a few risks, which inevitably leads to getting some things right and some things wrong. When mistakes are made, learn from them but don't be afraid to take a few risks again – it's one of the only ways to differentiate you from the crowd.

From early on, it would have been useful to see example essays … During one of our lectures, we were given four extracts from different essays and asked to mark them individually. We then had a group feedback session about what and why we had given the marks we had. We then did a show of hands to understand if we had marked similarly, which we had, although there were a few exceptions. Everyone found this a really useful task and we all learnt a lot about our own expectations and that of others.

Query: Were these answers similar to or different from your own? Have they made you think of some things to do straight away?

Discussion: One thing we noted was that there is so much confusion about getting the tone or level right, of knowing what is expected of you when you are a student. This is why we go on to write about each of the major assessment forms (essay, report, presentation and seminar) and give tips on how to do well in each of them. We also have a chapter on building your self-confidence (Chapter 9) because we, too, have found that having confidence can help you succeed more quickly, whereas

▶

having little confidence can mean that you do not push through problems, but may let yourself be defeated by them. Finally, we have addressed the point about having 'small manageable targets' in our ten-step approach to successful assignments. Here, we do break down assignment success to what we hope are manageable stages so that you, too, do not feel overwhelmed.

Assessment: what and why

Assessment is part of a measurable education system. If we have a system that is going to offer credits, certificates and other qualifications, we will also have assessment and the production of assignments. With an assignment, tutors get a piece of your work that is concrete and real – it exists as proof of your achievement. As we argue in Chapter 3, it proves that you have met all the learning outcomes of a particular module or course. Further, once they have given it a mark, tutors have the evidence, your work, to prove that the course was delivered appropriately and that their marking was rigorous.

Also, it has taken you time to produce an assignment and it will take your tutor time to mark it. Thus, assignments become products that are substantial and worthy of respect.

Furthermore, the assignment enables a dialogue between student and tutor. In a way, it is your feedback to them about what you learned from the course – and when they mark your work they can give you feedback about your communication strategies (written or oral) and the understanding of the topic that you demonstrated. Make use of this feedback – ask yourself what it tells you about your understanding of the topic and your ability to communicate effectively.

Write to learn

But more than this, it is intended that the process of preparing an assignment is heuristic – it brings about powerful active learning. That is, as you get to grips with a question, you will revise your course material so that you develop a better understanding of it, and you will research the topic further so that you extend your knowledge.

As you study, you will discover a whole range of differing arguments and opinions. When you think about all the different data, you work to synthesise what you have learned – you struggle to understand. As you then shape your data to answer a specific question, you will find that you are now struggling to communicate effectively. These are the academic practices of a successful student.

It is in the 'struggle to write' that your learning is refined. And we do mean struggle! As the typical writer says, 'Writing is easy – you just sit and stare at a blank piece of paper till your eyeballs bleed!'

Writing is hard for everyone! Not just you – or us! Once you accept that, you realise that writing is difficult because it is difficult. There does not have to be anything wrong with you if you are finding it difficult also.

However, there are some successful planning and preparation strategies that can help, and that is what we are going to look at now. It is here that much of the advice that we have given elsewhere in this book comes together.

Formative and summative assessment

In the education system, we often talk of formative and summative assessment. Formative is developmental – it is intended to measure a student's progress at a particular moment in a subject. With formative assessment, there should be an emphasis on tutor feedback, and that feedback is designed to help you do better in the summative assessment. Summative assessment usually occurs at the end of a programme of study, and it is designed to measure the student's overall achievement in the unit, course or programme.

Arguably, the best forms of assessment manage to bring about learning in the student as they engage in the assessment process. That is, while there is a product – the essay, report or presentation – that can be assessed, preparing and putting together the product is a learning process.

It can help if you view assessment in a more positive light. Try to see assessment as a chance to:

- learn your material
- show what you know.

And remember, assessment is not a trick – you will be assessed on material that you have covered on a programme of study.

Tips:
- Writing and planning both get easier with practice.
- Practise planning everything before you write, e.g. a letter to a friend.
- Write every day, even if it's only for 15 or 20 minutes.
- Write a lot!

How to write better assignments – ten steps to successful assessment

So, now that we have looked at the what and the why of assessment, we can move on to give you practical advice on how to prepare and write any assignment. We are going to consider everything from examining the question and preparing to research to using your tutor's feedback effectively. We have broken this down into ten key steps, and there is a photocopiable checklist below so that you can follow these ten steps with every assignment that you undertake.

Tip: Remember, studying is meant to be full time. You are supposed to be working between 35–40 hours every week when at university. Read something every day and write often.

The ten steps to success

Prepare
Actively research and read
Review notes
Plan structure
Write first draft
Leave it
Review, revise and edit
Proofread
Hand in and celebrate
Review work and progress

Tip: Think 35–40 hours per week, every week!

Step 1: Prepare to research

This is the longest section which reflects how important good preparation is. The trick with good preparation is to spend time working on the question. Do not try to answer the question – think about it first. This is where it is important to manage your time (Chapter 5), as it takes a significant amount of time to prepare a good assignment.

Tip: Start to work on an assignment as soon as possible (week one or two would be good!). Allow several weeks for reading and several more weeks to draft and re-draft your work.

Open a research folder

It is useful to have a folder for every assignment that you are doing. The folder becomes the place where you automatically put useful notes, press cuttings, thoughts and feelings on the assignment. Without a folder, your information can drift, and your thinking will too.

Open a research folder early and start collecting information from week one of your course.

The research folder itself can be simple or elaborate – you can re-cycle old A4 envelopes or buy something really swish and attractive that will inspire you just by looking at it. The point is to open the folder so that you focus on the question early, and gather information throughout a programme of study – not in the couple of days before the deadline!

> **Tip:** Open a folder for every module that you do, and every question that you have to answer. Make sure that you put something in each folder every week.

Look at the question

Write the whole question on the outside of the folder or envelope. Do not abbreviate: if you miss a bit of the question you will definitely miss an important part of the answer. When this happens, you are throwing marks away.

Examine the question: once you have written out the question (essay titles are often called questions, even when not phrased as such), analyse every word in it. Make sure that you understand exactly what and exactly how much the question is asking you to do.

Doing this early in a course of study tunes your brain into the course itself more effectively. In this way you 'hear' more in class and 'see' more in set texts; also, you may hear and see more as you read the papers and watch television. Note what you see and hear – put the notes in your research folder. This will give you more overall.

Each time you hear something in class, or read something related to the topic, and then put the notes that you make in your envelope, remember to write the source – author, date, title, publisher – on the outside of the envelope and you will build up your bibliography as you go.

> **Tips:**
> - Put the question in your own words and say it back to another student or a tutor.
> - Underline every important word in the question. Investigate every word underlined.
> - Every word in a question is a gift – use them all. Each one is there to be investigated, questioned, challenged, argued for or against.
> - Make sure that you do something about every word – don't leave any out.

Be creative

Consider every word in the question in a flexible, creative way. Don't forget to brainstorm and question-matrix every word in the question (see Chapter 8).

Performing a creative loosening-up activity like this allows you to cover the question in more depth and breadth. It should also reassure you – you do not need to know the answer when you look at a question, but you should know how to devise more questions.

Tip: Put your brainstorm or matrix on the outside of your research folder. Look at it before you go to a lecture or seminar, or before you start your reading.

Use the overview

Cross-reference the question with the aims and learning outcomes (see Chapter 3). Remember that when answering an assignment question, one brief comes from the question itself, while the wider brief comes from the course, module, programme or unit that set the question.

You must be very clear about the module aims and outcomes when researching and drafting your essay. You must shape your essay so that it answers the question, and also so that it demonstrates that you have met the learning outcomes (see example in Chapter 3).

Tip: Add key words from course aims and learning outcomes to your brainstorm or matrix. Brainstorm those words as well.

Action plan

In the light of your brainstorming and other thinking, you then have to decide exactly what you will have to do to research and produce your assignment. Things to consider include:
- What do you now have to do?
- Who will you speak to (tutor, study partner, subject librarian)?
- What will you read?
- When will you do these things?

Tip: It helps if you draw up a detailed and systematic list of everything that you will need to do and when you will do it. Allow a column for ticking off items as you complete them (see Figure 13.1).

A typical action plan might contain:

- which lecture notes to re-read
- which essential texts to read
- which additional texts to read
- dates – when you will do the work
- check off – space to tick once you have completed the work.

Step 2: Follow the action plan: systematic and targeted research and active reading

Follow the plan

Once you have devised your action plan, follow it through. Read actively and interactively, using your QOOQRRR technique (see Chapter 11). Remember to get physical with the

WHAT	WHY	WHERE	WHEN	CHECK
Note what you will research	Remind yourself *why* you are researching that topic	Note where you will look for the information	Set a date and keep to it	Check when you have done it
e.g. Key word from the assignment	e.g. It could be a word from the question or it could refer to a learning outcome.	e.g. Lecture notes, books, journals, etc.		
Research: Active learning	Part of question	Essential study skills Chap....	Thursday afternoon	

FIGURE 13.1   A sample action plan

texts – mark them up, annotate, make comments and cross-references as you go – you will get much more from your reading when you do this.

Read with a purpose

Don't forget that when you are reading, you are looking for the answers to the questions generated by your question matrix. Typically, you are looking for them one at a time – you are not looking for the whole answer to the question in any one piece of reading.

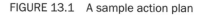

> **Tip:** When reading to find the answers to an assignment question, read about one word or phrase at a time. Do not look for the whole answer to the question.

Creative notes

Remember to make your creative pattern notes (see Chapter 12) on one side of the paper only: you do not want half of your information facing the table – you want it all facing you.

> **Tips: paragraph patterns**
> - Get really large sheets of paper – A1 rather than A4 – and put a key word from the question in the centre of each sheet.
> - Put the notes from all your reading about one topic onto one sheet of paper – this becomes a potential paragraph.
> - Put all the evidence on another paragraph topic on another sheet of paper.
> - Keep going till you have all the question words covered.
> - Remember to put author (date) title, publisher, town and page numbers in your notes.

Referencing tips and avoiding plagiarism

All the reading that you do to prepare for your assignments provides you with ideas, knowledge claims, arguments and evidence. It is really important that you note from where you got your ideas when you use them in your writing.

You are not supposed to be generating new knowledge – you are supposed to be using the knowledge that is already out there, and demonstrating that you are by citing correctly and constructing complete bibliographies.

If you do not give the source of an idea – even once you have put it into your own words – this is considered to be theft, it is called plagiarism and it is a serious academic offence.

> **Tip:** When you read, record your sources as you go, and in the correct format for your discipline's referencing system.

Harvard system: Author (date) Title. Location: publisher.

Paper-based sources
Author (by surname and initials) (Date of publication) Title (italic if a book, inverted commas if a journal article). Location of publisher: publisher.

For example:
Burns, T. and Sinfield S. (2008) *Essential Study Skills: The Complete Guide to Success @ University*. London: Sage.

Documents obtained from the Internet
All references begin with the same information that would be provided for a printed source (or as much of that information as possible): author (date) Title publisher. The WWW information is then placed at the end of the reference.

Note: It is important to give the date of access because documents on the Web may change in content, move, or be removed from a site altogether.

For example:
■ An article:
Jacobson, J.W., Mulick, J.A. and Schwartz, A.A. (1995) 'A history of facilitated communication: science, pseudoscience, and antiscience – science working group on facilitated communication', *American Psychologist*, 50:750–65. Retrieved 25 January 1996, from http://www.apa.org/journals/jacobson.html
■ A newspaper article:
Sleek, S. (1996, January) Psychologists build a culture of peace. APA Monitor, pp. 1, 33 [Newspaper, selected stories online]. Retrieved 25 January 1996, from http://www.apa.org/monitor/peacea.html

▶

- WWW document:

Li, X. and Crane, N. (1996, 20 May) Bibliographic formats for citing electronic information. Retrieved 10 March 1997, from http://www.uvm.edu/~xli/reference/estyles.html

- WWW document – corporate author:

American Psychological Association (1996) How to cite information from the World Wide Web. Retrieved 17 March 1997, from http://www.apa.org/journals/webref.html

- WWW document – no author:

A field guide to sources on the Internet: citation formats (1995, 18 December) Retrieved 7 February 1996, from http://www.cc.emory.edu/WHSCL/citation.formats.html

- WWW document – no author, no date:

GVU'S 8th WWW user survey (n.d.) Retrieved 8 August 2000, from http://www.cc.gatech.edu/gvu/usersurveys/survey1997-10/

- An abstract:

Rosenthal, R. (1995) State of New Jersey *v*. Margaret Kelly Michaels: An overview [Abstract]. *Psychology, Public Policy and Law*, I: 247–71. Retrieved 25 January 1996, from http://www.apa.org/journals/ab1.html

Film/video

Maas, J.B. (Producer) and Gluck, D.H. (Director) (1979) Deeper into hypnosis [Film]. Englewood Cliffs, NJ: Prentice Hall.

CD ROMS

- Newspaper or magazine on CD-ROM:

Gardner, H. (1981, December) Do babies sing a universal song? Psychology Today [CD-ROM], pp. 70–6.

- Abstract on CD-ROM:

Meyer, A.S. and Bock, K. (1992) The tip-of-the-tongue phenomenon: blocking or partial activation? [CD-ROM]. Memory Cognition, 20: 715–26. Abstract from: SilverPlatter File: PsycLIT Item: 80-16351.

- Article from CD-ROM encyclopedia:

Crime (1996) In Microsoft Encarta 1996 Encyclopedia [CD-ROM]. Redmond, WA: Microsoft Corporation.

- Dictionary on CD-ROM:

Oxford English dictionary computer file: on compact disc (1992) (2nd edn.) [CD-ROM]. Oxford: Oxford University Press.

Taken from: www.UEFAP.COM (writing/references)

Step 3: Review your notes

Once you have nearly finished your reading, remove your notes from your research folder and lay them out in front of you. Look at what you have gathered for each paragraph. For each paragraph, consider all the 'agreeing' points and all the 'disagreeing' points. Read them again. Reflect on what you have discovered – given all this information, what do you now think? Why?

Tips:
- Notice the evidence for and against your topic.
- Think what your argument will be, given the evidence.
- Discuss your evidence. Remember, when other people write, they are not answering your question. When you lasso their points, you will have to work on them to build them into your arguments. This is why we always have to discuss our quotes. Relate the quote to your argument; relate it to the question.
- See how we have discussed Rogers, Buzan and Gibbs in Chapter 8, on how to be creative in your learning.
- Index-surf to brush up your paragraphs. Once you have completed your major research, and you are happy with it, you can just index-surf to get little extra bits and pieces to take your work that little bit further.

Step 4: Plan

When you are ready, plan the body of your assignment (essay, report, presentation). Think of the different ideas that will go to answer the whole question. Think about building a logical case and all the different ideas that you will have to cover to answer the whole question.

Always remember that it is one main idea per paragraph. For each idea, think of a possible argument and think of the evidence that will support that argument. Think of the evidence that might work against that argument.

Remember that your reader will be thinking of the opposite evidence: do not just ignore inconvenient or contradictory evidence – know what it is and argue against it.

Once all the ideas are jotted down, you can examine them again and number them according to where they should come in the body of your answer – order them so that you are building a logical case.

Tip: Write all the ideas on separate pieces of paper. Move the pieces of paper around to discover the best structure for the answer.

Step 5: Write the first draft

Once you have the points (paragraph outlines) in a rough order, write the first draft of your answer. Use the paragraph questions to prompt your writing. For each paragraph, answer the following:
- What is this about?
- What exactly is that?

- What is your argument?
- What is the evidence? What does it mean?
- What is the opposing evidence? What does that mean?
- Therefore … ?
- What is your final point (in relation to the question)?

At the end of each section, remember to tie what you have written to the question. It is not down to your reader to guess what you are trying to say, or to think, 'I wonder how this relates to the question?' If your reader has to do that, then something is missing from your answer.

Intros and outros

If you write your introduction and conclusion at your first draft stage, remember that the introduction has to set the reader up to understand how your final piece (essay, report or presentation) will answer the question. Therefore, an introduction can have some general remarks about the question – how important it is, how it touches upon key issues – but you must also give the agenda, that is, the order in which you will be presenting your points. In the conclusion, you must re-state your main arguments and the points that you made.

> **Tip:** Write draft intros and outros, but change them when you have finished drafting your piece.

Go with the flow

As you write your first draft, try to build a flow in your writing – remember, it is a first draft and does not have to be perfect. If you try to be perfect, you will hit writing blocks.

So, when writing your first draft, do not try to answer all the paragraph questions the first go through. Leave gaps. Repeat yourself. Put in rough words rather than the 'best' words. Write messy sentences in poor English with no verbs. Write overlong sentences that hide the point you are trying to make. But remember also that you will be going back over this first draft several times.

Writing tips – get a computer:

- get a computer and draft and re-draft work straight to computer
- learn to touch-type
- use the format button to make your work look professional. Format leads you to

Font and paragraph
Font – think about:
- font type: Arial is nice and clean, while Times New Roman is the font used in academic books and journals
- font size – 10, 11 and 12 are good readable font sizes. Consider:

THIS IS AN 'ARIAL' TYPE FONT, SIZE 12

▶

THIS IS A 'TIMES NEW ROMAN' TYPE FONT, SIZE 14
THIS IS A 'GARAMOND' TYPE FONT, SIZE 16
THIS IS A 'COURIER NEW' TYPE FONT,
SIZE 18

Paragraph – think about:
- left-aligned or justified
- spacing – typically, 1.5 or double-line.

Step 6: Leave it!

Once you have written the first draft you feel great, your answer is great, your friends are great and life is great. Do not believe this! Put the work to one side and leave it for a while.

This will give you some distance and objectivity, but more than this: your unconscious mind will seek to close the gaps that you left.

In other chapters, we point out that we do have to train our brains to remember and learn the things that we want remembered and learned, but we also have to train ourselves to work with the way that our brains actually work. Typically, the brain likes closure. The brain will not be happy with all the gaps in your assignment. Thus, your brain will struggle to close the gaps that you have left. If you allow a break in your writing process, you are allowing the brain to close the gaps – you are working with your brain.

First draft tips

- You are not looking for the one right answer that already exists – there are usually several ways of tackling a question. As long as you were creative with the whole question, and you cross-referenced with course aims and outcomes, you are probably on the right track.
- Write the first draft, following the plan.
- Or write your 'favourite' paragraph first to get you started.
- Or free write your conclusion to get an idea of where you want your answer to go and change the conclusion later.
- Do not even try for perfection – this will cause writing blocks.
- Be boring, repeat yourself, and, most importantly of all, leave gaps.
- When you get stuck for an idea put . . . (dot, dot, dot – this is an ellipsis) and write on.
- Academic writing is always tentative rather than definite. You will get very familiar with: typically, it could be argued that, thus this makes a case for . . . , or, this suggests that . . .

▶

- It can be difficult to be tentative when you do care passionately about what you are writing. Practise.
- If you write the first draft straight onto your computer, it is easier to revise and edit.
- As you play with the ideas – and possibly re-arrange them – you will need to re-write your introduction and conclusion to reflect the changes that you make; that is why it is usually good to leave these till last.
- Use the paragraph questions.
- At the end of each paragraph, remember to make a point. Tell the reader what you have demonstrated or proven.
- Remember to tie in what you have written to the essay question. (If your reader could say, 'So?' or 'So what?' after reading your paragraph, you have not said enough.)

Step 7: Review, revise and edit

This is the stage where you go back over your work and struggle to make it the very best it can be. Here you have to re-read what you have written, and change it. Sometimes we have to change everything, and nothing of our first draft gets left. This does not matter. Remember, we are writing to learn, so our thoughts should change as we write. Also, we would never get to a good version if we did not go through our rough versions. So always be prepared to draft and re-draft your work: not only is it impossible to hit perfection on a first draft, you should not even try – it is bad technique and it can actually stop you writing anything.

Remember, once you have written something you have something to change, but a blank page stays a blank page for an awfully long time.

On your first review, you might start from the beginning of the answer and polish as you go. After that, try to concentrate on one paragraph at a time, not necessarily in the order it is written but in any order. Polishing one paragraph at a time is much better than always going back to the start. If you always go back to the beginning, you may never polish the end, and you can quickly become very bored with what you are doing.

Tips:
- Review, revise and edit – this struggle is the assignment-writing process.
- Allow plenty of time for this.
- Go through the whole answer when doing the first and last drafts, but in between, attack one paragraph at a time.
- This is where you go back and put in the 'best' word. This is where you put in the verbs. This is where you shorten long sentences so that you make clear, effective points.
- When you have finished polishing paragraphs, check the 'links' between paragraphs – make sure that they still connect with each other.

Step 8: Proofread

Once you are happy with your assignment, you are ready to stop revising it – you are ready to say, 'This is the best I can do'. At this point, you still have to proofread the final version. (Sometimes we are never really 'happy' with our work, but there still comes a time to stop and move on to the next task.)

Proofreading is not editing. At this stage, you are not looking to change what you have written – here you are going through looking for mistakes, grammatical errors, tense problems, spelling mistakes or typographical errors.

Note: You now know that when writing, it is useful to leave gaps, knowing that the brain likes closure – it will work to fill the gaps. This works against us when we are proofreading. The brain still likes closure – this means that our eyes will 'see' what should be there rather than what is there. To get over this, we have to make our proofreading 'strange', which we can do by having breaks in between our proofreading.

Tips:

- Read your assignment aloud (if it is a presentation, rehearse before a critical friend).
- Swap assignments with a friend – proofread each other's work.
- Cover the assignment with paper and proofread one sentence at a time.
- Proofread from back to front.
- Proofread from the bottom of the page to the top.
- Proofread several times, just checking for one of 'your' mistakes at a time.
- Like everything else we do, proofreading gets better with practice.

Step 9: Hand it in

You should now be ready to hand your work in, on or before the deadline. (And remember that deadline. On most university programmes, a late submission is awarded an automatic fail! This is serious.)

So, once your assignment is done – congratulations! – but before you rush off and celebrate: remember to always keep copies of your work. Never hand in the only copy. Obviously, if you are writing on a computer it is OK – save your work to the hard drive and to a memory stick.

If writing by hand, still photocopy. And if the assessment unit loses your assignment, do not hand in your last copy – photocopy that. A student of ours came back and told us that the assessment unit lost her essay – the same one – three times!

Step 10: Getting work back

When we get work back, we look at the grade, feel really happy or really unhappy, throw the work to one side and forget all about it. This is not a good idea. What is a good idea is to review what you have written, and see if you still think it is good. As an active learner, you should try to take control of your own work – you have to learn how to judge it for yourself and not just rely on the tutor's opinions.

At the same time, you should also utilise the feedback that you get from the tutor, and be prepared to use that feedback to write a better essay next time. So, a good thing to do is to perform a **SWOT** analysis of our own work, that is, look for the:

Strengths
Weaknesses
Opportunities
Threats.

When you SWOT your work, look for the things that you think you did well or not so well. Then look for the things that the tutor appears to be telling you that you did well or not so well. Resolve to do something about your strengths and your weaknesses.

Getting work back – a student's response

For an example of one student's response to receiving critical feedback, go to http://anessayevolves.blogspot.com/2007/08/experience-and-goal-irreconcilably.html We reproduce a bit of her commentary here:

> 'In the case of this essay, the assessor's final comment that the assignment, *"… could be improved by having a clearer focus and a stronger take-home message, which could perhaps be achieved by interpreting the title in a narrower way…"*, lends weight to this. I feel that in this case (and in some others!) I slipped away from my main task which is usually identified by a thorough question analysis. Looking back, instead of presenting the strengths and weaknesses of Freud's theory of personality as measured against the yardstick of evidential science, I decided at too early a point to become an advocate for it. I tried also to question the appropriateness of the paradigm often used to assess Freud when it might have profited me (in terms of more marks) to stick with it. It may have helped me achieve the stronger take-home message counselled by the assessor. And interestingly, in this case, I carried out my question analysis belatedly.' (accessed 14.08.07)

We were impressed by this student's response to her feedback. She had worked long and hard on the assignment and the mark was lower than she had hoped, however, she still managed to appreciate the tutor's comments and to take something away from the experience that will help her in future assignments.

Becoming a confident writer: free-writing exercises

The ten-step approach will help you with any assignment, so please put it into practice. Here, we are going to explore how to practise your writing. As we have argued above, writing for assessment is fraught with tension; because of this, we tend not to approach writing the way that we might approach other activities in which we wanted to develop our skills, techniques or practices.

For example, if we wanted to get better at cooking, driving or playing a musical instrument, we would know that we would need to practise – a lot – in order to do so. However, there is something about academic writing that makes it special and different in the minds of most people, and they tend to only do it when it is being assessed. In other words, they only engage in academic writing under the most stressful of conditions. Funnily enough, when engaged with in this way, academic writing continues to be stressful.

Students will only become confident writers if they practise writing, and if they are interested enough in their subjects to have something to say:

> '...The emphasis should be, I would argue, on getting students to become familiar with, and practised or rehearsed in, those practices which are associated with (a) being an undergraduate and then (b) being a graduate ...
>
> Particular forms of writing (and reading and talking) may be seen as examples of the practices associated with the identity of an undergraduate, and also of a graduate. Academic writing encompasses a range of types, particularly papers written for an academic audience – for a conference (or seminar, symposium, colloquium, etc.), for an academic journal, book, etc. The purpose is (or should be) to present an argument in support of a knowledge claim. The criteria for judging such an argument would include its location wrt [with respect to] existing, broadly accepted (and also contested) knowledge claims (the existing literature), the logical reasoning and the empirical evidence adduced. The style should be that which is generally accepted, including conventions for citations, etc.
>
> ...Above all, it requires the student to have something to say that is worth saying, their own voice wrt the issues at hand.'

Len Holmes by email, 2002

Included below are several free-writing activities that are designed to help you to review your own approaches to writing, and in the process to build your own writing confidence.

Writing development tips

- **Group writing:** form a group with some friends that you trust. Brainstorm and plan 'perfect' answers to your assignments. This is especially useful when preparing for exams.
- **Practise brainstorming:** sit down with a list of questions. Give yourselves ten minutes to brainstorm and plan each answer. Remember, brainstorming and planning get quicker with practice.
- **Write those paragraphs:** once you have an assignment plan, sit down and use the paragraph questions to prompt your paragraph writing.
- **Do not aim for perfection:** get something written and then change it.
- **Practise writing:** do not just write for assessment – get into the habit of writing something every week, even every day.

Activity 2: Overcoming writing blocks (OWB)

This is an activity you can try on your own, or with other people around you. Each person will need two pieces of paper plus pens and pencils.

1. Find a space in which you think that you would be able to write.
2. Settle down with two pieces of paper in front of you, and all the pens and pencils that you could want. Label one piece of paper – writing. Label the other piece of paper – commentary.
3. Give yourself a set time to write – at least 15 minutes and up to 30 minutes.
4. Settle down to write about anything that you can hear, see, feel or smell at the time of writing. Write continuously. Do not stop.

> **Tip:** Do not worry about this... just write. Do not put the exercise off – do it!

5. Every time you do stop writing, put the reason for stopping on the commentary sheet of paper. No matter what the reason is – how silly, or small or trivial – make a note of it.
6. After your set writing time, stop writing.
7. Review all the different reasons you gave for stopping. Notice what your reasons for stopping are.
8. If you have been working with other people, discuss all the different reasons given for stopping writing.
9. Work out what to 'do' about some of your different reasons for stopping.

Reasons that other students have given for stopping:
- Stopping to search for the right word
- Checking my spelling
- Wondering whether I've got the sentence right
- Checking my grammar and tenses
- I kept checking the time
- Thinking of a new idea
- I was trying to think of a better idea
- It was too hot
- I felt too cold
- I was uncomfortable; I kept wriggling in my chair
- I was thirsty
- I was hungry
- I heard a noise

▶

- Someone left the room and I wondered what they were doing
- I could not see the point of this activity – I felt stupid and wanted to stop.

Query: Do you notice anything about these points? Are they anything like your reasons for stopping?

Discussion: There appear to be certain 'sets' of reasons for stopping work:
- Searching for words and spellings, checking that the work is correct.
- Thinking of new or better ideas.
- Feeling uncomfortable physically or mentally; being hungry or thirsty or too hot or cold; checking the time; not feeling right in the chair; wondering what people are doing; doubting the point of the task.

Query: Is there anything we can 'do' about these things? Think about it first, then move on to our suggestions.

1. Thinking of words and spellings and generally getting it 'right'

We have mentioned above that you should be prepared to draft and re-draft your work. In first drafts, *you should not even try to go for perfection.* Put in the wrong word, and do not worry about getting the spellings and tenses right. When stuck for a word, put in an ellipsis (dot, dot, dot) or BLAH or a note to yourself, and move on. The trick with getting a first draft down is to keep the 'flow' going. Definitely do not interrupt your flow of ideas, for in doing that you will lose the thread of your thinking.

Tip: Practise using the ellipsis to keep your flow going. Accept the notion of drafting and re-drafting work.

2. Searching for ideas

We mention often that it is a good idea to brainstorm before you write. Even with a task like this, it is typically a good idea to jot a few ideas down before you start. At least brainstorm a few key ideas to get a rough shape to your work. Once you have a plan, write to your plan.

▶

> **Tip:** Practise brainstorming and planning.

3. General feelings of discomfort

This could mean that you have not yet sorted out 'where to write' or perhaps 'why' you are writing or studying.

Where: Perhaps you need to do a bit more work on your organisation – plan when, where and how you will study (Chapter 5). Or perhaps you need to explore your own individual learning style (Chapter 4). Remember, there is no one correct way of working. Some people like quiet, some like noise. Some like bright lights, some definitely do not. Some people like to sit still, some like to move around. Discover where you want to study and what learning conditions suit you. Next time you write, write in your study space.

Why: If you are feeling really resentful about the writing that you have to do on your course, or more generally about all the time that being a student is 'costing' you, perhaps you have not fully accepted that you are a student, or perhaps you have not chosen the right course or the right module? Being a student should be taking about 35–40 hours per week of your time, every week. You will not want to give this much time to something you are not interested in or motivated about, or if you do not want it. Have a look at Chapter 4 which explores how to be a successful learner.

After reflecting on these topics, plan what you need to do next, and when you need to do it.

> **Tips:** Complete a learning contract for the course that you are currently undertaking (Chapter 4). If you think you have chosen the wrong course after all, and that you will never be able to put in the effort that needs to be put in, make an appointment to see Careers or the student counsellors at your institution as soon as possible to discuss this.

Activity 3: Prompted writing – paper prompts

As with the OWB activity above, this is an activity you can try on your own, or with other people around you. Each person will need paper plus pens and pencils. Before you start to write, you need to collect together old cards – such as birthday, Christmas and old postcards; you could write quotes from philosophers or people you are studying on large index cards. The cards need to be shuffled and placed face down on a table so that no one can see what is on them.

1. Find a space in which you think that you would be able to write.
2. Settle down with your paper in front of you, and all the pens and pencils that you could want. Everybody chooses one 'prompt' card at random.

▶

3. Give yourself a set time to write – at least 15 minutes and up to 30 minutes.
4. Settle down to write about anything that pops into your head when viewing the prompt card. Write continuously. Do not stop.

> **Tip:** Do not worry about this... just write. Do not put the exercise off – do it!

5. After your set writing time, stop writing.
6. Review this writing process – how similar to or different from your academic writing process was it? Notice what was good about writing in this way. Notice if there was anything that you did not like about writing in this way.
7. If you have been working with other people, discuss what you liked and disliked about writing in this way.
8. Work out how you can learn about what encourages you to write from this activity, and build what you learn into ways of approaching your academic writing.

What other people have said:

- 'I just loved having other people in the room working at the same time as me. I did not know that about myself. I will work in the library more often now, as that will encourage me.'
- 'I started to write, then thought that everybody else had chosen a better card than me. I was convinced I'd chosen a bad card. . . This is the way I am on a course. I keep thinking I've made a bad choice and this gets in the way of me getting anything done at all. I have to choose wisely and then just get on with it.'
- 'I found that I wanted to write about two different things at once. So I just got two sheets of paper and did that. I do get like this with my essays too – I feel blocked because I really want to say something, but I know it's not really what the question wants. I think next time that happens I will just write out what I want to get off my chest – and then dump it.'

> *Query:* Are these comments anything like your own? Can you also 'learn' from these points and your own? What will you do with this information?

> *Discussion:* All sorts of little things can get in the way of our writing: we do or do not like having other people around us; we do or do not like the question that we have been set; we do or do not have something to say or, worse, we know that what we really want to say is not what the question wants from us. Notice how the other students, above, plan to deal with their issues, and think of some tips or tricks of your own that you think will help you with your writing in the future.

Activity 4: Prompted writing – physical prompts (being creative)

As with the OWB activity and the prompted writing activity, above, this is an activity you can try on your own, or with other people around you. Each person will again need paper plus pens and pencils. Before you start to write, you need to collect together physical objects that you will then use to prompt your writing: candles, pieces of wood, rock or machinery, statues or other interesting objects. Place all the objects in a sack. Everybody then chooses an object at random and uses this to prompt free writing, as above. Again, all the writing and reflection on that writing can be used to help you understand what helps or hinders you with respect to writing.

Tip: This activity is especially useful if you are a kinaesthetic learner (see Chapter 4) or if you want to develop your creative side (see also Chapter 8).

Free writing

Free writing is a bit like brainstorming; however, rather than looking at a title and jotting down all the random thoughts that occur to you, in free writing you read the title and then write briefly, but in a really focused way to the title. Write in a 'stream of consciousness', capturing everything that pops into your mind when you respond to the title.

In free writing, you are not trying to be right, you are plumbing your unconscious to see what comes out that might be valuable in your thinking around and preparation for writing the subsequent essay. As with other advice on writing a first draft, the free write is best if you just write. You do not check spellings, tense or grammar. You do not try to get the 'right' order. You just let everything out as quickly as possible on to your page. After some little time has elapsed, you can look at your free write to see if you have captured anything useful to use in the essay proper.

Free writing can really surprise you, often revealing that you know much more about a topic than you previously thought, and also revealing that you can communicate really effectively when you do not get in your own way. Some of our favourite chapters in this textbook started as free writing, where we just sat down and poured out everything that we thought and felt on a topic, later revising, shaping and otherwise improving what we captured the first go round.

All the writing activities set above have been versions of free writing – the trick now is to start free writing as part of your repertoire of academic writing techniques.

For an example of how another student has used free writing to approach an assignment go to: http://evolvingessay.pbwiki.com/FreudianFreewrite

This is the evolving essay website that we have already referred to. Have a look at the free write that this student did on the Freud essay question and consider the editing strategies she used to start her Freud essay journey.

Conclusion

We have considered the what, why and how of assessment. With 'what', we paid attention to assignments being substantial and tangible evidence that you have engaged with your programme of study; that you are demonstrating your learning. With 'why', we stressed the active learning aspects of assessment, stressing that while the product can be marked, your process, all the reading, thinking, discussing and struggling that you do to produce an assignment, is part of active learning – we really do write to learn rather than learn to write. With 'how', we looked at the ten steps to assignment preparation, breaking the process into ten manageable stages. We followed this with a series of practical exercises designed to build your awareness of ways in which you can improve your writing, including a section on free writing. We hope that you now feel in a better position to approach your assignments.

Review points

When reviewing your notes on this chapter, on how to become a more confident writer, you might realise that:

- you can now look at assessment in a more positive light
- you are prepared to engage in 'writing to learn' as opposed to writing up what you know
- you are ready for the 'struggle to write' – it does not mean that there is anything wrong with you
- you realise the importance of the ten-step plan, prepare and review strategy
- you have made links with the other sections of the book, especially managing your time, utilising the overview, being creative with a question, making pattern notes and engaging in targeted research and active reading
- you have realised the importance of practising writing, and of writing often
- you have enjoyed these free writing activities and you will attempt free writing with your next assignment
- you have realised more about your own approaches to both studying and writing, and you have noted some strategies to put into place immediately, to help you get more confident as a writer and more successful as a student

Ten stages to assessment success

Photocopy this assessment preparation checklist, and complete one for every assignment that you undertake.

- ☐ **Prepare:**
- ☐ Check you know the task (the whole question) and the form (essay, report, presentation, seminar, etc.)
- ☐ Open research folder – write the whole question on the folder
- ☐ Have the overview – fit the task to the module aims and learning outcomes
- ☐ Analyse the question – all of it
- ☐ Use creative brainstorming strategies to generate ideas
- ☐ Action plan – work out what to research, why, where and when!
- ☐ **Follow the action plan:** attend lectures and seminars in a positive frame of mind and undertake targeted research and active reading
- ☐ **Review your findings:** identify gaps and then plug the gaps
- ☐ **Plan the outline:** of the essay, report, seminar, presentation
- ☐ **Write the rough draft:** go with the flow and leave gaps
- ☐ **Leave a time lag:** allow the brain to close the gaps
- ☐ **Review, revise and edit:** struggle to write and then decide on a final draft
- ☐ **Proofread:** (rehearse, if it involves a presentation)
- ☐ **Hand in work:** on or before a deadline
- ☐ **SWOT:** your progress

14

How to write great essays

AIMS

To prepare you for successful academic writing – the essay.

LEARNING OUTCOMES

That after reading through this chapter, and engaging with the activities set, you will have:

- considered the value of writing to learn as opposed to learning to write
- considered the key academic assessment/communication form of the essay
- started the process of organising yourself for successful assessment, with an emphasis on planning, preparation, practising and reviewing techniques
- made links between assessment activities and other activities covered in this text: organisation and time management, using the overview, being creative, notemaking, targeted research and active reading.

The academic forms

In these chapters (14–18), we are going to explore the primary assessment forms – the essay, report, presentation and seminar, in terms of:

- **What:** the formal conventions of the essay, report, presentation, seminar. Knowing what these things are, what they should look like, and how they should be structured, can allow you to think about the question, rather than how to structure the answer.
- **Why:** the particular purpose of each activity – that is, each assessment engine or form is designed to bring about slightly different learning, or to demonstrate different aspects of your learning. In discussing the 'why' of assessment forms, we want to encourage you to ask that question in future: 'why have they set *this*?'
- **How:** successful planning and researching techniques, including the ten steps to a successful assessment (Chapter 13).

A quick look at the most common assessment forms

Each assessment form has its own structure and typically has its own function. Here, we are giving a very quick overview of some of the major forms used in universities at the moment. See if reading this helps you better understand what is going on and why, when you are being assessed.

An essay is typically a discursive tool, that is, it invites theoretical argument around a topic. You are supposed to research for an essay by reading the key knowledge claims in your subject, and use them, citing correctly, to build a series of arguments, supported by theoretical evidence, to answer the question set. One of the most formal academic tasks, essays are typically written in the third person and past tense, with extensive accurate reference to supporting arguments and evidence taken from the key players in your discipline.

A report (Chapter 16) is typically a practical tool: it invites investigation of real problems and the discovery of realistic solutions, c.f. the scientific experiment or business report. Reports are written for specific readers, in the third person and past tense, and are signposted with headings and sub-headings for easy navigation.

A presentation (Chapter 17) is very similar in structure to the essay and can be either discursive like the essay or more practical like the report. The purpose of the presentation is usually to demonstrate the student's oral communication skills.

A seminar (Chapter 18) is a combination of elements of the above with the presentation of a paper plus discussion among the 'audience'. The goal here is that research is shared with other students, and discussion by those students will be used by the seminar giver to develop their research/thinking further. This is also useful to students as a forum for testing ideas and gaining understanding of how an academic argument is built.

A reflective essay (Chapter 15) is designed to get the student to make links between theory and practice. In this way, you are invited to enrich practice (as a teacher or a social worker, say) with reference to theory. And to better understand

▶

theory by reference to practice. These days, the reflective essay is often used as a precursor to the research project (see end 15) or dissertation.

A dissertation is an extended piece of writing associated with Honours-level projects or Masters and PhD work. The dissertation comprises independent research to investigate specific phenomena in the world or to deepen understanding of key literature in a subject. The typical dissertation structure is like that of a formal report, with an extended literature review – see below.

An exam (see Chapter 20) is designed to test that understanding has accompanied learning, so that students can use information gathered over a programme of study in new ways, for themselves.

A reading record: Some tutors now set a reading record task rather than an essay proper. The reading record is designed to be the annotated record of all (or a specific part of) the reading a student has undertaken on a particular course or module. The annotations are not supposed to be descriptive (this book was about . . .) but analytical (this text is a key text for this topic outlining the major theoretical perspectives of . . . This text could be used to support the arguments of. . . However, Y and Z would take issue with the following aspects of the major arguments . . .). A tutor might set a reading record to test that students are in fact reading in an active and analytical way (see Chapter 11). Thus, your annotations should demonstrate that you are indeed being an analytical and critical reader.

An annotated bibliography: the annotated bibliography is a condensed version of the reading record. That is, typically, the student is expected to construct a bibliography in the conventional way – Author (date) *Title*. Location: Publisher – and note down, alongside each text cited, some points about its strengths or weaknesses: how useful it was and why, in relation to the aims and learning outcomes of the module and the key theoretical debates of the discipline.

A literature review occurs at the beginning of a dissertation; a short review might be placed at the beginning of a reflective essay or research project. The literature (or lit.) review typically constitutes coverage of the most up-to-date research in the field that you are studying. The process of reading for and writing a lit. review is designed to enable you to gain deep knowledge of your subject and the key issues and debates in that subject. This allows you to identify hot spots (areas that have not been researched so well – perhaps this could be a focus for your research?) and to discover how others have researched and written about the topic. It enables you to put together a substantial body of knowledge claims with which to compare your research findings. For extended pieces of writing, you will also be expected to justify your methodology in your lit. review.

For materials on all these assessment forms, and much more, go to www.learnhigher.ac.uk. Note especially that each learning area covered by Learn Higher has an associated **literature review**, so if you want to see models of these before you write one of your own, go there.

▶

Tip: When set a different type of academic task, like the reading record or annotated bibliography, or an exam where you are asked to write only 300 words rather than for 45 minutes for an answer, say, always ask yourself *why*, then make sure that you do something about that.

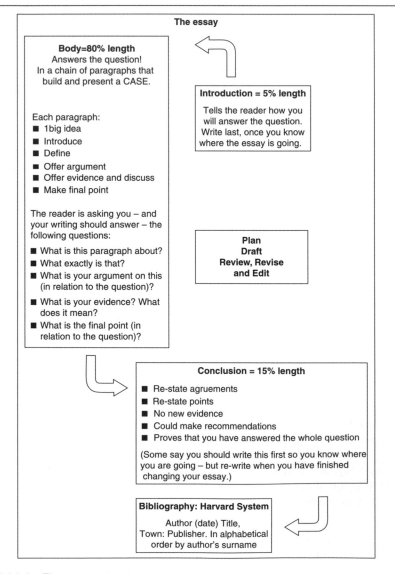

FIGURE 14.1   The essay structure

How to plan, prepare and draft great essays

What is an essay?

The word 'essay' comes from the Latin word exagium, which means the presentation of a case. When constructing an essay, you have to think of making a case, building a case, in a way that is appropriate for your subject. In some ways, it can help to think about a lawyer prosecuting or defending a client.

When defending a client, it is not enough for the defence to say, 'He didn't do it, your honour!' The defence has to construct a case to *prove* that the client did not do 'it'. To do this, the defence has to search for and gather the evidence to prove their case. The defence also has to anticipate the prosecution's evidence against the defendant. The defence has to then make the case for the defence in a series of arguments, presented one at a time. Each argument is supported by evidence. Have a look at the 'legal precedent' model, below (see also Figure 14.1 for a diagrammatic representation of the essay structure and 'what is an essay' box).

The essay – a legal precedent model

The defence might open thus:

'The defence will prove that the case against our client is utterly mistaken. In particular, we will prove that he could not have been identified as being at the scene of the crime for it was too dark to make a definite identification. We will tell you that the so-called witness suffers from poor vision and therefore could not identify our client. Finally, we will conclusively prove that our client was somewhere else at the time. *(Do you see how all the points have been separated out? And how they are all flagged up here in the introduction? The listeners are not left wondering, 'Where is all this going?' This is the same in an essay, and with an essay introduction.)*

The defence then elaborates upon those three key points:
1. The alley was too dark blah blah
2. The witness was not wearing his glasses . . . blah blah
3. My client has an alibi for the time . . . blah blah

The defence might conclude:
In conclusion, we argue that despite everything that the prosecution has said, you must find our client innocent because we have conclusively proven his innocence. He definitely could not have been identified as being at the scene of the crime. Firstly, it was too dark to positively identify anyone; further, the witness was too short-sighted to have any value placed upon his testimony, and finally we proved beyond a shadow of a doubt that our client was somewhere else at the time of the incident.' *(Here, in the conclusion, all the main arguments are re-visited, and all the main points are re-stated.)*

Tips: When it comes to searching for the answer to academic essay questions, you too – as with the legal precedent – will have to:

- break the whole question down into mini-points that can be covered one at a time
- search for evidence – things that other people have written – for and against your arguments
- think of a case that you want to make
- think of the separate arguments that would go to making your case
- make sure you have evidence for each argument.

And you would have to do this within the academic 'rules' of your subject – that is, the arguments you construct must build upon and use the arguments and evidence that already exist in your subject. So you will have to:

- re-read your lecture or class notes to get a starting point for your research
- read further – read around the topics looking for 'evidence'
- present your arguments in the correct way for your subject.

See Figure 14.1 on the essay structure.

The essay explained

An essay has a formal convention, a set style to which it must conform, or it is not an essay. The convention is as follows:

The body
This is the section of the essay where you do answer the question that you have been set. It can be 80 per cent of total length. You answer the question in a chain of paragraphs that you have organised to build a well-argued case. Note: This is typically written in the third person, past tense. That is: *It can be argued that* . . . . rather than *I think this* . . . .

Paragraph structure
Each paragraph also has a set convention: introduction; definition; argument; evidence plus discussion; final point. This is where it is useful to remember that you are communicating with a reader. When writing, imagine your reader asking you questions, and make sure that your writing answers them.

Paragraph as dialogue
- What is this paragraph about?
  Introduce your topic.

▶

- What exactly is that?
  Define, explain or clarify.
- What is your argument in relation to the question?
  Say something about your topic.
- What is your evidence? What does it mean?
  Say who or what supports your argument. Give evidence. Say what the evidence means.
- What is your final point? (How does this paragraph rtelate to the question as a whole?)
  Take the paragraph back to the question.

Sometimes your writing has to acknowledge contradictory evidence (the people that disagree with you) as you go – here are some questions to encourage you to address those.

The advanced paragraph questions:

- What is this paragraph about?
- What exactly is that?
- What is your argument in relation to the question?
- What is your evidence? What does it mean? That is:
  Who or what supports this view? What is the evidence? What does it mean?
  What is the opposing evidence? What does that mean?
  Therefore. . . ?
- What is your final point? (How does this paragraph relate to the question as a whole?)

(Again, while these questions address you, you write in the third person, past tense.)

> **Tip:** Write these questions out on an index card and stick them on your computer screen. Look at them when you write.

The introduction

This is the first paragraph of the essay. It can be between five and seven per cent of the total length. In the introduction, you tell the reader how you are going to answer the question. You write some introductory remarks that acknowledge the importance of the topic and then give the agenda of the essay.

> **Tip:** Write the introduction last, when you know where the essay is going. Writing it too soon will give you a writing block.

▶

The conclusion

This is the last, often long, paragraph of the essay. It can be 13–15 per cent of the length. In the conclusion, you re-state your main arguments and points in a way that proves that you have answered the whole question. You do not include new information or evidence, but you may make recommendations if appropriate.

> **Tip:** Use the words from the question in your conclusion to prove that you have answered the whole question.

Bibliography

Literally a book list, it is now a record of all the sources you have used to construct your essay.

> **Tips:**
> - Harvard System: Author (date) Title. Town: Publisher.
> - British Standard System: Author, Title, Publisher, date.
> - Alphabetical order by author's surname.
> - See also citations tips in Chapter 13.

Why write essays?

The essay is perhaps the most theoretical of the assessment forms. It is the assessment mode that invites you to read, understand and then use for yourself the major theories, knowledge claims, arguments and evidence of your subject. If all assignment production is designed to be heuristic, to bring about active learning, then the essay is the form that is designed to get you to undertake *deep* learning of your subject. Indeed, there are many who would say that the essay is one of the most powerful learning tools, and that students cannot be said to really understand their subjects until they have and can write essays within their discipline.

> **Tips:** Make the most of your essay-writing opportunities. Read the key people, in books and also in journal articles. Make notes that you can use again and again as you study your subject. Make key point notes of your essays to prepare for your exams.

How to prepare and write an essay

As always, we recommend that you use the full range of SOCCER activities covered in this text when undertaking assignments: be organised, plan and use your time well, have the overview, be creative, know how to communicate effectively, want to do well and reflect on your practice.

We also urge you to specifically follow the ten stages of advice given in Chapter 13, and summarised here. In this section of 'How to write great essays,' we are going to give additional tips and activities around these ten stages to assessment success (see page 189).

Activity 1: Preparing to research – question analysis

On the website 'An essay evolves' (http://evolvingessay.pbwiki.com/), a student volunteer undertook to think about, read for, plan, draft and revise an essay on the topic of Freud's theory of the personality. Please do visit that site to see how the whole essay evolved, the final draft of the essay and the mark and feedback that the essay received; also, all the discussion that took place around the task.

The site gives fascinating insights into how a real person has approached an assignment task, and we can learn much from seeing how other people operate in the world.

Here, we would like you to read the student's response to the essay question, and then to answer the questions set at the end. (Our thanks go to 'An essay evolves' and to Lisa Clughen from Nottingham Trent University for sharing this activity.)

Question: Evaluate Freud's theory of personality

I only have 1500 words in which to do this, so I will not be able to go into a long explanation of the ins and outs of the theory. How to reduce a life's work to 1500 words, though? Plus, I do not want to do the obvious thing where I explain all the theory and then evaluate it. Boring. Boring. I want to give a flavour of evaluation, of opinion, right from the off, as in take a critical view of the concept of personality. I also do not want to stick to purely scientific evaluation. There is not really enough of it. Evaluate to me suggests be even-handed in my assessment. Look at pros and cons, with evidence for both, and come to an opinion. OK, I already feel that Freud's ideas are unfairly and unreasonably dismissed. I need to limit myself to areas of theory that have something to say for and against. Also, the essentials: dynamic unconscious, psychological defences, id and ego, we develop through psychosexual stages. Personality quirks can arise from fixation. So also a discussion of libido. I notice in my argument list I mention libido late, and do not explain it. I need to get it in early, with the id. Then I need to finish by saying that contemporary scientists have seen fit to take Freudian theory and subject it to systematic appraisal. What is more, it has not been found as wanting as the hype would have us believe.

Query:
- How has this student approached the question? What has she done? What initial thinking can you see?
- How do you usually approach a question? List your successful strategies.
- Discuss your successful strategies with your partner. List five things to do before you start reading up on any assignment question.
- Take a real assignment question. Analyse the question. Make a list of – and then do – the five essential things that you need to do before you start to read.

Discussion: When we have undertaken this activity with students in class, they all noticed that this student was having fun with her assignment. For most of them, this was a revelation; they understood that assignments were hard work, they had not realised that you could enjoy that work.

Step 2: How much should I read?

Advice that we have from around our university is that you should dip into between three to five textbooks, five to ten journal articles and a couple of peer-reviewed websites when reading for an assignment.

Tips: Read for one word from the question at a time. Use the reading from one assignment in another; often, reading is transferable across several modules, so a canny student chooses to read texts that can be re-used in this way.

Step 3: Review your notes

Do not write on both sides of a sheet of paper when making notes or drafting essays – it is much easier to review *all* that you have written if you can lay it all out and see it all at once (that is, you do not want half of what you have written facing the table).

Step 4: Plan

Write the whole question out again in the middle of a large sheet of paper. Circle key words or phrases in the question, and draw a line from each word. Note key points from your reading against the key words or phrases in the question. Now number the different sections of your rough plan in the order in which you think you will mention them in your essay.

Tip: Write all the ideas you have generated onto separate pieces of paper. Move the pieces of paper around to discover the best structure for the essay. Now number the points on your plan.

Step 5: Write the first draft

Once you have your plan ready, sit down at your computer with your plan in front of you. Write straight from the plan as quickly as possible. Do not try to be perfect – just write. If you cannot think of a word or phrase, or if you get stuck in any way, do not search for the right word/spelling/tense. Put an ellipsis (three dots) or write something like: blah blah. Then move on. Continue like this until you have a first draft of your essay written. Once you have something, no matter how bad, written, you have something to work upon and change.

Tips:

Worried about your grammar? Apparently 91.5 per cent of all grammar mistakes boil down to just 20 typical errors. Go to: http://www.dartmouth. edu/~writing/materials/student/ac_paper/grammar.shtml to see what these errors are, or buy a really simple grammar book to help you get better – Lynne Truss's book, *Eats Shoots and Leaves,* is still really popular.

- Remember to have your paragraph questions on an index card and taped to the front of your computer. Write each paragraph of your essay – except for the introduction and conclusion – in answer to the questions:
  - What is this about?
  - What exactly is that?
  - What is your argument?
  - What is the evidence? What does it mean?
  - What is the opposing evidence? What does that mean?
  - Therefore . . . . ?
  - What is your final point?

Go with the flow – a first draft should not be perfect. Trying to get it right first go will lead to a writing block.

Step 6: Put it aside – worry about one thing at a time

Once you have the first draft of one assignment ready, you can have a rest, go out and celebrate or, much more likely in these days of over-assessment, you can get on with another assignment.

Tip: Learn how to concentrate on one thing at a time. Typically, you will be studying several courses or modules at the same time. In our university, students have to take four modules a semester. Each course will have several assignments attached to it – and often hand-in dates will be the same or very nearly so, such that in any one assessment week you may have to hand in four different assignments. So, if you are writing essay A, you need to be able to not worry about essay B, C and D; you need to be able to put the other essays on a mental shelf, and only take them down one at a time when you are going to concentrate on them. This is a trick that gets easier with practice.

Step 7: Review, revise and edit

One way to know what your final essay should look like is to read journal articles to see how they are written:

> 'So I learned how to write and I learned how to structure from my reading. Sometimes I used to copy from the book to see the way they just write it down … then through that experience I started knowing how to structure my phrases and my writing. It just… I don't know, it just got better through practising. That's the main thing.'

> **Tips:** Don't just write for an assignment, write little and often and you will see that your writing really does improve with practise. It is very similar to learning to play a musical instrument; you only get better if you practise. Use the essay checklist, below, when reviewing your work to check that you really have met all of your assignment targets. Use the exercises and advice on free writing (Chapter 13).

Step 8: Proofread

Proofreading can be easier if you use the proofreading symbols that publishers use when you go through various drafts of your work. So try using the following:

- ⊔⊓ TRS – Transpose words
- ≡ UC – Upper Case
- ≢ LC – Lower Case
- ⋏ Insert word or letter
- ᧐| Delete word
- ⌒ Close gap
- ⋎ Insert gap
- … Stet, leave as it is

Step 9: Hand it in

When handing your work in, always get and keep a receipt so that you have proof that you handed work in on or before a deadline. Never miss a deadline, even to improve your work, because a missed deadline tends to mean the work will be awarded a fail grade.

Step 10: Getting work back

Always make the effort to go and get your work back after it has had the mark confirmed. We know that often you are only really interested in the grade, but there is so much to learn from the thing itself, especially if you have a tutor who likes to scribble all over your assignments.

SWOTting your essay

- **S**trengths – Go through the essay very carefully; look at all the ticks and positive comments. These indicate that you have done something well. Note the good things you have done, and make a note to do them again.
- **W**eaknesses – Look at all the passages without ticks or with comments suggesting that something is missing or incorrect. Note these: do something about them. Go and find the missing information, and correct errors.
- **O**pportunities – Think what you can do now to learn the subject better or improve your grades. Think how to write a better essay in your next module.
- **T**hreats – Ask yourself if anything is stopping you from doing better work. Find out what it is and do something about it. (Sometimes we can be as frightened of success as of failure – is this you? What are you going to do about it?)

Tips:

- If you can answer an exam question on a topic previously covered in an assignment, put the assignment in your revision folder.
- If you improve the essay, then the exam answer will be even better. This is a good thing.
- Share it. Read each other's work, discover different writing styles and other ways to answer a question – this stretches our thinking.

Conclusion

So, we have considered the what, why and how of the essay. With 'what', we paid attention to getting the shape of the essay right, and to building a logical case using argument and evidence. We mentioned that each subject will have its own way of presenting information and encouraged you to discover what that is for your subject (read the journals and see how the textbooks do it). With 'why', we emphasised that the 'struggle to write' is a learning process – we really do write to learn rather than learn to write. With 'how', we looked at an effective plan, prepare and review strategy that draws on the various techniques recommended throughout the book (and which would thus help with all our academic tasks, not just the essay), and elaborated upon the ten steps to successful writing outlined in Chapter 13. We also referred you to useful websites, such as 'An essay evolves', so that you can see how another student has gone through the whole process from beginning to end. We hope that you now feel in a better position to approach your assignment essays.

Essay checklist

For every essay, check:

- ☐ Have you addressed the whole question?
- ☐ Have you addressed the aims and learning outcomes?
- ☐ Is there an introduction that acknowledges the significance of the question and gives the agenda of the essay?
- ☐ Would that agenda actually answer the question set?
- ☐ Are the paragraphs in the best possible order?
- ☐ Does each paragraph have its own introduction, definition, argument, evidence, and final point? Double-check that you have discussed your evidence.
- ☐ Is there a conclusion re-stating the main arguments and points? Do you use all the words from the question to prove that you have answered the whole question?
- ☐ Is there a comprehensive bibliography (referring to every source you have mentioned in the essay)? Is it in alphabetical order by author's surname?
- ☐ If anything is missing or imperfect, change it.

Tips:
- Print off a copy of your essay. Cut up the paragraphs, mix them up, and put them in the best order.
- Allow some time for reviewing your essay to make sure you have written a good essay that does indeed answer the whole question.
- Use a computer – even for your first draft – it is easier to cut and paste and re-write an essay that has been drafted on a computer.

Review points

When reviewing your notes on this chapter, you might realise that:
- essay writing is really an opportunity for learning and not the problem it is often imagined to be
- you are prepared to engage in 'writing to learn' as opposed to writing up what you know
- you are ready for the 'struggle to write' – you know that you should draft and re-draft your work
- you now think of communicating successfully in your essays, using the paragraph questions (in reports, you will think of reaching real readers and in presentations, you will consider the audience)
- you now feel ready to tackle the most theoretical assessment form: the essay
- you realise the importance of the ten-step plan, prepare and review strategy
- you have realised that preparing for an essay can be 'fun' and stimulating as well as an assessment activity.

15

How to write a great reflective essay and a brilliant research project

AIMS

To help you write great reflective essays. To make links between the reflective essay and the research project.

LEARNING OUTCOMES

That after reading through this chapter, and engaging with the activities set, you will have:
- made links between the reflective practitioner and yourself as a reflective student
- considered the what, why and how of the reflective essay, making links with the research project
- started the process of organising yourself for the successful planning, preparation and drafting of a reflective essay
- been guided towards the processes of setting a research project in motion.

Introduction

We discuss in Chapter 14 how the essay is one of the most theoretical of assessment forms, while in 16 we go on to unpack the academic report, a more practical document that allows exploration of real world phenomena. The reflective essay (sometimes also called the reflective account), and the even more formal research project (below), has the theory elements of the essay and the real world elements of the report. That is, in the reflective essay, you are expected to review how you have applied the theory that you are covering on your course to your real behaviour as a practitioner; and in a research project, you set up a real–world investigation of some aspect of the theory.

Reflective essays are especially appropriate for students who are also nurses, teachers, social workers or business people, and for people in the sciences: engineers, laboratory technicians or pharmacologists. All are expected to be reflective practitioners. That is, they are expected to continually keep up to date with research and developments in their relative fields, and apply new theory or developments in that theory to their own practice, i.e. the things they actually do on the job.

Indeed, you might also note that, as a student, you are already a reflective practitioner; you are expected to develop professionally (your understanding of your subject) and personally (your transferable skills or PDP). In this chapter, we are going to explore the reflective essay, giving examples that are of particular relevance to the reflection you are expected to undertake as a student, especially in early modules (see also Chapter 10 on the reflective learning log and Chapter 21 on PDP). We will also make links with the tasks involved in putting together a research project.

What is a reflective essay?

Introduction: This acknowledges the relevance of the question and gives the agenda of the essay.

Brief literature review: A paragraph or two on the relevant literature on the theory/ies being explored in your practice.

Critical assessment of practice (Theory into Practice): Paragraphs that explore how the theory was put into practice and how the practice illuminated or challenged the theory. Each element of practice described should be linked to relevant theory.

Conclusion: A final critical assessment of practice that re-states main arguments and points made in the essay, possibly with recommendations for future development of practice.

Bibliography: In a style appropriate for your subject.

FIGURE 15.1   The structure of the reflective essay or account

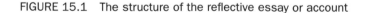

Why write reflective essays?

The reflective essay encourages the writer to make connections between the theory that they are studying and the practical world in which they will have to apply that theory. Thus, reflective essays are especially useful for people on vocational courses: teachers, social workers, nurses, engineers.

All these people are practitioners who, as part of their continuous professional development (CPD), will be expected to apply theory to their practice. That is, it is expected that what they do at work will be continually informed and improved by knowledge and understanding of relevant theory or developments.

The reflective essay or account:

- allows you to develop as a critical practitioner while a student
- prepares you for future research projects
- offers the opportunity to practise the thinking, writing and behaviour that you will adopt when working.

The reflective cycle

There are many explanations of reflective writing or reflective practice – for an overview have a look at Chapters 10 and 21 and also http://www.rlo-cetl.ac. uk:8080/rlo/reflective_writing/reflective_writing.html which has an animated audio–visual resource to explain the reflective process, with student examples.

The flow of theory, action and reflection that we are considering in the reflective essay, can be summed up thus:

➲ Theory – planned action – reflection on action (and theory) – theory (new theory sought) – action (new action planned)

OR

➲ Problem identified – theory – action – reflection
(See also Kolb's reflective cycle, in Chapter 21.).

> *Discussion:* It can be seen from these diagrams that the reflective practitioner is supposed to think critically about the theories with which they engage, the actions that they undertake and the experiences they have.
>
> They are expected to operate in an informed, critical and analytical cycle of thoughtful action and practical critique of theory

---

How to prepare and write a great reflective essay

See also Chapter 13 on effective communication and Chapter 10 which explores reflective writing in the reflective learning diary. We are going to discuss here the specific aspects of preparing and drafting a reflective essay – that is, a written account that tackles theory and practice.

A strategic use of time

You need to be especially strategic with your use of time when undertaking a reflective assignment, for you will have several key time-consuming stages to work through:

• Research the literature to discover the key theories and developments that you are going to explore in practice.
• Put theory into practice – as a student or in your work or work placement.
• Reflect on your practice and reflect back over the theory (literature).
• Discuss the relevance of the practice with respect to the literature.

   This requires even more systematic and strategic organisation of your time than usual because it is a complex process.

It starts with the reflective question

As always, write the whole question on the outside of a folder or envelope. Examine the question, asking yourself two sets of questions:
   Theory: Which theory will I be drawing on here? What have I already covered on this or a related topic? What additional reading will I be doing?
   Practice: What aspect of my practice relates to this theory? Am I already engaged in relevant activities at work, or will I have to set up some specific activity to allow me to investigate this theory?

Tips:
• Look back over the reading that you have already undertaken in that programme, especially in the modules that have introduced you to the key theoretical concepts in your subject or discipline. Ask yourself:
• What are the key issues?
• What interests you?
• What would you like to explore with respect to your practice?
• Dip into the essential reading on your reading list – these should highlight the key theories.
• Read between three to five textbooks on the theory, then review articles in about ten journals – perhaps articles written recently by the people who wrote the chapters in the textbooks. This keeps your theory up to date.
• If you will be applying theory to an aspect of your work that happens regularly, make sure that you do make notes everyday that record what has happened: what did you do to plan the activity? What resources were necessary? How did you set it up? How did you make sure people engaged? How did you get others to reflect on the activity? What follow-up action did you plan?

▶

- If you will be applying theory to an aspect of your work that you will need to make happen, make sure that you plan what that is and when it will happen. Consider the following: When will you undertake the activity? What will you need to do before the activity? What resources will be necessary? How will you set it up? How will you make sure people engage? How will you get others to reflect on the activity? What follow-up action will you undertake?
- Make sure you keep a notebook in your pocket or at your side everyday on placement or at work. Make notes of interesting things that happen, especially noting things that relate to the theory or theories that you are investigating in practice. Make notes of any problems and how you overcame them.
- Write brief commentaries on your practice notes – this initiates your reflective thinking.

A strategic action plan

In the light of all the thinking that you have undertaken on the above, draw up a strategic action plan of all the things that you need to do, read, make and prepare in order to get a reflective essay together.

Things to consider include:

- What do you now have to do?
- Who will you speak to (tutor, study partner, subject librarian, people at work)?
- What will you read?
- When will you do these things?

> **Tip:** Allow space in your action plan for inserting new targets as you think of them.

A typical action plan might contain:

- which lecture notes to re-read
- which set texts to read
- which additional texts you would utilise, which notes and assignments from relevant modules you would re-read
- when you will undertake your practice activities
- dates
- check–off.

Tips: Use these paragraph questions to prompt your writing:
- What is this about?
- What exactly is that?
- What does the theory indicate?
- What does your practice indicate?
- What does this mean?
- What is your final point?

Activity 1: A simple reflective essay for (first-year) students

In Chapter 2, we note that the first year at university allows you to build up your knowledge base of your subject, and also starts the process of you becoming a reflective practitioner as a student.

Many university courses or modules, including those associated with PDP (see also Chapter 21), encourage students to develop their awareness of their own practice by setting reflective writing assignments. This might include learning logs (see Chapter 10), a simple first-year reflective essay (like this) or a skills audit, perhaps before a research project or a Masters dissertation (Figure 15.1 gives a sample structure for a reflective essay, while 15.2 outlines the structure of a research project).

In this brief exercise, we want you to quickly brainstorm the sort of question that many first-year students are set, to get them thinking about their own development in study and academic skills, strategies and practice.

Please brainstorm the question for ten minutes. Number the points you might cover in the order in which you would raise them in a *reflective* essay on this topic.

Once you have a possible outline for an essay of your own on this topic, please compare with our sample structure below.

The question
Write a reflective essay to answer the following question: 'Discuss the study and academic skills or strategies that you have learned this semester that will help you in your studies. Give reasons for your answers'.

Brainstorm/plan for ten minutes, and then move on to the sample plan below.

Sample plan:
Introduction: I will acknowledge the importance of the topic, that is, it is good to be a reflective practitioner as a student, and that study and academic skills are important and can be learned and rehearsed. I will focus on the three things that have helped me the most: saying something like this essay will explore how pattern notes (Chapters 8 and 12), positive thinking (Chapter 9) and organisation and time management (Chapter 5) are essential for successful study. (In Chapter 8, there is a brainstorm on pattern notes and a question matrix on positive thinking – these might help here.)

▶

Brief literature review: I will make reference to key study and academic skills authors who argue that constituent study and academic skills and practices exist, and that learning these skills will make a difference to the student (in terms of grades, self-confidence, time or whatever . . .). Perhaps pick out themes that recur in different texts. Will re-read Burns and Sinfield, Buzan, Susan Jeffers, and explore the literature reviews on www.learnhigher.ac.uk.

Critical assessment of practice – application of theory to practice, with the self as the case study: I know that this part of the essay could be a set of arguments exploring how different skills or strategies have improved my practice. There has to be a flow between theory – practice – reflection – perhaps more theory – perhaps how I improved practice.

I must make notes of what has happened in real life in respect to the three areas that I am exploring, and give examples to make my case:

1. Pattern notes: theory – my own practice – what happened – conclusion and recommendation.
2. Positive thinking: theory – my own practice – what happened – conclusion and recommendation.
3. Organisation and time management: theory – my own practice – what happened – conclusion and recommendation.

Conclusion: A final critical assessment of my practice that re-states the main arguments and points of the essay. I could possibly make recommendations about how development could continue, including which areas I would inves-tigate next.

Bibliography – I will look at:
- Burns and Sinfield
- www.learnhigher.ac.uk
- Buzan on mind maps
- Susan Jeffers on fear.

Query: Was the sample plan above similar to or different from your own? Are the differences so great that you are confused? Did we select different aspects of study and academic skills practice to investigate?

Discussion: If you have actually been left confused by this exercise, it might be that you would benefit from discussing the question with another student, or with someone from the learning or writing development team in your university. If you have just chosen different topics to investigate, then fine – it means that different things are important to you as a reflective student (practitioner).

▶

Query: Can you see how the above plan could take you towards a reflective essay on this topic? Can you see why this would be a *reflective* essay rather than an academic essay?

Discussion: This would be a reflective essay, because the student writing it would be writing about their own real study-skills practice, rather than writing a purely theoretical essay on the notion that you could become a better or more successful student by developing certain academic skills and practices.

The brilliant research project

The purpose of the research project that you might undertake in your second or third year as an undergraduate is to further develop your rigorous critical and analytical thinking as you explore a real-world situation relevant to your chosen profession. Here, we are going to briefly explore some of the things that you will have to think about to get your research project started.

Research is what you do as a student

Many people think of research as something special and different, something 'other' that is associated with a project or dissertation, and only with that level of student work.

But research is about investigating or searching for ideas to increase your knowledge, therefore, all of your studies constitute research for you. Listening in class and/or lectures, reading textbooks and journals – these all involve research, for they are all opportunities for you to deepen your knowledge by engaging with the theories and knowledge claims that already exist in your subject area.

Therefore, when it comes to preparing a research project you should continue to use the successful study and academic practices that you already use, and that we cover throughout this text.

Tip: A research project is typically instigated, run and evaluated by the student – you. Thus, you have to ensure that you review sufficient literature, and engage with sufficient primary and secondary sources, to enable you to identify the existing knowledge claims and a suitable area for research. You will also have to decide how you will research your topic; you will have to determine and justify your methodology.

Primary and secondary sources – and your methodology

When asking people for research data (information), we often talk about using primary and secondary sources. As the names imply, primary means first-hand and secondary means 'second-hand', that is, moving away from primary data to the arguments and opinions that people have drawn by using primary evidence. Things to think about:

Primary sources

- Original documents – e.g. birth certificates, treaties, and testimonies – might be used in History.
- One's own observations – for example, if training to be a teacher, you would note what students actually do in the classroom, and attempt to analyse it.
- One's own investigations – for example, Science practicals or using questionnaires or interview techniques to gather data for almost any subject.
- Case studies – for example, in Business Studies, students will often be given or will use an account of a real-life business venture, or in Social Sciences an account of a real-life scenario. The student is supposed to analyse the case study using theories covered on the course.
- Poetry and novels – for example, in Literature Studies, the poetry and prose that is actually studied constitutes primary material. (Critics produce secondary-source material.)
- Films and television programmes can be primary sources in Media or Film Studies, but might constitute secondary sources if used for evidence as part of other subjects, such as Sociology.

Secondary sources

- Write-ups of other people's observations, experiments, interviews and questionnaires become secondary-sources for you.
- The subject literature – articles, chapters, textbooks where people write up their arguments – are all secondary sources.

Methodology

Quantitative research: Encompasses a group of methods focusing on quantities, on numbers. It is argued to be more objective and rational than qualitative research, because it is not supposed to involve personal or subjective judgements but the rational, accurate noting of facts, of realities. It includes randomised controlled trials, cohort studies and controlled studies.

Qualitative research: Founded on the belief that social phenomena (beliefs and experiences) can be explained with reference to the wider contexts of lived lives. Adopts the position that people have knowledge of their own lives and that they can talk about them. Is criticised for being non-factual and subjective – that is, people may not tell the truth about their lives – and that what they reveal requires interpretation by a researcher with their own beliefs and values.

For resources on methodology and the presentation and interpretation of data

Quantitative/qualitative research methods, with explanation, quizzes and resources:
http://www.nottingham.ac.uk/nursing/sonet/rlos/ebp/qvq/index.html

See also the Wikipedia entries on quats/quals. Note, while tutors often dislike Wikipedia as a source of information, these links take you to references regarding research methodologies:
http://en.wikipedia.org/wiki/Qualitative_research
http://en.wikipedia.org/wiki/Quantitative

Probability associated with inferential statistics, with explanation, quizzes and resources:
http://www.nottingham.ac.uk/nursing/sonet/rlos/statistics/probability/3.html

Descriptive statistics for interval and ratio scale: includes mean, mode, median, measures of dispersion and standard deviation, with explanation, quizzes and resources:
http://www.nottingham.ac.uk/nursing/sonet/rlos/statistics/descriptive_stats/index.html

Real data-sets combined with worksheets to create authentic scenario-based learning activities around the analysis of data. Examples relate to the subject areas of Business, Health and Psychology:
http://stars.ac.uk/

Animated resource demonstrating how to convert survey or experimental data into cross-tabular data and the steps involved in this process:
http://www.ucel.ac.uk/rlos/cross_tab_data/main.html

For brief revision courses on Mathematics, including percentages and fractions:
http://www.mathtutor.ac.uk

Why undertake research projects?

The more formal research project, especially for the practitioners noted above – nurses, teachers, social workers, engineers – can be understood as a more formal, extended version of the reflective essay, or a version of a formal academic paper – see Chapter 16.

As argued, these allow you to develop as an analytical, critical, reflective practitioner in your chosen field or subject. The project allows you to discover an area of your subject that really interests you, and to take forward research into that area, such that you develop deep and intimate knowledge of that subject, and of how to undertake research in your field.

You are supposed to read the existing literature to discover the most up-to-date knowledge claims on that topic. This review of the literature should reveal to you areas that are either contentious or under-researched; these would be the areas that you would follow up on in your own research. Specifically, you have to design a research activity that would allow you to investigate that area further in the real world.

Title page

Abstract: Summary of every part of the project – write it last.

Contents page: The sections of the project clearly labelled – with page numbers.

Introduction:
– Acknowledges significance of the area under research.
– May give the background or context to this project (why it was undertaken).
– Gives the terms of reference, the aims and scope (see Chapter 17) of the project.

Literature review: A significant section critiquing the relevant literature on the theory/ies being explored in the project (see Chapter 14 for a brief account of the purpose of the literature review). **Tip:** See www.learnhigher. ac.uk for a range of literature reviews.

Typically also includes a section reviewing literature on the methodology utilised in the project (academic justification for the approach taken). Typically you will utilise similar methodological approaches to those used by the theorists that you cite.

Methodology: Justifies the approach that you took in your research – whether you used quantitative or qualitative data and why. **Tip:** PhD theses in your subject area will typically have justified their methodological approaches – note how they did this.

Results/findings: Presentation of the data acquired during the research phase. **Tip**: Go to the Web addresses on data suggested in the resource box.

Discussion: This is your discussion of your findings and it reveals the significance of your findings. **Tip:** Again, go to journal articles/PhD theses to see how academics in your field discuss their findings.

Conclusion: This lays out the conclusions that can be drawn from the research undertaken, the findings and your discussion.

Recommendations (if appropriate): Lays out the recommendations that can be drawn from the conclusions.

Bibliography: In the correct format.

Appendices: As with reports, see Chapter 16.

Tips:
For more information on how to put a research project together, go to the following:
  The LearnHigher 'Doing Research' pages which have links to excellent learning resources, including those that will help you build your research project focus, and think about the data that you will want to collect, and how to analyse that data:
  http://www.learnhigher.ac.uk/resourcepages/doingresearch/doingresearch.html
  This site is a comprehensive web textbook on undertaking research projects:
  http://www.socialresearchmethods.net/kb/

FIGURE 15.2   How to undertake and structure a research project

Conclusion

In this chapter, we have explored the reflective essay as part of the continual professional development you would do as a reflective practitioner in the field (as teacher, nurse, social worker, engineer) and as a reflective student and active learner. We also discussed the reflective essay as a precursor to the research project.

We looked at the structures of the reflective essay and the research project (what) and we discussed the value of reflection (why) for the practitioner. Here we stressed that the critical application of theory to practice is a powerful learning and self-development tool.

With 'how', we noted that this exercise in applying theory to practice, and subsequent analysis of both, requires you to be very strategic with your time.

We made links with other key sections of *ESS2*: Chapters 10 and 21 that also explore reflection; 14 that covers the theoretical form of the essay, and describes the literature review; and 16 that looks at the more practical report, where the formal academic report or paper is very similar in structure to a research project.

As always, we emphasised that in the process of putting your reflective essay together, you will be involved in very powerful 'writing to learn', and that you are in fact practising for your research project.

We hope that you now feel in a better position to approach your reflective essays and your research projects.

Review points

When reviewing your notes on how to write great reflective essays and brilliant research projects, you might realise that:

- you can now look at both these forms in a more positive light; they are powerful learning tools that encourage you to interrogate theory through practice, and to improve practice with reference to theory
- you are prepared to engage in 'writing to learn' with respect to the reflective essay
- you not only better understand the what, why and how of the reflective essay and research project, you can see the role that reflection plays in your life as a student and as a practitioner (see also Chapters 10 & 21)
- you now feel ready to tackle your reflective essay
- you have made links between the reflective essay, the report (Chapter 16) and the research project – you are ready to undertake your research project.

Reflective essay, checklist

For every essay, check:

- ☐ Have you addressed the whole question?
- ☐ Have you addressed the aims and learning outcomes?
- ☐ Is there an introduction that acknowledges the importance of the question and gives the agenda of the essay?
- ☐ Would that agenda actually answer the question set?
- ☐ Is there a brief literature review (relevant to the topic or topics to be covered in the review of practice)?
- ☐ Is there a critical assessment of practice?
- ☐ Are the paragraphs in the best possible order?
- ☐ Does each paragraph have its own introduction, reference to theory, examples from practice, argument and final point?
- ☐ Is there a conclusion re-stating the main theories, arguments and points?
- ☐ Is there a comprehensive bibliography (referring to every source you have mentioned in the essay)? Is it in alphabetical order by author's surname?
- ☐ If anything is missing or imperfect, change it.
- ☐ Have you proofread the final draft?

16

How to produce excellent reports

AIMS

To enable you to plan, prepare and produce excellent reports.

LEARNING OUTCOMES

That after reading through this chapter, and engaging with the activities set, you will have:
- considered the what, why and how to the academic report
- started the process of organising yourself for successful report writing, with an emphasis on planning, preparation, practising and reviewing techniques
- made links between assessment activities and other activities covered in this text, especially Chapter 13 (the ten steps . . .).

The academic forms

In these chapters, we explore the major ways of communicating in terms of:

- What: the formal conventions of assessment – essay, report, presentation, seminar. Each form or genre has its own rules – knowing the rules is one step towards communicating effectively.
- Why: the particular purpose of each activity. Once you know why a specific form has been set, you can meet that form's targets (see descriptions, in Chapter 14).
- How: successful planning and researching techniques that will draw on the strategies and techniques introduced elsewhere in this book.

Introduction

Report writing is becoming an increasingly popular academic assessment activity. Superficially, students often appear more familiar with the academic report; they might have already written reports at work or perhaps have, incorrectly, used headlines and straplines in their academic essays. In this chapter, we will be looking at the what, why and how of reports. We will also be referring back to the basic ten-stage approach to assessment (Chapter 13) which works with all your assignments.

Thinking about reports

Reports are very popular on both business and science courses; further, the project write-up, the dissertation structure and the journal article are very similar to the formal academic report. Whatever your subject, if you do not feel comfortable about report writing, please go on to work through the 'thinking about reports' activity.

Tips:
- Read the journals for your subject. Note the way they structure arguments, the way that they use evidence, and the layout and style of their articles. This will tell you how to structure arguments and present evidence in your subject – it will also be the report model that you ought to follow.
- Find old dissertations that have been written by students in your department; often these are kept in the library. Read one or two of these that are relevant to your subject area to see how good dissertations and academic reports are written in your subject.

Activity 1: Thinking about reports

When thinking about academic reports, it can be helpful to think about other reports that we might have dealt with in our lives, as long as we remember to use the proper academic and subject conventions when we come to write our report assignments.

Have you ever read a school report, a surveyor's report or a *Which* magazine report? School report – allows the child's carer to understand how the child is doing at school. The carer can use the information to judge whether or not the child is progressing as they think they should. They can then take action if they wish.
Surveyor's report – for the potential homebuyer. Gives factual information on the status of a property. The buyer can then decide on purchase, depending on the risks that they are prepared to take, judged against the information that they have been given.
Which report – for a readership typically interested in purchase. Information given allows readers to judge different items against disclosed criteria – they can then decide on what to do, depending on their own criteria for action.

Query: What do they have in common?

It could be argued that what these reports have in common includes the following:
– Each report is designed to give specific information to specific readers.
– Each writer of a report knows what sort of reader they are writing for.
– The writer will expect the reader to act on the information in the report.

Query: Will knowing this help you to write better reports? How?

What is a report?

The essence of the report is that it is a document designed to deal with the real world – specifically, a report is a practical document that describes, details or analyses a situation in the real world, such that the reader can make decisions or take specific actions about that situation.

Here we call it a paper

Some university tutors refuse to speak of essays or reports. They think essays smack of school compositions and that the notion of a report is too simplistic. These tutors might speak of writing academic *papers*.

If you have a tutor like this, ask them exactly what sort of structure they require. They will probably be expecting you to lay out your writing in the journal article format. This is very much like a report.

The structure(s) of a report

Typical report structures

Simple structure:

Complex structure:

Simple structure	Complex structure
• Title page	• Title page
• Contents	• Synopsis/Abstract
• Introduction	• Contents page
• Methodology	• Introduction
	(+/− some review of the literature)
• Findings	• Methodology
	• Findings
	• Discussion
• Conclusion	• Conclusion
• Recommendations	• Recommendations
• Bibliography	• Bibliography
• Appendices	• Appendices
• Glossary	• Glossary

Figures 16.1 and 16.2 show science report structures.

The report

Title page

This is the front sheet of the report. This should include: title, sub-title; date; author's name and position; distribution list (reader(s)' name(s) and positions(s)); reference number/course details/ statements of confidentiality:

- Title and sub-title: usually divided by a colon. The title gives the big picture of the report, while the sub-title narrows this down. Thus, the title gives a focus of the report and the sub-title indicates the scope of the report – the 'terms of reference' of the report.
- Date: places the report in real time.
- Author's name and position: when you write a college report, you are often told to assume a position – public relations expert, tax consultant . . . You have to write the report as though you were that person. Revealing who you 'are' tells the reader where the report is 'coming from', and thus it reveals what angle you might be expected to adopt on the topic.
- Distribution list: as your position as writer might be revealing with respect to the report, so might the list of readers and their positions. You would write a different report for the bank manager than for the trade union rep.

Abstract

The abstract – synopsis or summary – is the essence or gist of your report. The abstract might include:

- overall aims
- specific objectives

- problem or task
- methodology or procedures
- key findings
- main conclusions
- key recommendations.

Tips:
- Journal articles typically begin with an abstract – read the journals and see how they do it.
- Check with your tutors to see what they expect.
- As the abstract refers to the whole report, write it last!

Contents page
The contents clearly list all the major sections of the report, including sub-sections and appendices, with page numbers.

The contents page allows the reader to navigate your report. Thus, use detailed, clear headings in the report, and put them all in the contents.

Tip: Check out the contents pages of books. Do they help you as a reader? How? Make yours just as useful.

Introduction
The introduction should help the reader understand the what, why and how of your report. It needs:
- a background to the report: either why you were interested in the topic or why the report was necessary
- terms of reference: the focus, aims and scope of the investigation – its purpose or goal, any specific limitations
- the methodology: the research methods you used to put the report together – a literature review or something more practical: interviews, questionnaires, etc.

Findings (The body of the report)
This small word refers to the major part of your report. You sometimes do call this section 'Findings', but you *do not* call this section 'the body'. The different sections of this part of the report need clear headings. Each section gets its own large number, and each sub-section gets its decimal point. *Note:* When writing reports, as with essays, we have to use clear but formal English – there is no room for abbreviations or slang.

The conclusion
Each finding should have a conclusion. Conclusions point out the implications of your findings, that is, you tell your reader what they mean, tactfully.

Recommendations
Each conclusion should lead to a recommendation. While the conclusions tell us what the findings mean, the recommendations tell the reader what to do about them (or, more tactfully, suggests a range of things that might be possible).

Appendices
An appendix is something added on or attached to something. 'Appendices' is the plural of this. In this section, you can show your reader some of the things that you have used to compile your report. For example, if you used interviews, you would place the interview questions there. If you circulated a questionnaire, you would place a sample questionnaire there.

> **Tip:** Appendices do not count in the word limit for your report, but this does not mean that you can just put everything in there. Only put useful things there, and only things that you direct the reader to.

Bibliography
As with the essay:
Harvard System: Author (date) Title. Town of publication: Publisher.
British Standard System: Author, Title, Publisher, date.

Glossary
A glossary is literally a list of unusual words. This is especially useful in a report accessible to more than one reader: for example, a technical report that will also have to be read by a layperson (member of the public).

Presentation and style
Make sure your text:

- is neat and easy to read
- is word-processed
- has a consistent style: a simple basic layout used consistently throughout your whole report.

> **Tip:** Decide where you will number, underline, embolden, italicise; save a template (pattern) and use it every time you start work; check for a department style and use that.

Why write reports?

A basic 'why' of report writing is that reports are another form of written assessment, thus they give you practice at developing different aspects of your written communication skills.

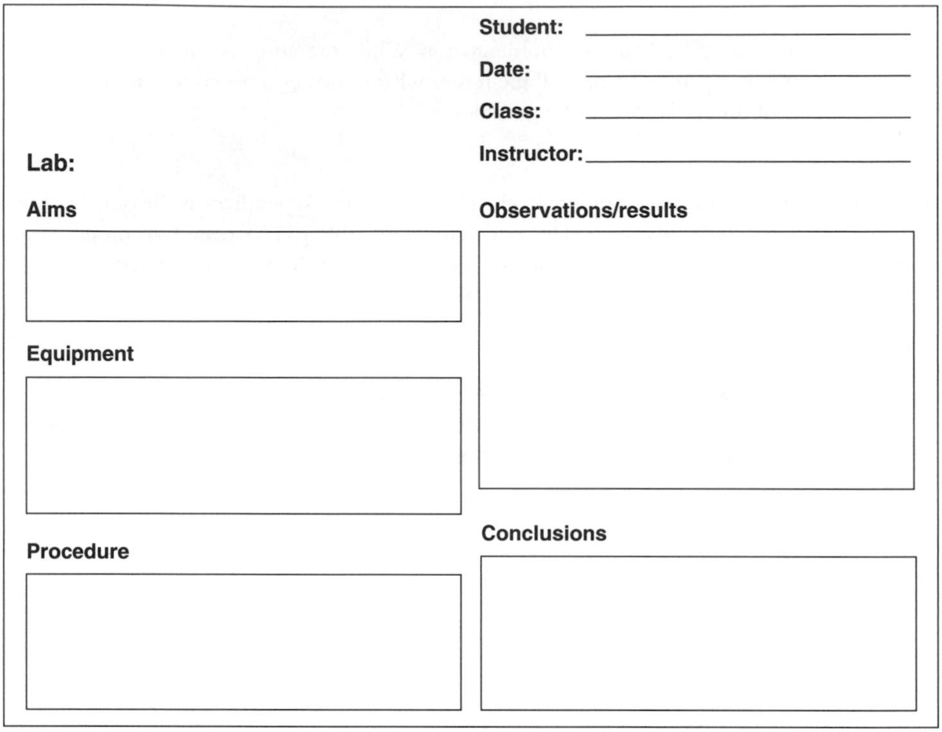

	Student: _____
	Date: _____
	Class: _____
Lab:	**Instructor:** _____

Aims

Observations/results

Equipment

Procedure

Conclusions

FIGURE 16.1   Structure of a typical science report

More importantly perhaps, there are two characteristics to reports that make them significant for you:

- Reports on courses model the reports we will write in our jobs. Writing reports at university therefore prepares us for the work we will do.
- Reports also model academic journal articles. Writing reports at university can be academically challenging and may prepare us for publishing our own research.

Thinking about the 'why' of individual reports

However, each report that we are set to write at university is designed to investigate a particular topic, to be read by a particular reader, and to achieve a particular purpose with respect to that reader. If we focus on these things, we can see some other 'whys' to writing each specific report that we write, and this gives us two useful questions to keep in mind when we write:

- Why am I writing this report – what am I trying to achieve?
- Why am I writing this report – what do I want my reader to think and do after reading my report?

Student: _____

Date: _____

Class: _____

Lab: Title of Experiment

Instructor: _____

Introduction

Include the date the experiment was performed and the date the report was submitted. State aim of experiment.

Results

Results should be recorded directly in the practical book at the time of measurement. Calculations can be included in this section.

Risk Assessment

List all the chemicals used in the experiment indicating the known hazards of each and the precaution you will be taking when using the chemical. (e.g. Acid Corrosive. Avoid skin contact, wear gloves when handling)

Conclusions

This should relete to your AIM. Clearly and briefly state your main conclusions from your own results.

Procedure

The procedure should clearly and simply outline what you did so that another student reading the report and familiar with the subject would be able to understand how you did the experiment.

Discussion

Discuss the significance of your results; you may like to compare them to theoretical results or other results. Only do this when you are sure of the origin of the comparisons. Include any problems you had when performing the practical or in acheiving the original aims.

FIGURE 16.2   Structure of a more advanced science report

Why write reports – what am I trying to achieve?

Arguably, there are three main forms of reports: factual, instructional and persuasive; each has a different purpose. Think about what you are trying to achieve before you start your report.

- Factual: The factual or informative report is expected to define or establish a current situation. The school report might fall into this category.
- Instructional: The instructional, explanatory, report is supposed to explore a situation and suggest a range of options for further action. The *Which* report might fall into this category.
- Persuasive: The persuasive or leading report is supposed to investigate a problem and suggest a specific course of action. A surveyor's report might fall into this category.

The line between these reports does become blurred at times, but do try to at least clarify your aims for yourself before you start.

Query: Are you writing a report right now? Is it factual, instructional, persuasive? Will this affect you in any way?

Tips:

- If your report is factual, you will be gathering information to fully explain or define a situation.
- If your report is instructional, you will be gathering the information to explain a problem and offer a range of solutions.
- If your report is persuasive, you will be gathering the information to explain a problem and recommend just one solution.

What do I want my reader to think and do after reading my report?

Unlike an essay – which is often written as though for an intelligent, interested member of the public – a report is written for a specific reader or readers. These are real people.

The thing with real people is that they have different wants, needs and beliefs; a head of Human Resources will be influenced by different arguments than the staff representative, for example. Therefore, if you want to influence a real reader, and make them think and do what you want, you must consider the reader when planning and writing your report.

Key questions to consider here might be:

- Who is my reader?
- What can I expect my reader to already know about this topic?
- How can I deal with this in my report?
- What can I expect my reader to believe about my topic?
- How can I deal with this in my report?
- What can I expect my reader to want from this report?
- How can I deal with this in my report?
- What will I want my reader to think and do after reading my report?
- What language, tone and style will my reader respond to?

Tips: When drafting reports, think of the language, evidence and examples that will influence real readers.

How to plan and prepare a report

The ten-step process (Chapter 13) is equally valid for the report, with a few extra questions thrown in. We are going to cover them here:

Additional things to consider when preparing your report

Think about the practical dimension:

- Why am I writing this report? What are the conditions that instigated the report? What interesting situation makes the report necessary?
- What is the purpose (factual/instructional/persuasive)? What am I trying to do or achieve with this report?
- Who is my reader?
- What do they know on this topic?
- What are their beliefs/attitudes?
- What will they want from my report?
- What will I want my reader to think?
- What will I want my reader to do?
- How will I make that happen?

If using interviews and questionnaires to gather information for your report, you will need to design and conduct interviews and design, circulate and collect questionnaires. You will then need to critically analyse the data that you collect. How will you do this?

> **Tip:** Go to http://stars.ac.uk/ for real data-sets/worksheets around the analysis of data for Business, Health and Psychology.

If undertaking second- or third-year research, you will need to investigate the merits of quantitative research (statistically significant data) and qualitative research (typically involves focus groups or interviews, the gaining of more personal responses). You will have to justify your methodology, that is, you will have to argue a case for why you have chosen a quantitative or a qualitative approach to your research.

> **Tip:** Read relevant journal articles and see how they justify their methodological approaches.

- Think of all the sections that the body of your report will need.
- Think of clear titles – headings and sub-headings that you can use. Make sure that they reveal what is going on to your reader.
- Think of the language, tone and style that will impress your potential reader.
- Make sure that there is a conclusion for each section of the body of your report.
- Write a recommendation for each conclusion.
- When proofreading, do not look for all your mistakes at once, or you will miss many errors. Keep a record of all the mistakes that you commonly make. Look for one of 'your' mistakes at a time. For example, perhaps you know you 'always' get your tenses wrong, plus you 'always' spell certain words wrong. Go through once looking for tenses; go through again looking for spellings.

Tip: When you get your work back, note three things that you do particularly well and three things that could be improved upon.

Conclusion

We have looked in some detail at the academic report, making clear links to the plan, prepare and review strategies necessary for any successful academic assignment. We have also directed you to a useful website that gives you information and activities around the analysis of data. As always, we recommend that you reflect on everything that you have read here about the report – make brief, pattern notes to remind yourself of all the things that you will now follow up on and do to plan for, research and write a really great report.

Review points

When reviewing your notes on this chapter you might realise that (above checklist):
- you can now look at report writing in a more positive light
- you now feel ready to tackle your academic report
- you realise the importance of the 10-step plan, prepare and review strategy
- you have realised the importance of journal articles as models for your report writing.

Report checklist

Photocopy this checklist and complete a copy for every report that you write.

- ☐ What was my aim in writing this report? Have I achieved my goals?
- ☐ Is the title page adequate: title and sub-title; author and position; reader and position? Date?
- ☐ Is the title/sub-title appropriate?
- ☐ Was an abstract necessary? Is there one? Is it clear?
- ☐ Is there a contents page? Is it clear?
- ☐ Is there an introduction? Does it reveal: background? Terms of reference? Methodology?
- ☐ Are the sections and sub-sections of the body clearly labelled?
- ☐ Does the reader get sufficient information to make the decisions I desire?
- ☐ Is all the information necessary or have I written too much?
- ☐ Can the reader follow the development of my ideas? Are they laid out logically?
- ☐ Is the layout simple and consistent?
- ☐ Are the language and tone suitable for the actual reader?
- ☐ Is the style appropriate to the subject and reader?
- ☐ Do I offer sufficient evidence to 'prove' my points? Do I discuss my evidence/data?
- ☐ Does my conclusion follow logically from my arguments? Is there a 'conclusion' for every section of the body?
- ☐ Have I really laid the groundwork for my recommendations? Is there a recommendation for each conclusion?
- ☐ Should there be a glossary? If there is one, is it comprehensive?
- ☐ Are the appendices clearly labelled? Is the reader directed to each appendix in the body of the report?
- ☐ Is the bibliography adequate? Is it laid out in the correct way? (Remember, alphabetical order by author's surname.)

Obviously, if the answer to any of these questions is 'no', then you must make the necessary changes.

17

How to deliver excellent presentations

AIMS

To enable you to prepare and deliver excellent presentations.

LEARNING OUTCOMES

That after reading through this chapter, and engaging with the activities set, you will have:
- considered the what, why and how of presentations
- considered the nature of oral communication and issues surrounding communicating effectively, especially in presentations
- started the process of organising yourself for successful presentations
- made links between preparing a presentation and other activities covered in this text: organisation and time management, using the overview, being creative, notemaking, targeted research and active reading.

Oral communications: the presentation

Presentations are becoming an increasingly popular assessment tool with tutors. Typically, presentations were introduced onto academic programmes to acknowledge that most of us are much better at speaking than we are at writing, especially academic writing.

Of course, what this growth in popularity glosses over is that students, like every normal human being on the planet, tend to be terrified of public speaking, or presentations.

We cannot make all the fear go away, but we can help you to realise that you can get really good at presentations. Motivated students who do what is recommended here tend to get high grades for their presentations. It is as simple as that.

We are going to look at the what, why and how of presentations. With the 'how' – while it will help you to cross-reference with our ten-step strategy in Chapter 13 – here, we will refer to the four presentation Ps: plan, prepare, practise and present.

> **Tip:** For a detailed literature review on the role of oral communication in HE, go to: http://www.learnhigher.ac.uk/Literature/Oral_Communication.pdf

What is a presentation?

There are several 'whats' to a presentation that we are going to cover here and they are all true. The trick for you, as always, is to think 'How will knowing this help me to give better presentations?'

It's just talking, isn't it?

A presentation is a formal talk of a set length, usually on a set topic, given to a set (that is a knowable) audience. When preparing your presentation, you have to think about all these factors: time, topic, audience. That is, you have to fit the topic into the time you have been given – there is no point in saying that it could not fit into five minutes. If that was the task, then that is what you have to do. You also have to pitch the topic at your actual audience. Again, as with the report, these are real people with real knowledge, thoughts and feelings. You have to make sure that your language, style and tone are just right for the real people that you are going to address. Finally, you have to make sure that any audio-visual aids (AVA) – that is, supporting material like handouts, OHTs (overhead transparencies), PowerPoint, photographs, posters, etc. – are appropriate and will connect with your actual audience.

> 'I remember this presentation – it was on breast cancer, a really frightening topic, and the students had left all the funny noises on their PowerPoint. So, there they were giving life and death statistics and scaring everyone silly, and all the while there are explosions, and whistles, flying noises and breaking glass!'

It's all an act

No matter what anyone else tells you, remember that a presentation is a performance. You are standing in front of people and talking to them: they are looking at and listening to you – this is a performance. Therefore, you are a performer. Use this! Like any performance, a presentation is an act. To make it work for you, act happy, confident and interested, even if you are bored silly.

If you are happy, your audience can be happy; if you are not, they cannot. And if you are not interested in the topic, why should your audience be? And if your audience is not interested, then this fails as oral communication. So act your socks off.

It's an act – positive body language

Remember the performance aspect of the presentation and resolve to use positive body language:

- do face the audience
- do not only look at the board behind you
- do stand or sit straight
- do not hold anything in front of your face
- do smile
- do not tap your foot or hand or make chopping motions with your hands
- do draw people calmly into your presentation with brief welcoming gestures
- do not hold your arms defensively in front of your body
- do stand in a relaxed manner
- do not stand there with clenched fists or looking as if you want to be somewhere else
- do dress for success
- (in a group presentation) do not act as if you hate everybody else on the team
- do ACT calm, confident and in control.

It's communication

As a performer, you will have to build a rapport with your audience, and create a relationship with them. You will also have to communicate and interact with them. This means that you will need to look at them, and you will have to make eye contact with everybody in your audience.

So do not listen to those who advise you to look at the ceiling at the back of the room. That may be OK if you have an audience of 1000 or more people, but in a small group it looks weird, and not in a good way. You will need to look at people to draw them into your talk and take them with you. You will also need to check that they are following what you say. This will tell you whether or not to repeat or explain something, and you will never discover this if you do not look at your audience.

Further, to be a successful performer, just like an actor on the stage, you must never, ever speak from a script. You must not read a presentation. You must learn your presentation and then deliver it fresh, as though for the first time. Reading a presentation is the quickest way to lose your audience and lose any marks that were available for good communication.

The formal convention

The presentation has the same form (formal convention) as the essay, and it has the same need to address real audiences as the report. Therefore, you should have a sense of the presentation already from what you now know about essays and reports. Figure 17.1 shows the specific details of the presentation.

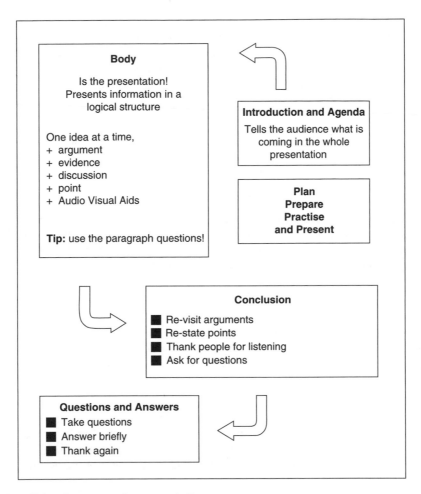

FIGURE 17.1:   Structure of a presentation

What is a presentation?

Firstly, have an introduction, with a clear agenda:

- introduce yourself
- give the topic title
- make opening remarks
- give the agenda of the talk.

The *introduction* is where you acknowledge the question and hook the audience and tell them why they should be listening to you. Are you going to be interesting, useful or funny? Will it help them pass an exam or get better grades? Will it save them time or effort? Think of something.

▶

The *agenda* is where you tell the audience exactly what is coming in your presentation. Without an agenda, the audience does not know where the talk is going. This is unsettling and confusing. A confused audience is not a happy audience. Tell them what is coming . . . and this simple technique will dramatically improve the presentation itself and your marks.

The body
This is the presentation. This is where you answer the question that you were set. As with the essay, think about one big idea at a time, supported by argument and evidence and AVA. Think about building a logical case.

> **Tip:** Use the paragraph questions to structure the sections of your presentation: What is this section about? What exactly is that? Tell me more. What is your evidence? What does it mean? How does this relate back to the question as a whole?

The conclusion
As with the essay conclusion, this is where you draw the whole presentation together. Re-visit your main arguments, re-emphasise your main points, and use all the words from the question to prove that you have answered the whole question.

> **Tips:**
> - Write introductions and conclusions last.
> - Accept that this is a repetitive structure: tell them what is coming; tell them; tell them what you told them. This can feel silly, obvious or uncomfortable, especially in a short presentation. But this is what is required, so bite the bullet and do it!

The question and answer session
It's over – you want to rush out screaming! Don't. You now have to thank the audience for listening and ask them for questions.

> **Tips:**
> - Do re-phrase difficult questions and check that you have understood.
> - Do keep answers short.
> - Do keep answers good-natured.
> - Do notice when people put their hands up and take questions in order.

▶

- Do not start fighting your audience.
- Do not try to make everyone agree with you.
- Do not think that you have to know everything (unless it is a job interview or an oral exam).
- If you cannot answer, why not try: 'That is a very good question – what does everyone else think?' If no one else knows, 'Well, that has given us all something to think about. Thank you again for listening!'.
- Do bring the question and answer session to a firm end. The audience likes to know when it is all over safely.

Why do we set presentations?

As with planning and preparing any assignment, the process of preparing a presentation is designed to be an active learning process. As you plan, prepare, practise, perform and finally reflect on your presentations, you are really getting to grips with and learning the material. As you think about how to communicate a topic effectively to your audience, you are synthesizing and using information. Effective communication of what you have learned leads you to develop a familiarity with the way your subject actually works, and you become familiar with the academic practices of your subject.

It's an opportunity

And, yes, presentations really do extend the range of assessment opportunities open to you. Before you have successfully delivered and survived your first presentation, you may find this hard to believe, but once you have done this, you may find that given the choice between an essay and a presentation, you would choose the presentation every time. Once you have cracked how to do presentations well, you will realise that it is easier to get good grades for a presentation than for a piece of writing.

'I did everything you said and practised again and again. The tutor said I was a natural – if only she knew.'

And a job skill

Further, good oral communication skills are definitely required by employers – some even require a formal presentation as part of the interviewing process. Developing good presentation skills over your time at university can make the difference between getting that job you want – or not.

What a gas – self-esteem rises

Finally, once you can do presentations, your self-esteem really improves. From the very first one that you plan, prepare, practise and present, you start to feel better about yourself as a student. This is not just something that we are telling you here to make you feel better – this is something that all our students have fed backto us – succeeding in presentations is one of the best confidence-boosters they have ever had. More than that, an increase in self-confidence enriches all your studies.

'I really hated the thought of presentations, but once they were over, I felt so good about myself. In the end, I wanted more of them.'

How to succeed in presentations – the 4 Ps

Here, we will be looking at the four presentation Ps: plan, prepare, practise and present.

P1 – Plan

Think about your time limit, your topic and your audience:

Time limit: How can you fit the topic into the time you have been allowed? What will you have to put in and what will you have to leave out?

Topic and audience: Remember, an audience is made up of real people with real knowledge and expectations of their own.

Planning Tips and Questions

Some things to think about:

- What can I expect my audience to know about this topic before I start?
- What will I want them to know when I have finished (this can give you the aims of your presentation)?
- How will I get them from where they are to where I want them to be (this can suggest a logical structure to your presentation)?
- What language, tone and style will be right for this audience?
- What arguments and evidence will they understand and relate to?
- What audio-visual aids will help and will work with this audience? Think of visual aids to illustrate the topic – photographs, charts, diagrams, key quotes. Think of visual aids that will help people follow your presentation – have the agenda on an OHT or write it on the board, or make a large pattern note of your presentation and display it!
- How will my audience react to this topic? Will they be resistant, happy, frightened, interested, or not? What will I have to do to get them to respond positively?
- What questions might they ask me? What answers will I give?

Action plan: Now that you have considered all these things, what will you do, read, find and make to get your presentation ready?

P2 – Prepare

Preparing a presentation requires the same research and hard work that an essay does, and you have to think about making audio–visual aids as well:

- Remember the ten stages: brainstorm the topic, link to the learning outcomes, follow your action plan, etc.
- Read actively and interactively.
- Remember to make your AVA with back-ups (e.g. handouts of PowerPoint slides).

> 'I knew someone who went all the way to Japan to deliver a presentation based on a video. The technologies were incompatible, so they couldn't show the video. The whole thing was a huge and expensive disaster!'

- Review your notes.
- Review your AVA – which will you use? Which don't you need?
- Plan the body of your presentation – this will give introduction/agenda and conclusion.
- Remember to convince yourself first. If you can act as though you believe it, it will help the audience to believe you.
- Prepare a script: Once you have collected all your data and made your overall plan, you may wish to prepare a script for the presentation. A script draft can give you a sense that you have taken control of your presentation and organised your material to your satisfaction. That is OK, if you remember that you must not read from your script. So at some point you should destroy your script.
- Prepare your prompts: Make cue cards or prompt sheets to guide you through the presentation itself. This could include:
  - key words
  - key examples
  - key names and dates
  - notes of the key AVA.
    - Number your cue cards and your points.
    - Destroy your script.

Tips:
- You must not read from your script – you will be boring and dull and you will lose your audience.
- Recreate your presentation from the key words on your cue cards.

P3 – Practise: rehearse, rehearse, rehearse

Once you have a shape to your presentation, with your prompts prepared, you are now ready to review, revise, edit and learn your presentation, and this comes through practising or rehearsing your presentation.

Rehearsal is vital to a successful presentation

You must not say the presentation for the first time in front of an audience – it will not be 'polished' and the words will sound extremely strange to you. This is not a good thing. You must learn and be comfortable with your presentation.

There are several key stages to your rehearsal:

1. Refine and polish

Your first rehearsals allow you to review, revise and edit your presentation – to refine and finish it. This is very similar to going over your essay, so that all the gaps are closed, the boring bits are tidied up and the overlong sentences are shortened so that they become clear and effective.

This is especially important in a presentation, as you move from a script (a written communication form) to the presentation proper (an oral communication form). What works in writing rarely works in speaking. So you need to hear your presentation and shape it again, so that it works as spoken rather than written communication. This can take time.

It will help to refine your presentation if you rehearse in front of a critical friend who will give you useful feedback.

Tip: Do not rehearse in front of your children. Our mature students always say that their children tend to say 'it's boring, it's silly' . . . leaving them feeling really discouraged.

A critical friend can tell you what is good about your presentation. They can tell you what is working, what is easy to follow and understand. But they can also tell you what is not working, where they do not follow you or your meaning is unclear.

Tip: Listen to this feedback. Do not argue with the critical friend and tell them that they do not understand. If they cannot understand, neither will your audience. You are not yet communicating effectively. Change your presentation until it can be understood.

2. Learn the presentation

Once your presentation is as good as it can be, you need to rehearse to learn it. Here you need to practise with your cue cards and your AVA. You need to do this until you know your presentation really well, until you could do it in your sleep.

Tip: Walk around your home delivering the presentation to your cat or a chair. Make yourself feel comfortable speaking those words out loud.

3. Give it life
Once you are comfortable with speaking out loud and you know your presentation by heart, then you need to practise some more until you can say it every time as though you are saying it for the first time. This will keep your presentation fresh and alive, and hence it will appeal to and grip your audience.

> **Tips:** Video it: For really important presentations, assessed ones that carry a high percentage of your course marks – oral exams, vivas – and for job interviews, videotape your rehearsals and check how good you are. When rehearsing, use the presentation checklist to mark yourself.

P4 – Present (Perform)

To make sure that your presentation proper is as good as it can be, we have boxed some tips and tricks of things to do before and during your presentation.

Presentation day – tips and tricks

OK, you are going to be nervous. Do not focus on that – think positive and get on with it. Here are some things to do:

Before

- Work on being positive!

> **Tip:** Read Chapter 9 on how to deal with your emotions. Practise your positive thinking. Keep saying: 'I am prepared' or 'This is a great presentation.'

- Travelling to your presentation, run through your main points, with and without your cue cards. Reassure yourself that you do know it.
- Get to the room early so you will be as cool, calm and collected as you can be. Rushing in late will increase your stress levels.
- Organise the seating and take control of the environment. Where will you want people to sit so that you feel good and they can all hear you? Do you want them in rows, in a semi-circle, sitting on the floor?

> **Tip:** Arrange to stand behind a desk or a lectern. This small barrier between you and your audience will help you feel safe and in control.

▶

- Check that the equipment is working.

> **Tip:** Have a back-up system in place – have some photocopies of your OHT pages or printouts of your PowerPoint slides to circulate as handouts if the OHP (overhead projector) or computer does not work.

- Use your adrenalin – it will help you think on your feet.
- Be positive again: Say, 'I am prepared' and 'I can handle this.'
- If too stressed (before or during a presentation):
  - Stop.
  - Sigh.
  - Drop your shoulders. (We hold our shoulders up when tense and this increases tension.)
  - Wriggle your toes. (We clench our feet when stressed and this increases our blood pressure and hence our stress levels.)
  - Unclench your fists – this is a typical anger/fear reaction – let it go.
  - Take a few deep, slow breaths (deep quick ones and you will pass out).
  - Start again more slowly.
- Write your agenda on the board, on a handout, on an OHT or on the flip chart.

During your presentation

- Introduce yourself and your topic.
- Give a brief introduction and say your agenda even if it is written up.
- Speak slowly and clearly. Let people hear and follow you.
- If you get lost, don't panic! Pause, look at your prompts, and carry on.
- Remember to use linguistic markers: we have looked at. . . . now we are going to cover . . . moving on to . . . .
- Make good eye contact – look at everyone in the room.

> **Tip:** Do stand so that you can see everyone and everyone can see you. Don't stare fixedly at one person so that they want to get up and leave!

- Use your AVA with confidence. Make sure everyone can see everything. Allow people to notice what is there before you take it away.
- Remember your conclusion – re-visit and re-state . . . no matter how silly it seems. Your audience does not know the topic as well as you do – they will need to be reminded of what you have talked about and what it means.
- Thank people for listening and ask for questions.
- Chair the Q&A session fairly and keep those answers short and sweet. Bring the Q&A to a firm conclusion. Thank people again.
- After your presentation, review your performance.

SWOTting your presentation

As with the essay and the report, it is useful for you to be able to review and evaluate your own presentations. However, because of the especially emotional dimension of presentations, we recommend that you undertake this in two stages:

1. Immediately after your presentation, tell yourself what a wonderful presentation it was and how brave you were for giving it. Try not to dwell on anything that went wrong; this just makes it harder to do a presentation next time. So make this first review a very positive one.
2. As with your writing, after some time has elapsed, it becomes useful for you to undertake a more detailed SWOT analysis of your presentation.

SWOTting your presentation:
- What were your strengths? What did you do very well? What sections of the presentation were you particularly pleased with? Why? Sometimes we are so busy correcting our faults that we forget to repeat our strengths. Make notes so that you remember.
- What were your weaknesses? What did not go so well? Why was this? Was it form – perhaps it was not structured or presented properly? Was it content – was it a poor argument unsupported by evidence? Did you forget to discuss your evidence? Did you forget to refer back to the question? Make notes.
- Opportunities: Now, go on; try to think of just how good you can become at presentations and of all the opportunities this gives you, both as a student and in future employment. Make notes.
- Threats: If you are still feeling threatened by presentations, what are you going to do next? Will you practise more? Do you need more support with your positive thinking? Do you need to find a study partner? Do you need to seek out the learning development or support team and get some more help? Make notes.

> **Tips:**
> - Make notes of your strengths and repeat them
> - Make notes of your weaknesses and repair them
> - Use your tutor feedback
> - Use video playback to refine your performance.

Conclusion

We have now looked in some detail at the academic presentation, paying particular attention to 'what' – that they are talks of set length, on set topics, to set audiences. Here we stressed how particular audiences have to be predicted and catered for. We looked at why we set, and you do, presentations. As always, we considered the heuristic (active learning) dimension of presentations. We also emphasised that developing good presentation skills will prepare you for employment and increase your self-confidence, while encouraging you to access an assessment mode in which you should be able to

▶

shine relatively quickly. With 'how', we referred you to the ten stages (Chapter 13), but here we focused on the four Ps of the presentation: plan, prepare, practise and present, emphasising the specific aspects of oral rather than written communication.

(Now, that was a conclusion – see how it re-visits the main arguments and then highlights the main points? It is as simple as that.)

As always, please make your own key-word pattern notes of the points that you wish to remember and use. None of this will make a difference unless and until you put it into practice!

Presentation strategies

Some things to think about and do to improve your presentation skills.

1. The three-minute presentation: Before giving a presentation for your course work, prepare and deliver a three-minute presentation to your study partner or study group. Choose a simple topic like a hobby or a holiday, just to get you started.

    With this presentation, just get the form right – introduction, agenda; body (logical structure and AVA); conclusion; Q&A. This will build your confidence for your assignment.

> **Tip:** Use the presentation checklist to evaluate yourself, and ask your friend to complete one for you, too.

2. Practise with a critical friend. Before an assignment presentation, practise in front of your study partner. Use their feedback.

3. Teamwork: If asked to prepare and deliver a group presentation, remember to practise with your group.

> **Tips:** Do look like a group – this could mean dressing in similar colours. Do act as though you were a good group that workedreally well together (even if you dislike each other).

4. Role play: Consider building some element of dramatic performance into your presentation, especially with a group. We have seen that when students act out a scenario or role-play a point to illustrate it, tutors are usually really impressed and give higher marks.

> **Tips:**
> - Think about writing up your agenda and speaking it.
> - Never pass anything around because that really disrupts a presentation.
> - Make handouts simple and clear, if they are too detailed, people will start reading and they will not listen.
> - Make handouts simple and clear, if they are too detailed, people will start reading and they will not listen.

►

- Put only a few words on OHTs, PowerPoint slides or flip charts, and make them big enough for everybody to see. Too many words and they will read and not listen.
- Let people see what you are showing them before you take visual aids away.
- Remove visuals when you are finished with them, so that they do not distract the audience from your next point.
- If you want people to see and then make notes, you will have to stop speaking long enough for them to do so.

Examine your practice presentation and improve it.

'One student presentation that really impressed me was one on Fibonacci numbers in maths. The students used real flowers and fruit – a pineapple – to illustrate the numbers in nature. One played the flute to illustrate the link between maths and music . . . I thought it was excellent!'

Review points

When reviewing your notes on this chapter, you might realise that:

- you can now think about presentations with excitement rather than dread
- you have considered the what, why and how of successfully preparing and delivering presentations
- you have thought about the what, why and how of presentations, and you understand how knowing these will help you to deliver better presentations in future
- you are aware of the importance of oral communications in HE and for future employment
- you are ready to tackle that presentation!

Presentation checklist

Photocopy the following checklist and use it to review your own presentations.

☐ Check the introduction. Does it tell the audience what you are talking about and why? Does it have a 'hook' telling the audience why they should listen to you? Does it give a clear agenda telling people the 'order' of your talk?

☐ Do you have a logical structure?

☐ Does each part of the presentation answer the paragraph questions? Do you discuss your evidence? Do you make points?

☐ Do you signpost clearly? That is, do you tell people what is happening and where you are going? (Also known as using the linguistic or discourse markers – put more simply, this means: do you clearly indicate your progress through the presentation – we have looked at this . . . now we are moving on to . . . ?)

☐ Do you have a conclusion that revisits your main arguments and re-states your main points?

☐ Do you have any strange mannerisms or gestures that you might like to get rid of (do not fiddle with a pen or scratch your nose).

☐ Will your AVA support your talk or distract from it? Will everybody be able to see at once?

18

How to run and participate in seminars

AIMS

To prepare you for running and participating in successful academic seminars.

LEARNING OUTCOMES

That after reading through this chapter, and engaging with the activities set, you will have:
- considered the nature of the academic seminar (what, why and how)
- considered the nature of successful communication with respect to the seminar
- considered the value of sharing research information with peers
- started the process of organising yourself for successful seminar participation
- made links between preparing a seminar and other activities covered in this text: preparing an essay or report, delivering an excellent presentation.

Introduction

The academic seminar is typically used as a formative device designed to help students develop their research, data collection and review techniques as part of working on a real academic paper. This may be an H-level project or report, a Masters dissertation or even a PhD, upon which a student is really working.

The idea is that at some point in your research, you draft a research paper that you present to a group of your fellow students, your peers. Your peers discuss your research in some way determined by you. That is, you set the topics for discussion, and you make sure that these topics will take your work forward.

After the discussion, you draw together the points raised in your paper and presentation and all the issues raised in the discussion. You also try to give some indication of the direction your research will now take, or what further work you will now do, in the light of the seminar itself.

Thus, the seminar is a real opportunity for interdependent, collegiate learning and for students to work to extend and deepen each other's understanding.

The seminar itself may or may not be assessed as part of the assessment proper of a particular course or module. While seminars are often used at high levels of university study, this form of student engagement and collaboration can work at any education level. In this chapter, we are going to look briefly at the what, why and how of the academic seminar.

Seminars are an opportunity, not a problem

If you are asked to prepare a seminar on a topic about which you are also writing, make sure that you get the most from the opportunity.

Remember that at some point in your research, you will be expected to offer the ideas that you have formed (so far) to your peers for discussion. Think about at which stage you would most benefit from help – at the beginning or end of your process.

Usually, you will be expected to write an academic paper, deliver a presentation and lead a discussion among a group of your peers. You will then use the discussion to seed further research of your own, or to better shape and present your final paper.

If you are set a seminar on your programme of study, embrace it; if you get a good discussion going, you will end up with a really improved final paper.

You will be fully prepared for your seminar if you both refer back to our sections on the essay, report and presentation, and utilise the tips below.

What is a seminar?

Typically, a seminar is made up of four parts:

1. **Paper** – prepared by you (seminar leader) and circulated in advance to all participants.

Tip: Check with the tutor as to what form the paper should take – essay, report, journal article. Check when it has to be ready for circulation.

2. **Presentation** – given by you on the seminar topic. Not just the paper read aloud, but a proper presentation that captures the key aspects of your research to date (see Chapter 17).

3. **Discussion** – this is beyond the question and answer session that normally succeeds a presentation. Here, you must make sure that the audience engages with your ideas in some way.

> **Tip:** Set useful discussion topics for the audience. Ensure that the audience actually does engage in a discussion.

4. **Summative conclusion** – that is, you, the seminar leader, have to draw together everything that was covered in the paper, in the presentation and in the group discussion. You should also be aware of how the seminar will help to shape the next step of your research or improve your final paper.

Why engage in seminars?

As we have indicated in the opening remarks above, the seminar is a highly developed university activity. It is designed to feed individual student research into a collaborative learning process.

If you are giving a seminar, you will have to organise your thinking in order to present your ideas in both written and oral form. This will develop your communication strategies. You will have to consider which areas of your research or writing will benefit from group discussion; this helps you to take control of your own learning and better manage your learning processes. You will have to set topics for discussion and then manage that discussion; this will develop your analytical and critical faculties and your communication, teamwork, interpersonal and leadership skills.

For those attending a seminar, it is a chance to participate in their colleagues' research; it can be an interesting and intense, active and interactive learning experience. It can model good practice for participants as they get to read other students' papers and hear other students' presentations, which is a very good thing. Finally, as this is a high-level university activity, engaging in seminars allows and enables you to refine your academic practice.

How to plan, prepare and benefit from seminars

We are covering this in key-point summary format, with annotations that highlight specific seminar points. See also Chapter 13 for effective communication tips; Chapters 14 and 16 for guidance on writing essays and reports; and Chapter 17 on putting together a successful presentation.

Things to think about:

1. When to give your seminar
Seminars often form part of programmes of study that happen over a whole semester or even longer. Typically, if you volunteer to run your seminar early, you will have very little data ready for review by your peers, but you may have encountered many interesting issues or even problems with which you would like some help. If you volunteer to run your seminar late,

your research may be almost over, and you may not be expecting your peers to suggest further research sources, but you may want them to discuss your findings and conclusions. Input from your peers may help you refine your interpretation of your data and improve the presentation of your final paper.

Tips: Things to think about:
- Are you researching a topic about which you know very little? If so, go early and hope that your peers will suggest further avenues to explore and further sources to read
- Are you confident about your ability to find sources, but unclear as to how best to interpret or present data? If so, go late, present your data in rough format and invite critical commentary on your analysis, even on your writing style.

---

2. Plan the whole seminar

Remember, the seminar has four parts to it – paper, presentation, discussion, and conclusion. Things to think about here include:

- **Plan the paper:** if you are delivering your paper early, it may consist of quite brief notes of what you are going to do in your research and why. You might note the context of your research (what makes it a valuable or interesting topic – what gaps there are already in this field) and the reading and other research activities (interviews, questionnaires) that you have already undertaken. If you are going late, your paper may very well look like a nearly finished draft of what you would expect to hand in. Think about highlighting the areas of the paper upon which you would appreciate critical feedback.

Tips:
- Think about what the paper could look like: on some courses, you may have to present papers that look very similar to journal articles, in others, you may be allowed to be more creative. We have seen students who have presented papers in poem format; while this was a very creative strategy, it might not be appropriate in some cases.
- Write your 'discussion' questions at the end of your paper. As the paper is typically circulated in advance, it should mean that people will have already read and thought about your questions before they attend your seminar.

- **Plan the presentation:** Whatever style of paper you have circulated in advance, you should expect your audience to have read it, thus, there is no need to cover the whole paper again in your presentation. So in your presentation, perhaps you could just outline the aims and purpose of your research, why you were interested in that topic, why you took the approach that you did, any problems that you encountered, and either detail how you overcame them, or invite solutions from your audience.

> **Tips:** Make your presentation interesting, keep your voice lively, display real enthusiasm for your subject and invite real collaboration from your audience. If you have managed to engage and keep the interest of your audience, they may well give you really good advice about how to extend, develop or refine your research or how to improve your paper.

- **Plan the discussion topics and discussion strategy.** It is very easy to waste the seminar opportunity by just seeing it as an ordeal to get through rather than the collaborative learning event that it can be. If you want to benefit from your seminar, think really hard about your discussion topics. Set real questions upon which you want your audience to think, and the answers to which could take your own research further forward.

> **Tips:** Do set questions that will help your own research. Do divide the audience into small groups and give each group a question (different or the same). Allow a set time for discussion. Hold a plenary to get feedback from the groups.

- **Plan the overall conclusion.** You may not know what the outcome of discussion upon your topics will be, but you do know what your paper and presentation will cover. So, have key points already drafted that sum up your own contribution to the seminar, and make sure that you make notes as your audience discuss your topics.

> **Tip:** Give flip chart paper to your audience (either individually or in small groups). Invite people to write key points on the flip chart pages and collect these in at the end. Sum up the key points, but keep the pages to make sure that you keep the ideas to use in your research.

3. Refine your paper, rehearse your presentation and test your discussion topics on a critical friend

Do not forget that any academic endeavour in which you engage gets better if you review, refine and edit first drafts. Do not expect to be perfect first go but draft and re-draft your work. This also applies to each part of the seminar.

4. Run your seminar with confidence and enthusiasm

> **Tips:** If getting students to discuss your questions in groups, move among the groups to check that they really are discussing your topics. Give flip chart markers out as well as the paper, so the writing can be seen. Allow a plenary session where everyone can briefly discuss each others' points. Give that overall conclusion! Think about how what you have learned really will help you with your research.

5. Review your own strengths and weaknesses overall

When reflecting on your seminar, think about your:

- paper
- presentation
- choice of topics and management of the discussion
- summative conclusion
- and then, in the light of the discussion that you managed, and the summative conclusion that you gave, decide what to do and read to improve your research and write a better final paper.

The advantages and disadvantages of seminars

As with any group or collaborative learning experience, there are advantages and disadvantages to the seminar.

Advantages:

- collaborative, collegiate learning
- active and interactive learning
- intense learning experience
- extends knowledge of a topic
- models good practice – paper, presentation, discussion techniques
- develops research angles
- improves grades in associated dissertation and essay work
- develops personal, interpersonal and communication skills
- develops organisation and time-management skills.

Disadvantages:

- lack of commitment in the seminar leader produces an uncomfortable event
- poor techniques – e.g. reading a paper instead of giving a presentation switches audiences off
- ill-prepared discussions become embarrassing
- ill-managed discussions can become exclusive, alienating or confrontational
- lack of commitment in an audience can mean that little or no learning actually takes place.

Obviously, all the disadvantages can be turned into advantages with the proper planning and commitment.

Conclusion

The academic seminar draws together oral and written communication strategies to form powerful interactive learning experiences for all involved. We really want you to engage positively and enthusiastically in your seminars and to make the most of them. To that

▶

effect, we have covered the what, why and how of seminars. In the 'what' of the seminar, we emphasised the importance of utilising what you already know about preparing essays, reports and presentations. We also stressed the importance of organising and managing a good discussion that will both interest your audience and seed your own research. In 'why', we stressed that the seminar is an active, interactive learning event that will benefit both seminar-giver and the other seminar participants, if they are all committed to the venture. In 'how', we paid particular attention to the importance of the discussion and the summative conclusion. Further, we emphasised how reviewing the seminar should seed your research, so that your final paper is significantly better than it would have been without the seminar itself.

As always, please make your key-word pattern notes on this chapter, considering: what do you want to take away about the seminar? What will you do with the information? When will you do it?

Review points

- When reviewing your notes on this chapter, you might realise that you have:
- understood the nature of the academic seminar (what, why and how)
- reflected on the nature of communication and issues surrounding communicating effectively in seminars (through writing and speaking)
- understood the positive benefits of sharing research information with peers
- started the process of organising yourself for successful seminar participation.

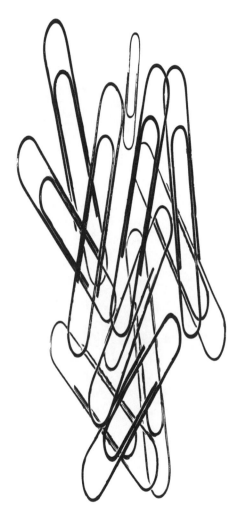

SECTION 4

Effective Revision, Exams
and PDP

19

How to build your memory and revise effectively

AIMS

To re-visit learning style and explore memory and revision techniques, such that you will be able to succeed in your exams. (See also Chapter 4 on effective learning and Chapter 20 on how to understand and pass exams.)

LEARNING OUTCOMES

That after reading this chapter and engaging with the activities, you will have:
- considered your own memory and memorisation strategies
- considered the difference between short-and long-term memory
- re-visited learning styles and made decisions about your own learning strategies
- been introduced to successful memory, learning and revision strategies.

Memory and learning style

This whole book is dedicated to active learning. If you put active learning techniques into practice, you will learn. This is especially so if you actually want to learn specific material (hence our stress on effective learning, learning styles and the learning contract, in Chapter 4). Here, we are going to actively tackle issues around memory, briefly re-visiting learning styles, such that you can focus on how to utilise your learning style when memorising information and revising for exams.

> *Query*: Do you think that you have a good memory?

Whenever we ask that question of a group of students, the majority always responds that they have a bad memory. However, there is an argument that everyone can develop a good memory with practice.

Memory

Tony Buzan has explored the psychology and dynamics of memory with respect to learning. His work on remembering and forgetting curves has led him to argue that we need to actively revise everything that we want to remember if we want to learn it: learning does not happen by accident or chance. Buzan states that, without active revision, we forget 98 per cent of what we encounter after just three weeks. This means that if we do not act to remember what we want to remember (our course work), we forget it all, almost immediately.

This is obviously a real problem for those students who revise only three weeks before an exam. For what these people are doing is not revision – it is learning it all from scratch. And, no, you cannot possibly do that in three weeks.

The revision cycle

Buzan recommends an active revision cycle when encountering new and important material:

1   The same day that you encountered the new material, spend ten minutes making a short, dynamic version of your notes. Build in memory triggers. Memory triggers might be cartoons or illustrations that make a particular page of notes easier to remember for you.
2   A day later, spend two minutes recalling your memory trigger and the notes attached. You might mentally recall the information or actually re-draw the notes. The more active you are the better.
3   A week later spend another two minutes re-activating the memory.
4   A month later spend another two minutes re-activating the memory.
5   Re-activate every six months for as long as you want to keep the memory alive.

You can see that the revision cycle is a sort of 'use it or lose it' cycle. It is a system based on transferring information from our relatively ineffectual short-term memories

▶

into our infinitely more useful long-term memories. In the process of doing this, we are actually building memories chemically into our brains.

> **Tip:** we get quicker with these revision strategies with practice.

Short- and long-term memory

Buzan's research adds to what is believed about our short- and long-term memories (see Figure 19.1). The belief is that the short-term memory is a very small and immediate working memory. This allows us to function day-to-day. However, our long-term memories are memories that we create and build. It could be argued that these allow us to function in our lives – they become who we are. In terms of our studying, the short-term memory is good for picking up pieces of information, but we need to get that information into our long-term memories if it is to be of any use to us.

Getting information into our long-term memories does not happen by accident or chance. It does not happen quickly, but over time. It does not happen unless we do something to make it happen. Basically, if we do want to learn something, then we have to:

- choose what to remember
- decide how we are going to remember it (our memory triggers)
- be prepared to re-activate the memory immediately, then a day, a week and a month later (use the revision cycle)
- make yet another commitment of time and effort to our studies.

Short-term memory	Attribute	Long-term memory
Relatively small – holds 5–9 pieces of information	Capacity – size	Infinite – can build an infinite number of memories in the brain
Brief – piece of information number 8 comes along – and a piece of information falls out	Persistence – how long information stays	Infinite – with reactivation and barring brain trauma – information can stay there forever
Is immediate – either it goes in or it does not	Input – how to get information in	Relatively slow – see revision cycle. It takes time and effort to build memories
Is immediate – if it is there you can access it	Access – how to get information out	Depends on input. How you put it in is how get it out (alphabet song)

FIGURE 19.1   The main attributes of short- and long-term memory

Activity 1: Think back to how you learned things in primary school or kindergarten

Spend five minutes jotting down how you learned things in your earliest days at school.

Now compare your list with points taken from other students:

- I learned the alphabet by singing a little alphabet song. It is still the way I remember the alphabet.
- We were taught our sums by reciting the times tables. But I don't actually remember them now. I don't think I wanted to learn my tables, so that didn't work so well.
- I remember the colours of the rainbow, you know: Richard of York Gained Battle In Vain. If you take the first letters, you can get back to Red, Orange, Yellow, Green, Blue, Indigo, Violet.
- One that my little girl came home with the other day was the spelling of 'because' – **b**ig **e**lephants **c**an **a**lways **u**nderstand **s**mall **e**lephants.
- And then there is that other one – Never Eat Shredded Wheat – which gives you the points of the compass: North, East, South, West.
- I went to a Montessori school, where we would see it, hear it, say it and do it.

Query: How do these memory systems compare with the ones that you have noted down?

Discussion: What is actually happening here is that the teacher, typically, is designing mnemonics (memory systems or triggers) for the students. Where the trigger involves rhythm and rhyme (the alphabet song) – and the student wants to remember – it seems to be more successful. Where the trigger involves something unusual or bizarre (Richard of York or the big elephants), it is also more memorable.

We put aside childish things

Unfortunately, what seems to happen as we get older is that we stop using these successful memory strategies, strategies that work with the way that our brains actually work. It seems that as we grow to be adults, instead of becoming more proficient learners, we put aside successful learning strategies – it is as if we deliberately forget how to learn. What we need to do once we are students, is to re-learn how to learn. When we apply learning strategies to our studies, we will have to be active learners: working out *what* it is that we want to remember, and deciding *how* we are going to remember that, using the systems that work with our brains.

Tips:

- Design your own mnemonic systems for all the things that you need to remember.
- Use rhythm and rhyme.
- Use the bizarre.
- Reduce key information onto index cards, and carry them about and revise in odd moments.

Learning is key

So, we are emphasising just how active you have to be in your own learning and remembering, choosing what and how to learn. However, we are not saying that you have to learn textbooks or essays by heart. Indeed, a key to successful learning is not to try to remember whole chunks of information. It really is not an advantage to try for word-for-word recall of whole lectures or seminars, of whole essays that you or other students have written, or of whole passages from books. This is ineffective: you are remembering padding rather than key information; you are being passive rather than active; and it can trap you in the way that other people have used information, and stop you from being able to use it yourself.

To be both active and effective in our learning, we have to develop our ability to strip back what we need to learn to the bare essentials: to the skeleton. Once we have learned key data, we need to be able to use it ourselves: in discussion, in presentations and in our writing, including our exam writing. If we simply remember how other people have used the information – in lectures or in textbooks, for example – it will never be our own.

'I saw this student in the library, preparing for the exam by trying to learn the PowerPoint slides from the lectures, in the same order that I had delivered them! I tried to explain that it's not about learning my lectures – it's about understanding and extending them – and then using the data to answer the questions set in the exam.'

Add flesh to the bones later

So, the trick is to reduce information to its bare essentials: the skeleton, which we do then learn by heart. We then need to practise using the information for ourselves over the whole programme of study. We do this by talking, reading, listening and writing – not just by rote-learning handouts or lecture notes.

What we can do as we move through a course towards the exams is, week by week, to reduce handouts, lecture notes and notes from our reading to ever fewer words. And we understand these key words because we have been using them constantly over the course itself (more on this in Chapter 20 [SQP4]). Thus, we reduce the quantity of what we have to learn (the amount) but improve the quality (we can use it ourselves, with confidence).

Tips: As you reduce information to the bare essentials, utilise 'see, hear, say and do' strategies to ensure that you are going to remember that which you need to. That is, you can use the information on learning styles to develop your revision strategies.

Use your learning style to learn your key words

See

If you are visual, you may enjoy learning by reading and using visual aids (television, film or video). It would help if you made revision notes as colourful as possible, and visual triggers would definitely help you to remember.

Hear/say

If you prefer an auditory learning style, then lectures, discussion and audio-tapes would all help you to learn. For revision purposes, it would help if you put your key-word data into jingles or songs, and if you used funny voices when revising.

Feel/do

If you favour a kinaesthetic learning approach, you will benefit from building a physical dimension into your learning – this could be really simple, like moving about as you study (very different from the notion of the good student sitting quietly in one place for hours on end). Your learning and revision would benefit from *making* your pattern notes, perhaps cutting out memory triggers from magazines and physically pasting them onto your notes.

Activity 2: Have some fun! (revision games)

A good tip with respect to learning material is to make a game of it, in order to inject some fun into the proceedings. Designing revision games for programmes really helps learning.

Activity: If you had to design a revision game for one of your programmes of study, what would you do? (Think for five minutes, then compare your ideas with those below.)

Typically, students have designed:

- **Quizzes** – here the students researched a specific programme (sociology, psychology, history, etc.) examining the aims and learning outcomes. Once they identified the key data (names, dates, information) that ought to be learned by the end of the course, they designed questions and answers that covered all the ground on that course. A competitive edge was set up for the quiz by having several teams competing against each other. Answering the questions or not

▶

revealed to the players both the information they had learned and that which they had forgotten.

■ **Board games** – here again, the students researched a programme examining the aims and learning outcomes. They again constructed questions and answers that covered all the learning outcomes (the key data, such as names, dates and information). But here they designed a colourful board game that could be played as the questions were answered.

> *Discussion*: Both these strategies are very effective with respect to learning the key information on a course.
>
> The quiz utilises 'see, hear and say' strategies, and the playing of the quiz can become an emotional and even a physical experience. The board game scenario is especially good, for to play the game, you will see, hear, say and do!

Conclusion

How to build your memory and revise effectively explored how to develop your memory and utilise your learning style, as part of your successful revision and learning strategies. Read Chapter 20 to see how to draw on all these things together in the SQP4 process: a whole course strategy for success. Be aware that you can build your memory, whatever you think of it now, and enjoy learning your course material and passing those exams.

Further reading

If you are interested in taking the ideas in this chapter further, the following might help:
Buzan, T. (1989) *Use Your Head*. London: BBC publications.
Buzan, B. and Buzan, T. (1999) *The Mind Map Book*. London: BBC publications.
Rogers, C. (1992) *Freedom to Learn*. Upper Saddle River, NJ: Merrill.
Rose, C. and Goll, L. (1992) *Accelerate Your Learning*. Aylesbury: Accelerated Learning Systems.

Activity 3: *ESS2* revision game

Choose one section of this book. Reduce the information to key-word points. Design a revision game that would help you learn the material. Play the game with your study partner.

Activity 4: If you have not already done so, complete the (Getting ready for your exams) checklist, Chapter 20 for each course that you are studying.

Review points

When reviewing this chapter, you might realise that you now have:
- a better understanding of the role of memory in learning
- a sense of how to utilise learning style information to develop your memory and learn course material
- an understanding of successful learning and revision strategies
- a sense of how to inject some fun into your learning.

20

How to understand and pass exams

AIMS

To explore exams and exam techniques, such that you will be able to succeed in your exams.

LEARNING OUTCOMES

That after reading this chapter and engaging with the activities, you will have:
- considered the nature of exams and some typical student responses to exams
- been introduced to a whole course approach to exam success
- been introduced to successful learning, revision and exam strategies.

Introduction

A sub-title for this chapter could be 'big picture – small steps'. This would indicate that while a course does have a big picture – an overall shape, purpose and direction – we typically take small steps through that course. That is, we generally make sense of and learn a course one piece at a time.

In this section, we are going to explore how the big picture allows you to take small steps to learning course content and ultimately pass exams. In the process of doing this, we will consider examinations – fact and fiction – and we will also look at successful exam strategies. Memory, learning style and revision are covered in Chapter 19; see also Chapter 4 on effective learning. We will start this off with a quick look at typical responses to exams.

Activity 1: Goal setting

As always, before you progress through the chapter, pause and reflect quickly on the chapter topics, asking yourself:
- What do I already know about exams?
- What would I like to know?
- What do I like about exam techniques?
- What would I like to improve?

Once you have brainstormed and set your own goals, you are ready to move on as an active learner.

Small steps: preparing for exams

While some aspects of studying will always fill some students with horror, examinations (exams) are typically loathed by most people. We believe that this situation arises because of early schooling and exam experiences. We are going to explore some reasons why students may not like exams. Finally, we shall give very specific and practical advice, entitled SQP4 – a whole course approach to passing exams.

So, what's wrong with exams?

Firstly, the problem is not necessarily with exams at all, but often lies in approaches to teaching and learning, and in how we are taught, at school, college and even in universities. That is, while we are taught subject content, we are not necessarily taught how to learn that content.

Some teachers believe that just presenting students with information will guarantee that those students will pass the exams. But presentation is not learning. It is good to know what we ought to learn, but in the end the student has to somehow learn the material for him or herself, if they want to use that information successfully to pass an exam. For it is the student that has to pass the exam, not the tutor.

How do we learn course material?

Carl Rogers, psychologist and teacher, believed that what the tutor has to do is facilitate significant learning in the student. That is, the tutor has to set up a learning situation, but the student has to then actively decide to learn. He described this process as the student reaching out for what they want and need. Most of the activities in this book are designed to help you, the student, reach out for what you want and need, initially from this very book itself and then from all your studies. But in this section we will be specifically focusing on how to learn course material in order that you do pass your exams.

Why haven't we done this before?

It can be really frustrating for students to turn up at university and realise that they have to take all the responsibility for their own learning, when they have not actually been taught how to do this. This can be especially galling when it comes to passing university exams. The grades that they get in their exams will determine what class of degree they receive, and typically while they do really want to do well, they do not know how to do well. If this is how you feel, then you know what we mean.

I'd be fine if it wasn't for the exams!

Often, the most motivated student still does not know how to do well in exams. Naturally enough, this guarantees that the majority of people never perform very well in their exams. Thus, a vicious circle of unpreparedness and exam failure sets in. Eventually, many people just give up on exams. These people tend to think that the problem lies with them – they are not clever enough, they are not suited to exams, or whatever it is. The reality is that they have often not been taught how to learn or how to approach exams.

Exams are simply misunderstood

The nature of how we prepare for exams, or not, leads to the second point about exams – they are often misunderstood. Many people have criticised exams for the high failure rates in this country, for not being educationally sound, for being set in hay-fever season, for disadvantaging people with high stress levels, and so forth. But it could be argued that what these people are doing is attacking the symptom – the high failure rates in exams – rather than the problem, which is that we do not teach people how to learn.

For there is a sound educational purpose to exams. Exams are designed not just to test your memory of key facts and data, your surface learning (though remember that these are often very important, too.) Exams are there to test your deep learning, your knowledge and understanding of material. That is, to test how you use the information that you have learned – and that you have made your own through reorganisation and understanding – over a whole course of study.

If we refer back to our earlier points on learning (Chapter 4), it is about being able to:

- gather
- record
- organise
- understand
- remember, and
- use . . . information.

Then, perhaps you can see that exams are designed to force you to demonstrate that you have indeed learned your material, so that you can flexibly use the information again in an examination. Yes, this does all occur in a time-controlled situation and this can feel very stressful, but the overall idea is not to trick you, but to test you. If you can accept that, then you are on your way to dealing more positively with the exam situation.

Further, some people do actually enjoy the idea of being tested, finding it a challenge. So if you really, really hate exams at the moment, work on changing your attitude. Try to see exams as a challenge, an opportunity to demonstrate what you do know, rather than a problem. It really will help you, if you could look at exams in a more positive light.

'I know I'm unusual, but I really love exams and hate coursework. With exams I get to pace myself throughout the whole year, as opposed to everything I write counting! Then I can psych myself up to perform really well for three hours or so. It's brilliant!'

It's a trick

Many people are so stressed by the idea of exams that they can only see the negative aspects. Exams feel like trickery – evil things designed to catch you out. Fear means that it is difficult to see that the exam is a test, not a trick. It is often fear itself that prevents these people from preparing for exams. Even if they do prepare, fear can have such a negative effect on the brain (release of the stress hormones cortisol and adrenalin which reduce short-term memory) that they cannot remember what they are trying to learn.

If this describes how you feel about exams, you really will have to change your basic negative approach before you will be able to move forward.

Tips:
- Have a look at material on positive thinking – see Chapter 9 to start you off.
- Understand that exams are a test, not a trick.
- Work towards particular exams with a study partner.
- Use the learning development (sometimes called learning support, study skills or study development) people at your college or university to help you prepare for exams.
- Use the counselling service to help you get over your fear of exams.

I'm dyslexic and I write really slowly

Many students ask us how long an exam answer should be. What can we tell them? There really is no right or wrong answer, because in the end there is only what you can write in the time you have been allowed. So every student has to discover how much they can write (how many words) in the time allowed, and then get better at answering an exam question in that many words.

This problem can be exacerbated for the dyslexic student who probably writes more slowly than most. However, there are still some positive things that you can do. First, if you think that you are dyslexic, you must get a proper test done. Go to the Student Support Services at your college or university to find out how this happens.

You can then use the test results to lobby for extra time in exams. Typically, the dyslexic student is allowed another ten minutes per hour in an exam. This does have some value. However, if you also lobby to take exams on a word processor or computer, this can have a marked effect on your grades. Students we know who have done this have turned the exam situation around dramatically, moving from an automatic fail in exams to gaining upper-second and even first-class grades.

There are several reasons why this could be the case:

- Word-processed work looks so much neater, and it overcomes any unconscious prejudice in the mind of the examiner towards untidy handwriting.
- The student feels so much more confident on the computer that they do indeed produce better work.
- The student actually practises more.

Tips:
- Practise timed writing.
- Practise answering assignment questions, but where you would normally be allowed upwards of 1500 words, give yourself half an hour.
- Practise preparing perfect answers with your study partner.
- If using a computer, learn to touch-type.
- Practise timed writing on the computer.

How can you learn a whole year's work in three weeks?

Contrary to popular opinion, revision is not something that you should be doing just before your exams. As we are constantly reiterating here, revision is part of active learning. You should be learning material as you go through your course – not just before the exams. What you do just before the exams is practise that timed writing.

Tip: Read the section on SQP4 – this will give a whole course approach to passing exams.

But I've got a really bad memory

Many people feel that they have a bad memory – often, this is because they have not actually learned how to use their memories (they have not learned how to learn). There is also the argument that, especially as we get older, we focus more on what we are forgetting, instead of noticing what we are remembering.

Everyone can develop a good memory. London cab drivers, for example, have measurably larger cortexes to their brains, because they have had to teach themselves to remember all the streets, alleys and roads in London. What the London cabby can do, you can do! The trick is to learn how to remember.

Tips:
- Check out Chapter 19 on memory.
- Get the overview of the course and use the learning outcomes.
- Check out Chapter 4 on effective learning and learning styles.
- Learn key points on any course as you go.

SQP4: Putting it all together – a practical guide to exam success

In this section, we will bring information about the use of the overview, memory and learning style together into our very practical revision and exam technique advice – SQP4: survey, question, predict, plan, prepare and practise. We will close with a look at 'examination day'.

Activity 2: Thinking about exams

Some people are so frightened of exams that they do not prepare for them at all – is this you? Obviously, we believe this is a bad idea: if you never prepare, you will probably always do quite badly, and this could keep you feeling bad about exams for the rest of your life. So let us compare exams to other things that you might choose to do. Compare exams to:
■ running a marathon
■ passing a driving test
■ entering a dance competition.
Choose one of these and think how you would prepare for it. (5 minutes)
Now compare your answer with that given by a student below:

'When planning for my driving test, I sorted out the written test first. I got the book with the key questions in and tested myself till I thought I'd got them right. Then I got my friends to test me till I was sure I'd got it right. I only lost two points in the test itself.

'With the driving part, I had lessons till my instructor thought I was ready. When I was confident that I knew how to do it, I booked the test. Then my instructor and I practised all the things that would definitely come up in the test – you know, emergency stop, three-point turn, and parking properly.

When I could drive a car in my sleep, I took the test and passed first time.'

> *Discussion*: When it comes to the sorts of 'test' that we choose to do in our everyday life, we do know what to do. We:
> ■ find out exactly what will be required of us in the test
> ■ learn the things that we need to learn
> ■ practise often.
> That is the essence of the SQP4 system.

Survey

As soon as you start on a course, get the overview of the course as a whole (see Chapter 3). This is the big-picture part of your whole-course approach to exam success.

• If you have a course booklet or handbook, check the aims and learning outcomes. Make key-word notes summarising all the things that will be assessed.

- If supplied with a syllabus, read it through and note which weeks are dedicated to which of the learning outcomes and mark them up. See how many weeks are set to cover each topic, and use that to try and gain a sense of how important each thing is.
- Read the assignment question for more information on what to do and learn on the course. Further, this reveals the sorts of questions that you could be asked on the course itself. Cross-reference the different parts of the assignment question with different weeks on the course. This helps you to take control of course content and delivery.
- Look for past exam papers to see exactly the style of the paper. Discover how long the exam will be, how many questions you will be expected to answer and the sorts of topics that come up all the time. Notice the way questions are written on an exam paper so that the real paper cannot frighten you!

Where are my papers?

Sometimes past papers are actually given to students, sometimes they are not. When they are not, you have to discover where they are kept.

With national exams taken by college students, past papers are sometimes kept in the college library. Sample papers may be kept on the online website designed to support the course.

Universities operate many different systems for storing exam papers, even across a single university. Some departments put papers online, some hold them in the university library, and others place them with the departmental secretary. It is your task both to find out where they are kept, and to actually have a good look at them. Photocopy the papers and put them into your subject file.

'I have a website for all my students to use, and I put many resources up there. I also have a counter to see which pages students look at the most. I suppose you've guessed it – they look at past exam papers and model answers the least! Why?'

Tip: Write an 'exam' list for each course that you are taking, noting:
- how long the exam will be
- how many questions you will have to answer
- whether it is a seen or unseen exam (where you get the paper in advance)
- whether or not it is an open-book exam (whether or not you will be allowed to take textbooks into the exam).

Question

Once you have spent real time surveying the course to gain your overview, you are ready to move on to Q for question. That is, very early on in a course, you need to reflect on all the information that you have gathered from your overview – your active surveying of the course. You need to sit down and ask yourself: what exactly do I need to do and learn to pass this course?

Make a list of all the things that you will need to do and learn to pass the course, and pin it up in your study space. Do this for every course or module or unit that you are taking.

> **Tips:**
> - Draw up your lists with your study partner.
> - For each exam, make a list of the topics that will come up.
> - Link to learning outcomes.
> - Link to course weeks.
> - Link to the assignment question.
> - Put the lists on your wall and in your coursework folders.

Predict

Once you have examined all the course information that you have been given and all the past papers that you can find, predict the questions that will come up on the exam paper attached to your programme. Then decide which questions you think you would be most interested in and that you will therefore plan to answer in the exam proper. It does help you to learn if you follow your interests and enthusiasms through a course and, conversely, it is very difficult to learn that in which we are totally uninterested.

> **Tips:**
> - Where possible, choose to do the assignment question that leads to an exam topic. (If the course booklet specifically states that if you answer an assignment question on one thing, then you must answer an exam question on something else, think about working out a strategy with your study partner. For example, you can both research for two topics (say) – let us call them A and B. One of you will use the A research for their assignment, while the other will use the A research for the exam. And the other way round for the B research.)
> - Open a revision folder on each exam topic that you intend to answer.

Plan

Once you have chosen your exam topics, you must plan your learning and revision strategy for each topic. This is your strategy for learning all you must know to answer an exam question on that topic, drawing on what you now know about effective learning, memory and learning style (Chapters 4 and 19). We have covered this in a list of useful things to plan to do throughout a whole course. This is definitely not something to do just before your exams.

> **Tip:** If you want to get a really good grade, you will have to do more than the basic minimum amount of work: you must read around the subject, you must think for yourself. If you only give back to tutors what you hear in class and you only use their examples and handouts, then you will only get an average grade. The choice is yours (for more information on this, go to Chapter 8 on creative learning).

Things you should plan to do

☐   Have a revision folder for each topic in each exam.
☐   Put relevant class, lecture and reading notes into each folder.
☐   Answer assignment questions linked to exam topics.
☐   Put assignment notes into the relevant folders.
☐   Put the assignments into the folders.
☐   Put any extra work that you do – say, following your tutor's feedback on your assignment – in the folders.
☐   Put in press cuttings.
☐   Start a revision cycle for each of the topics that you want to learn, from week one of each course!
☐   Build a big-picture, pattern note for each topic (see Chapter 12).
☐   Add information to your own 'big picture' every week.
☐   Spend a few minutes reviewing your big picture every week.
☐   Put key information onto index cards. Carry them with you and learn them in a supermarket checkout queue, learn them on the bus, learn them in the lift.
☐   Fill in the 'Get ready for your exams' checklist.

Prepare

It is not enough to plan to do well in your exams – you must actually do everything that you have planned to do. In this way, you really will prepare for your exams. So to prepare properly, you have to:

•   keep a revision cycle going for each exam topic
•   keep your revision folders and your big-picture revision pattern in order and up to date
•   go through each revision folder from time to time, throwing out excess material
•   each week add key points and illustrations to your big picture
•   keep your portable index cards up to date. As you learn the material, reduce your notes, and make your index card notes shorter

Tip: Each time you make your notes shorter, you are actually revising the material.

•   illustrate your notes with memorable cartoons
•   make key-word tapes using rhyme and music. Play these as you go over your big-picture notes
•   design quizzes and test your friends.

Successful exam preparation – tips and tricks

■   Want to do well: be interested, know what you want from the course, know why you want to get a good grade.

- Learn the bones: only learn key-word points, otherwise you fill your memory with padding. You want the skeleton, not the whole body.
- Memorise: take time each week to memorise key facts.
- Practise turning key words into essays.
- Study partner: make sure you do have a study partner. Plan and prepare perfect answers together.
- Board games! Get Trivial Pursuit or some other board game. Put the questions to one side. Devise question and answer cards for all your exam topics and play the game with your study partner.
- See it, hear it, say it, do it!

Practise

At last, we have come to something that you can do three weeks before your exams! All the above strategies emphasise learning key data – names, dates, key points of information – from the beginning of each course. What you need to do just before the exam is to practise using the information that you are learning, under exam conditions. Typically, this involves practising planning and writing essays under timed conditions.

It's different in exams

Over your programme of study, you use key information in class discussion, in group-based learning activities, in presentations and other assignments. You have time to plan and research your answers. You have anything from 1000 to 3000 or more words in which to answer a question. Suddenly in an exam, you have just half an hour or an hour to plan and write a perfect answer.

You now have to work completely differently to the way you have worked before. As with a driving test, you will not be able to do this unless you have practised doing it. You will not be able to plan and write a good essay in a time limit, unless you have practised both planning and writing under timed conditions. It is as simple as that.

Practising for exams – Tips

- Practise brainstorming and planning – develop the ten-minute brainstorm technique.
- Go through all the questions in your course handbook – allowing ten minutes per brainstorm, plan an answer for each one.
- Find past exam papers – allowing ten minutes per brainstorm, brainstorm every question on the paper.
- See how much you can write in half an hour.
- Practise writing something good in half an hour.

▶

- Practise timed writing: When you have finished a long assignment essay, practise writing a half-hour version of the same essay.
- Practise timed writing with notes.
- Practise timed writing without notes.
- Practise preparing and writing 'perfect' answers with your study partner.

Using time in exams

Each exam is different. For each, you will have to know how long the whole exam is, how many questions you will have to answer, and therefore how long you will have for each question. Time per question needs to be divided between preparation time, writing time and reviewing time.

This will mean allocating overall exam time to:
- **Reading the paper:** Always read the questions carefully. That is another reason why it is important to see past papers, so that the actual wording of the question does not intimidate or confuse you.
- **Planning each answer** (allow ten minutes per plan): As with your assignment questions, analyse all the key words in the question and brainstorm each word in the question. Use the brainstorm to plan the answer: at the most basic level, you can number the different points in your brainstorm in the order that you think you will raise them in your essay. Always plan before you write. Time spent planning is never wasted. Time spent writing without planning can be very wasted indeed.
- **Start each answer:** You must begin to answer every question that you are supposed to.
- **Writing each answer:** You ought to divide time equally between the questions. You must write to time. Time yourself.
- **Review what you have written.** A few minutes checking your answer can make a phenomenal difference to your marks!
- This all takes practice!

Handling the exam

Read the paper, identify which questions you will answer, then try the following:
1 Brainstorm and plan each answer before you write anything. The advantage of this is that as you brainstorm one question, you may recall additional information for another question.
2 Brainstorm/plan and write your favourite question. Then brainstorm/plan all the others and then write in order of preference. The advantage of this is that you feel good once you have a whole question out of the way.
3 Brainstorm/plan and then write one question at a time.

▶

> **Tips:**
> - Always start all the questions, never leave one out.
> - Maximum marks are picked up at the beginning of your answers.
> - Never answer more questions than you are asked – extra questions are just not marked.
> - If you run out of time, refer the marker to your plan and/or finish in note form. This allows you to pick up points for key facts.
> - Always cross out material that you do not want the examiner to mark.

And finally . . . examination day!

No writing on revision and exam techniques is complete without a look at the actual exams themselves. Here we are going to give some practical advice for the examination days. So, whatever you normally do around exam time, next time you have an exam, try to do some of the following.

Think smart – think positive

You need to mentally prepare for exams. You must want to do well, and you do have to work at believing in yourself. Read Chapter 9 on dealing with your emotions and building self-confidence, but here are a few tips for examination time:
- Remember that fear is normal – it does not mean that you cannot do well.
- Enjoy your fear – it means you are facing a new challenge.
- Think positive thoughts – I can handle this! I'm looking forward to this exam! I'm so well prepared!
- Act positive – find out what it would take to do well in your exam and then do it. Give 100 per cent.
- Have a positive study partner – encourage and support each other, with no moaning!

Relaxation

We recommend earlier that, as a student, you build in stress-relief activities from the beginning of your course, if not throughout your life. If you are in the habit of running or exercising, of meditating or doing yoga, then it will be easy for you to just do more of this around exam time.

If you are not in that habit, it is unlikely that you will suddenly develop good habits in the nick of time! So here we would just like to reiterate our advice – build some stress-relief activities into your programme from the start. Further, if you feel that you will become sleepless around exam time, why not practise using a sleep audio-tape before the exams come up? Then your body will know how to use the tape when you really need it.

The night before

If you have been putting SQP4 techniques into practice over your course of studies, you should feel confident that you do know your material, and that you can plan and write an answer in the time allowed. So the night before the exam, you should not be trying to cram in new information, and neither should you be panicking.

You should be quietly confident. You may wish to go over your key-word notes, whether you have them on a big pattern on the wall, index cards or summarised onto sheets of paper. You may wish to practise a few ten-minute brainstorms, but the essence is on quiet confidence and rest. Have an early night.

On examination day

Get up early and have a light breakfast, even if you do not feel like eating. Exams are hard work and you will need energy. But do not eat so much that all your blood goes to your stomach – you need a good supply getting to your brain.

Arrive at the examination room in good time. Do not cram in new information. Avoid people who are acting nervous or scared – they will only unsettle you and it is too late to help them now. Worse, we have heard of students who deliberately behave negatively in order to unsettle others so that they do badly in the exam. They feel that this increases their chances of doing well.

Make sure you have working pens and a watch. Take some chocolate with you or a glucose drink, for that extra energy boost mid-exam.

Think positive thoughts. Read through the paper carefully and choose your questions with confidence. Brainstorm and plan before you write. Recall your revision notes by sight, sound or feel. Time yourself through each question, and *start* every question. Leave time to quickly review what you have written.

Tip: The law of diminishing returns means that it is better to start every answer than to finish most and leave some out. More marks are picked up at the beginning of an answer.

What examiners like to see:

- Correct use of key words, phrases, terms and concepts from your subject.
- Questions answered in the correct format, with essays where they want essays and reports where they want reports.
- Not writing 'all you know' on the topic, but identifying the key words in the question and addressing those in your answer.
- Focus on the question set, appropriately drawing on course material.
- Discussing course material critically.
- Using the time well.
- Neat presentation.

After the exam

Try to avoid discussing the exam with other people, especially if you have another exam later that same day or the next day. Comparing answers with others can lead to panic, and you do not need that if you have other exams for which to prepare. If you do have another exam the following day, treat yourself to another relaxed evening and an early night.

Conclusion

How to pass exams links several of the active and effective learning strategies covered elsewhere in this text with exam success. Specifically, we focused on exams themselves, some responses to exams and then we discussed the SQP4 process – a whole course strategy for success. We finished with a quick look at examination day. You should now be ready to put these ideas into practice in your own learning. Do use the various checklists that have been included to help you. Good luck with your exams!

Further reading

If you are interested in taking the ideas in this chapter further, the following might help:
Buzan, T. (1989) *Use Your Head*. London: BBC publications.
Buzan, B. and Buzan, T. (1999) *The Mind Map Book*. London: BBC publications.
Rogers, C. (1992) *Freedom to Learn*. Upper Saddle River NJ: Merrill.
Rose, C. and Goll, L. (1992) *Accelerate Your Learning*. Aylesbury: Accelerated Learning Systems.

Activity 3: The three-minute test

Settle down and give yourself just three minutes to work through this short test.
Three-minute test
Name:
Date:
Read the paper carefully before answering any questions. This is a timed test – you have three minutes to complete the paper.

1 Before answering any questions, read through the whole paper.
2 Print your name, and date in the appropriate sections of this paper.
3 Draw five small squares in the bottom right-hand corner of this sheet.
4 Circle the word 'name' in question 2.

▶

5   Put an 'x' in each of the five squares.
6   Sign your name at the top of this paper.
7   In front of your name, write 'YES, YES, YES'.
8   *Loudly*, so that everyone can hear you, call out your name.
9   Put a circle around question number 3.
10 Put an 'x' in the lower left-hand corner of this paper.
11 Draw a triangle around the 'x' that you have just put down.
12 In your normal speaking voice, count down from ten to one.
13 Loudly call out, 'I am nearly finished, I have followed directions!'
14 Now that you have finished reading everything, do only questions one and
    two.

End of exam.

Query: Well, how did you do? Were you that student bobbing up and down and calling things out? What does that tell you?

> Discussion: Another name for this test is 'Can you follow directions?' It is a simple way of illustrating that you really do need to read an exam paper carefully before you start to answer the questions. The problem with not following directions in an exam could be that you do the wrong things. Typically, this would be in the sort of exam that asks you to answer one question in section A and then one in B, and then to choose one question from either section, or something like that. If you do not read these instructions very carefully, you can answer the wrong questions and throw marks away!

Review points

When reviewing this chapter, you might realise that you now have:
- an understanding of the role that exams play in the learning cycle
- a sense of how understanding exams can improve your attitude to them
- an introduction to SQP4 – a whole course strategy for success
- a sense of how to handle the examination day.

Note: For a practice exam, see Chapter 10.

Activity 4: Get ready for your exams checklist

This is a checklist that you could follow for each course that you do that has exams. Why not photocopy this checklist, and then fill it in for each exam that you have to sit?

Subject ....

Survey: I have:

☐ received the course outline

☐ read the course aims and learning outcomes

☐ read the outline and thought about the course structure and design

☐ found and analysed past exam papers

☐ learnt that the paper is... hours

☐ learnt that I have to answer... questions

☐ Come to know the typical language used

☐ Come to know the topics that come up every year.

Question: I have thought about this programme.

I need to know ....

I need to learn ....

Predict: I have:

☐ predicted the likely questions for this subject

☐ chosen .... topics to revise in depth.

Plan: I have:

☐ opened a revision folder on:

    ☐ Topic 1:........................

    ☐ Topic 2:........................

    ☐ Topic 3:........................

    ☐ Topic 4:........................

    ☐ Topic 5:........................

    ☐ Topic 6:........................

☐ made links between learning outcomes, coursework, assignments and my revision topic

☐ placed coursework notes, press cuttings, assignment notes and assignments into the topic folders; on a big pattern on the wall; and on my index cards

☐ discovered that I prefer learning:

    ☐ by sight

    ☐ by sound

    ☐ by feel/movement

Thus, my preferred revision system will utilise mainly:

    ☐ pattern notes of the key points

    ☐ tapes of me reciting the key points

    ☐ making condensed charts of the key points

    ☐ I will *see it, hear it, say it, do it.*

▶

Prepare:

- [ ] I have gone through my exam folders and have prepared condensed notes of everything that I need to remember for the exam for:
  - [ ] Topic 1:.......................
  - [ ] Topic 2:.......................
  - [ ] Topic 3:.......................
  - [ ] Topic 4:.......................
  - [ ] Topic 5:.......................
  - [ ] Topic 6:.......................
- [ ] I am learning this by:
  - [ ] memorising my key-point patterns/charts
  - [ ] reciting my key points along with my tape
  - [ ] testing myself and friends
  - [ ] carrying index cards with the key points on them.

Practise:

- [ ] I have drawn up a revision timetable for this exam subject. It includes practicing the following:
- [ ] positive thinking
- [ ] brainstorming and planning answers
- [ ] planning and writing 'perfect' answers with friends
- [ ] writing with notes
- [ ] writing without notes
- [ ] timed writing without notes

I am ready and confident!

21

How to make the most of Personal Development Planning (PDP) - Christine Keenan

AIMS

To explore how engaging with PDP can help you to help yourself, and to be successful in your academic, personal and professional life.

LEARNING OUTCOMES

That after reading this chapter and engaging with the activities, you will have:
- started to develop your own ideas of what PDP is all about
- understood how engaging with PDP can give you a clear idea about the kind of life and work that you want for yourself
- linked the idea of PDP to developing confidence in your skills, qualities and attributes
- thought about how to articulate your skills, personal qualities and competencies with potential employers
- developed a positive attitude and approach associated with success
- understood many of the terms associated with PDP.

Introduction

In many ways, this whole book is about Personal Development Planning. Each chapter has a number of learning activities, such as:

- how to learn and study – where you complete a personal study skills review
- organising yourself – where you think about the skills you have and what you would like to improve on
- how to research and read academically and how to use computers and e-learning – where you think about how to access and analyse the information you need, often called research skills, information literacy or ICT skills
- how to understand your course – where you examined how the overview or, big picture, helps you to become a more effective student by really understanding what your course is all about, including how it will be assessed
- how to pass exams – including goal-setting and thinking about learning styles
- how to work with others in groups
- how to build your confidence and how you feel about things.

If you stop to think about it, you will see that these activities are about:
- understanding yourself and personal organisation
- the management and handling of information
- managing tasks, including academic work
- managing and working with others.
- And, these involve:

  - reflection
  - goal-setting, objective-setting and forward-planning
  - collaboration and negotiation
  - being able to respond to different situations, contexts and people
  - persuasion
  - managing time
  - critical thinking.

Already, you are probably thinking that there are some terms and phrases that are unfamiliar to you. It is important that you feel comfortable with these, as they will continue to be used during the chapter. If you come across terms that you do not fully understand, jot them down and develop your own definitions for them.

Activity 1: Learning about terms and phrases often associated with PDP

Reflection:
What is reflection? Generally, we learn through experience, thinking about that experience and then making adjustments for the future. Some professional bodies require reflective practice to be included in the curriculum.

▶

But what is it? Think about a new recent experience. It might have been travelling abroad on your own for the first time, or learning to drive a car.

Reflect back on how you felt about it. Were you nervous? What planning and preparation did you do? How did you feel about it later? What will make for a better experience next time? There have been a number of attempts to help describe this process. One of the most famous is what is known as the 'Kolb' cycle.

The Kolb Cycle suggests that learning is a process, and that there are no fixed timescales for each phase, but that they all flow into each other in a cyclical way. There are many criticisms of this model, for example, some suggest that it is too simplistic in trying to describe a very complex process. Nevertheless, the model is quite useful in attempting an explanation of the role of reflection in learning.

There are four phases to the Kolb Cycle:

Concrete experience – What happened? What took place? What was the experience?

Reflection – Your own personal analysis. What skills, attributes, competencies did you draw on? Reviewing what happened, thinking about how you, and others, felt about it.

Abstract conceptualisation – Coming to an understanding of what happened. Being able to make generalisations from the experience, and thinking about whether more information is needed before coming to conclusions.

Active experimentation – Planning for the future, based on experience and reflection. What would you do differently next time and why? What would you do in exactly the same way, and why? Who could you get help from next time to improve something? What resources do you need?

Leading on to the next concrete experience . . .

(Source: Kolb, D.A. (1984) *Experiential Learning: Experience as the Source of Learning and development*. Upper Saddle River, NJ: Prentice-Hall)

If you come across other terms that are new to you, jot them down and find out about them in a similar way. You can then come to your own definitions and conclusions about what they mean, for you.

(See also Chapters 10 and 15 on the reflective learning diary and the reflective essay).

What is Personal Development Planning?

It's interesting to think about the term 'Personal Development Planning.' This can indeed be very 'personal', something that you 'do' for yourself, in order to think more deeply about your life, how you do things, your goals, ambitions and how you perceive yourself. 'Development' implies that PDP is a process that happens over time. If you really work with it, it will become a way of life and not just an add-on that you are required to do. 'Planning' suggests that you will be careful to make sure you have the right information to be working with, that you know who can help you achieve your goals and what resources you may need. From this 'reflection', you can plan for developing the knowledge and skills that you will need, in order to help you to achieve your ambitions and hopes.

Sometimes, PDP may be a process required by a tutor, or an employer, in which case your development plans will be developed often in consultation with others, and it can be very helpful to share your reflections with others. For example, you may find that your university covers aspects of PDP in tutorial sessions. Also, many employers, and professional bodies, have clearly defined activities that you may be required to work through in order to progress.

Whatever your motivation, active engagement with the process of PDP will ensure that you have a clear idea of:

- who you are
- how you like to learn
- your strengths and weaknesses
- how to achieve your desired goals, whether they be personal, academic, or professional.

Activity 2: Benefits of PDP

Jot down what you think the benefits of PDP would be to you. You may feel that you have limited time to do PDP, you may find that you have to engage with it as part of your course – perhaps it is assessed – or you may feel that it is something that you want to make part of your lifelong planning. Consider the following questions:

- How do you want to get started?
- What are your priorities at the moment?
- How can you maximise your own potential and how will PDP help you to do this?
- What are your timescales?

This can be the start of a general action plan.

Time

Engaging with PDP can be a very time-consuming exercise.

> *A quote from a service industries' first-year student:*
> 'I can imagine the reflecting on my strengths and weaknesses would be useful, but it's the rest of the work around it which I find a bit scary, such as action plans, listings, e.g. hobbies, etc.'

So, you might well be asking:

What's in it for me?

PDP can be seen as a set of building blocks on which to build your academic understanding, deepen your knowledge and understanding of yourself, and build your self-awareness and self-confidence.

To get the most from your studies and be really effective, you can probably start to see that by taking control and responsibility for your own learning, you can develop yourself as a self-confident and independent learner.

Whether you view PDP as an investment, or a waste of time, is entirely up to you. Engaging with PDP can be time-consuming and also challenging, but the pay-off is that you will find out more about yourself, you will get more out of your studies, and you will be better prepared as a graduate seeking employment.

A quote from a first-year computing student:
'I wish I had known about this at the start of the year. It is something that I will definitely get involved with now that I am more aware about it.'

If you think about it, it is actually a framework for life. Throughout life, we face new challenges and when doing so, we reflect on previous experiences, we think about what went well and what didn't go so well, and on what we might want to do differently in future. This can apply across any situation and at any time in our life, and underpinning this are what are often termed 'transferable skills,' when we apply the skills or competencies that we learn from one situation to another.

These are lifelong strengths that will help with your studies, your personal relationships and in your professional life.

The rest of this chapter will give some ideas on how to do this.

Why do we think PDP is important?

Each of us wants to be successful and, elsewhere, this book talks about motivation and commitment and visualising yourself as a successful person. You have already made a commitment to studying at university, and reading this book indicates that you have the motivation to succeed. But, have you stopped to think about, or reflect on, what 'success' means to you?

Activity 3: Planning to succeed

- Before you read further, jot down your own definition of 'success' – you might find that you have more than one!
- If you are just starting out at university, jot down how you think it will be different from school or college, what you want to get out of the next three or four years there, what you think your strengths are and where you think you can improve, and what you enjoy doing now (for example, hobbies, sports, pastimes) that you want to keep on doing.
- Then, jot down a quick plan of what you need to do next.
- Finally, keep this in a safe place and refer back to it from time to time.

Query: What is the point of this?

Discussion: Well, what is happening here is that you are taking time to pause, and reflect on what you want for yourself, what is happening to you right now, what your aims and goals for yourself are, and reflecting on your strengths and acknowledging any weaknesses that you might want to work on as well.

▶

This is the basis of PDP. You will see that it reflects on you as a person in your own right, you develop an honest self-evaluation and, in doing so, will have the basis for an action plan or personal progress file, or portfolio. Your definition of success might have concentrated on your own academic development, or you might have mentioned making friends and making the most of university life, or you might have mentioned getting a good job after graduation. These are all legitimate and form the basis of this chapter. In other words, PDP is not just about ticking the boxes in your academic life, but is all about becoming the whole person that you want to be.

Being positive

We know that many students think that PDP is boring, and that many may feel disenchanted because of their previous experiences. But, the aim of this chapter is to try and turn that perception around, and help you to see that it can be a very positive, exciting, illuminating and yes, also, a challenging process with many positive outcomes.

A quote from a psychology student:
'. . . will be appropriate when designing my CV as personal development will help me look back at what I have achieved.'

Does PDP happen at all universities?

Every UK university is required to provide PDP opportunities to its students, and all universities are free to interpret this in their own way.

In 1997, a far-reaching document that became known as the Dearing Report was published. This made a number of significant recommendations, including several in connection with providing structured support to students in developing lifelong learning skills.

In 2003, the government published a White Paper, entitled 'The Future of Higher Education', which set out its plans for HE. These plans included enabling 'learners to understand and reflect on their achievements and to present those achievements to employers, institutions and other stakeholders'.

This definition, provided by the Quality Assurance Agency for Higher Education, is probably the most widely used:

'a structured and supported process undertaken by an individual to reflect upon their own learning, performance and/or achievement and to plan for their personal, educational and career development.'

The primary objective for PDP is to improve the capacity of individuals to understand what and how they are learning, and to review, plan and take responsibility for their own learning, helping students:

- become more effective, independent and confident self-directed learners
- understand how they are learning and relate their learning to a wider context
- improve their general skills for study and career management
- articulate personal goals and evaluate progress towards their achievement
- develop a positive attitude to learning throughout life.

Source: Recommendations for Policy on Personal Development Planning, QAA, (2000)

Activity 4: How does your university tackle PDP?

- How is PDP referred to in your university prospectus, on your university website and in your course documentation?
- Look at the detailed information provided about each of the units or modules that you will be taking on your course, and list all the references to PDP activity, e.g. group project (working in groups), research skills (information handling), etc.
- Jot these down and think about your previous experiences, think about what went well last time you worked in a team, what didn't go so well, what you could do to make yourself a more effective group member, what resources or support you need to do this.
- You may also find that your university provides you with a progress file, or portfolio, where you can record your goal-setting, skills audits, action plans, transcripts, etc. This is a very useful way of recording your reflections, action plans and achievements, and can be drawn upon when preparing your CV or planning for an interview. For example, you could record the contribution you made to a group project and think about the particular skills that you have that made the project a success. Find out if your university has an e-portfolio – if not, find out whether they can support you in setting one up for yourself or, alternatively, create your own paper or online record.
- In some universities, the Student Union is actively engaged with facilitating PDP activities, e.g. leadership courses, volunteering, representation, etc. These extra-curricular activities are an excellent way of 'adding value' to your time at university – find out what happens where you are and perhaps get involved.

Transferable Skills

Universities often develop their PDP resources around what are known as 'transferable skills'. You may find that your university has a list of the transferable skills on its website. The term 'skills' can sometimes be contentious in higher education, so some prefer the term 'attributes' or 'competencies'. Nevertheless, the development of these 'skills' will continue throughout your life and will also contribute hugely to your employability.

Employers often look for a range of skills which will transfer from your experience of higher education into the world of work. Remember also that there are transferable skills within the curriculum (often termed academic skills) and outside of the curriculum (often termed life skills) – you have probably started to think about this already.

It might be useful now to have a think about a range of transferable skills typically referred to in higher education, and then carry out a personal audit – and remember it is important that you provide the evidence (the record associated with the activity) that you can refer to. This is where your progress file, or portfolio, comes in useful.

Transferable skill — learning

At university, learning is about building up valid knowledge for a particular situation while remaining open to other views, and being able to:

- extract general concepts, principles and procedures
- critically evaluate, select and present ideas/arguments/evidence
- connect ideas and knowledge
- form your own ideas
- apply theory to practice
- seek and use feedback
- evaluate your own work according to the relevant criteria
- find and adopt study techniques that work for you
- identify learning needs.

Let's think about this in the context of academic learning. At university in the UK, students are encouraged to formulate their own ideas by critically evaluating a range of ideas, scholarship and theoretical concepts and approaches. There is more about this in other chapters in this book. But, in terms of learning as a lifelong transferable skill, you might want to think about this a little more. How do you learn? How do you have confidence in what you are learning? Where do ideas come from? How do abstract ideas transfer into experience, and how can reflecting on experience lead to abstract ideas and concepts? All learners, whatever level they are at, need to be able to reflect on feedback to their work — how do you feel and react to feedback on your performance? Have you stopped to think about how you learn best? Have you identified areas of your learning that you need support with? Learning is often described as 'transformational', so why not record and reflect on the journey that you are undertaking?

You might not previously have thought about this as a transferable skill, but it is an area of development that is really interesting to reflect on once you get started on it.

Transferable skill — information technology

This refers to using electronic means to find, record, manipulate and present information. You could, for example:

- use a word processor to create documents and use functions to add value to work, e.g. Word
- create and use a spreadsheet and manipulate data within it, e.g. Excel
- create a database from a set of data, or work with it to produce reports, e.g. Access
- create effective presentations using a graphics package, e.g. PowerPoint
- produce transparencies or visual aids for a presentation
- research topics of interest on the Internet
- use email to maintain effective links with colleagues and clients.

▶

It is very difficult these days to think about any aspect of our lives that does not interact with Information Technology. This is a very broad life skill that is seen as being very necessary in our everyday interactions. Even those who do not consider themselves to be IT-literate will usually be comfortable with email and simple Web searching. Most universities will have workshops and tutorials available to help less confident students develop these essential skills.

Transferable skill—self-management

This is about understanding, using and developing our own abilities to effect good outcomes in life and work. You could look to:
- set appropriate targets and goals
- organise tasks to meet deadlines – prioritise and plan
- know your own strengths and weaknesses
- apply strengths to weaker areas
- reflect on progress and outcomes
- find support or develop new strategies where necessary
- accept and act on feedback
- evaluate your own performance.

Now, some hints on how to apply this. Your transferable skills audit may have highlighted a weakness in the area of self-management. Your action plan will help you to address these weaknesses, and identify resources and help that may be needed. But, why is this an important skill to develop? Being able to set manageable and achievable targets and stick to them, and having a clear understanding of your strengths and weaknesses, can help you maintain control over your life. The evidence you collect in your portfolio or progress file can be drawn on as a reminder to yourself of the journey you have undertaken to improve, enhance, or develop that skill. It will also provide a reminder of an achievement that you can include in a job application or in preparation for a job interview.

A recent job advert, for a worker with young people, called for candidates with an 'excellent skills base, including communication, organisational and group work skills'. Of course, in this case, they were looking for someone with understanding of the particular requirements of that area of work, policy and experience, but, why did this job advert, and many others, emphasise these particular skills? What does it reveal about the sort of person they are looking for, and what is the 'something extra' that would make you stand out as a candidate for this post?

If you are going to be looking at job adverts that emphasise these skills, why not start right now by making a record of your starting points. Did your audit reveal that communication is a weakness for you? What did it tell you about your organisational and group-work skills? What have you done to improve these, and have you attended any workshops or tutorials to help you? Can you provide examples of how you have improved your organisation skills through a better understanding of self-management?

▶

Transferable skill – critical thinking

This is often a difficult concept to grapple with. Critical thinking is about the development of logical thoughts and ideas about a subject, or coming to a reasoned solution of a problem or dilemma. When you think about it, we do this all the time in our daily lives. We make decisions about important things – for example, what were the things that you took into account when choosing your course and university? Critical thinking involves being able to:

- critically analyse a line of reasoning
- identify bias, distortion, illogical reasoning in arguments and texts
- challenge taken-for-granted assumptions and existing practice
- evaluate evidence presented in support of a conclusion
- identify and address gaps in knowledge or understanding
- identify and analyse key points/issues within a problem
- generate creative/innovative ideas using techniques such as brainstorming, mind mapping, critical path analysis
- consider alternatives/implications/wider or local contexts
- plan/implement a course of action
- take calculated risks as necessary to achieve goals
- organise sub-tasks appropriately
- monitor/control activities
- assess outcomes and incorporate the lessons into future planning.

Many of our day-to-day decisions are based on thinking about the pros and cons of something – for example, what influences us to open an account with one bank rather than another? What influences us to buy our groceries from a particular supermarket? There are other important considerations as well. Most people over the age of 18 have the right to vote. How do we choose the causes we want to support and follow? How do we differentiate between political ideals? Do we know enough about ethical shopping to help us make purchasing decisions that our conscience is comfortable with, or don't we care? Critical thinking allows us to recognise bias and take this into account when coming to our own decisions, whether they be decisions about lifestyle, politics or education.

In academic life, we are encouraged to review or evaluate competing ideas or approaches, and come to a conclusion based on our analysis and evaluation of them.

Critical thinking helps us come to an understanding of where we stand in relation to something, whether it be challenging the status quo, or evaluating a number of sources of evidence, in order to make our own mind up about something.

This is why critical thinking is often considered to be a key transferable skill, and one that is very important in enabling us to identify key issues, analyse them, and come to a conclusion based on them.

Transferable skill – information handling

This includes being able to:

- locate and use a variety of sources – print, electronic, people
- exploit bibliographic databases – search screens, keywords

▶

- sift through information to identify key points
- appraise information using relevant criteria
- reference material correctly and understand plagiarism
- organise and store information so it can be retrieved when needed
- organise information into a logical and cohesive format that can be communicated easily to others.

This transferable skill is often quite tricky. In a world where there is so much information at our fingertips, how can we possibly manage, handle and store information in a way that makes sense to us? This is a huge area, and you may decide that you need to break it down into manageable chunks.

A way to start may be to speak to your subject librarian and ask them to give you an introduction to searching for information relevant to your subject. In this way, you can learn to get the most out of the electronic resources available to you through your library.

Don't forget to record what you are doing and how the new skills that you are acquiring are facilitating your personal development.

Transferable skill – numeracy

This is about understanding and applying mathematical techniques when handling problems and projects. It includes being able to:

- make fundamental calculations – estimating, adding, subtracting, multiplying and dividing
- use a calculator confidently
- have a grasp of statistics and percentages, fractions, decimals and ratios
- derive conclusions and reason with the use of numerical data
- create and interpret spreadsheets, graphs, charts, tables and diagrams
- develop mathematical models using complex equations in order to find solutions to problems.

Many university courses and professional bodies have a basic requirement of maths or numeracy, but how important is numeracy to you? You may find that people are often quite comfortable admitting that they have a weakness with numbers and maths, but would be reluctant to admit a weakness with literacy. Why is this and does it matter?

Well, you need to think about this for yourself. Even those people whose daily lives do not involve the requirement of working with mathematical formulae or concepts still need to have a basic understanding of how to calculate their change and how to understand their utility bills and their bank statements.

Numeracy and literacy are often quite emotive topics and many adult education centres offer short courses in them – this tends to suggest that this is a skill worth thinking about and addressing, particularly if working with numbers is problematic for you.

Many universities recognise this and offer support sessions in numeracy and maths. If your skills audit demonstrates a weakness in this area, why not challenge yourself to tackle this area and beat this problem?

▶

Transferable skill – career management

Here, you will need to have:

- good organisational awareness
- an awareness of trends that are emerging in the business or professional world
- effective communication of your skills and experience to others, in order to gain employment or develop a career
- future targets in mind regarding your career and education.

It's never too early to start being aware of career opportunities and to start thinking about directions in which you might want your future career to develop.

Often, we think about a general area of a career, for example, teaching, working with computers, health and social care, but we may not exactly know quite how that will materialise yet. This is fine, and university careers offices will always be on hand to help alert you to the range of opportunities within a particular field. For example, emerging technologies may present opportunities that you had not thought of when you set out on your computing degree.

But, whether your goals are already firmly established, or whether you are still unsure about your career aspirations, you can start thinking now about who you are, and the sort of career that will suit you. Are you a vocational person with a passion for social justice, for working with people in difficulties? Very often, these jobs attract relatively low salaries. Do you consider yourself to be highly ambitious and aspirational, or something else all together?

An understanding of the broad aspects of PDP, and how this can help you to understand who you are, will help you to be comfortable with and validate the decisions you make. You can start now by keeping a note of what your goals and ambitions are for yourself, and how these might change and adapt over a period of time. You will then find that the evidence you collect in your portfolio or progress file will begin to help you picture the sort of career that you want for yourself. What skills are you developing, how do you get on with people, how well do you interact with technology, and so on?

Transferable skill – team working

This is about being able to:

- understand the basis of group behaviour and team roles
- motivate self and others to the achievement of common goals
- respect feelings, views and values of others, and take on board other opinions
- assist and support others
- collaborate and negotiate
- take the initiative when necessary
- delegate where necessary

▶

- review progress and alter a plan if necessary
- accept and carry out agreed or delegated tasks.

This is not easy for everyone, and very often, it might feel much quicker and simpler to just get the job done yourself. But, if you scan the situations vacant columns, you will soon see how important teamworking is. Many large organisations hold assessment days as part of their recruitment process, where applicants are required to demonstrate their teamworking capabilities.

Often at university, you will get the opportunity to develop these skills by working on group projects, and many students will engage with extra-curricular activities where working together in teams is a key principle in getting the job done.

Your transferable skills audit results will give you an indication of your strengths and weaknesses in this area. It is important sometimes to be able to achieve common goals in cooperation with others, and requires a number of the skills described in the list above.

Transferable skill – communicating

Communication is about being able to:
- use a variety of modern communication tools
- listen positively and respond to both verbal and non-verbal messages
- present a well-structured and evidenced argument
- express self and ideas clearly, concisely and logically in speech and writing
- influence others and gain agreement or acceptance of your plan/idea/activity
- understand other viewpoints and appreciate cultural differences
- evaluate how well your message is received.

There have already been a number of examples indicating how important this transferable skill is. It is difficult to imagine the opposite – it is doubtful that you will see a job advert that does not highlight the importance of good communication skills. It is also doubtful that you will be able to persuade, influence, encourage, motivate or engage others, without confidence in your communication skills. Some things to consider:

- Who do you need to communicate with? Depending on the context you are in, you may be required to deal with members of the public (and will probably have been developing these skills if you have had part-time jobs to help fund your studies), you may be required to deal with other professionals, you may be required to communicate with a range of people in a range of positions in your own organisation.
- What do you need to communicate? Are you able to present what you need to communicate in a clear and well-structured way?
- How do you need to communicate? You will need to be able to adapt your communication styles to meet the needs of your 'audience'.
(*Source*: www.pdp.bournemouth.ac.uk)

Activity 5: Conduct your own PDP Skills audit

Now, try an on-line activity in order to 'audit' yourself in these transferable skills, go to: http://pdp.bournemouth.ac.uk/documents/u-transferable_skills-self_assessment.doc

Because we all develop and grow all the time, it is useful to carry out a regular reflective review of your transferable skills:

http://pdp.bournemouth.ac.uk/documents/u-transferable_skills-reflective_review-question_bank.doc

Then, you can create an action plan to help you plan for improving areas of weakness, and to maintain and develop your strengths. You should also consider how you will do this, and what resources you need to help you achieve your goals. It is important that you give yourself timescales that are manageable.

For an example of an action plan, although you may prefer to design your own, go to: http://pdp.bournemouth.ac.uk/documents/u-my_goals-goal_setting_and_action_planning.doc

Tips:

You may decide that some of the transferable skills described above are more important in your life than others – you may also think that it would be very time-consuming to develop all of them.

Depending on your own plans, you might want to:
- scan job opportunities in the press (including jobs and careers that you are not necessarily interested in), and get an impression of which are the most regularly sought after
- have a look at the websites of the professional bodies, particularly where they express their mission and values to see how they articulate the skills and values you are interested in. Here are two examples:

✓ The British Computer Society (www.bcs.org) values include:
  - respecting the individual
  - advocating fair treatment
  - rewarding exceptional performance
  - showing commitment to personal and professional growth
  - encouraging teamwork.

If you are an aspiring computing professional, you will find that these values can be developed, recorded and evidenced through your own attention to your personal development planning.

✓ The website of the Royal Institute of British Architects describes the role of architects as:

'working closely with other members of the construction industry, including engineers, builders, surveyors, local authority planners and building control officers. Much of their time will be spent visiting sites in the UK and abroad, assessing the feasibility of a project,

▶

inspecting building work or managing the construction process. They will also spend time
researching old records and drawings, and testing new ideas and construction techniques.'
(http://www.architecture.com/)

From this, you will see that job adverts in this career area also include a
requirement of strong communication skills, skills of analysis, information
handling, and working with others.
The notion of transferable skills then works in a range of ways: applying learning
from one area to another and across all disciplines and areas of life.

Conclusion

Be your own person. Think about other things that are important to you:
- Check out your course documentation for PDP opportunities.
- Do you have paid work? If so, what skills are you developing when balancing work
  and study? Reflect on how these can be transferred to other aspects of your life.
- Do you play sport? Reflect on the many ways that playing sports can enhance your
  life, and think about the skills and qualities that you are acquiring.
- Are you a member of any clubs and societies?
- What extra contributions are you making in your local community?
- Are you prepared to get involved? For example, are you an elected course representative,
  or elected Student Union official?
- What hobbies do you have and how do these contribute to the whole you?

A quote from a first-year media production student:

'PDP encouraged me to take greater advantage of resources to improve my skills and capabilities.'

PDP really is an opportunity, not a problem. Think about how you want to
record your reflections, achievements and goals and ambitions. This may be in your
own personal journal, or your university may well offer a template for a progress file
or portfolio. It is really important to remember to keep examples as evidence of what
you have done and what you have achieved.

Engaging with personal development planning at university will help you to reflect
on the skills you are developing within your programme of study. It will also enable
you to reflect on your strengths and weaknesses in relation to academic work and plan
for improvement. PDP can be time-consuming and hard work. However, PDP is much
more than just a reflection on your academic work.

Everything you do and all your achievements, disappointments, ambitions and
aspirations are key to you being who you are. Reflecting on all of these experiences
can help towards your future growth. It's also important to remember that the whole
university experience, and making the most of all aspects of your life, will contribute
to your overall development.

If you have worked through all the activities, you will start to see how much time
this can take up, but it does become second nature with practice. Find ways of engaging
with PDP that suit you and your work, study and personal commitments. The rewards
will become clear and obvious over time.

▶

Further Reading

Recommendations for Policy on Personal Development Planning, QAA, 2000.

Resources

Carrying out your own searches within your university and on the Internet generally will provide you with further information. Further useful information about PDP can be found at:

Bournemouth University:
pdp.bournemouth.ac.uk
Centre for Recording Achievement:
http://www.recordingachievement.org/
Higher Education Academy:
http://www.heacademy.ac.uk/ourwork/learning/pdp
National Union of Students:
http://www.nusonline.co.uk/about/StudentCharter/11701.aspx
The Quality Assurance Agency for Higher Education:
http://www.qaa.ac.uk/students/guides/UnderstandProgFiles.asp
The University of Exeter:
http://www.services.ex.ac.uk/cas/employability/pdp/students/index.php

Review points

When reviewing this chapter, you might notice that you:
- have started to think constructively about yourself as an independent, self-confident and motivated learner and how to achieve this through PDP
- have a much better understanding of yourself as a person in your own right
- have started to think constructively about how to reflect on your experiences and plan for the future
- have a much clearer idea about your skills, personal qualities and competencies and how to articulate them to potential employers
- have a clear set of personal, academic and professional goals, a positive attitude and a clear sense of who you want to be
- have a better understanding of some of the terms associated with PDP and know where to find out more if you wish to.

With thanks to Bournemouth University and Exeter University for allowing the use of their PDP websites to provide a basis for much of the content of this chapter.

Index

weekly plan 79
wesites, Furl (bookmarking) 94
Wiki farms 88
Wikipedia (Wiki) 87–9
word processing 196–7
work placement or volunteering 32, 34
World Wide Web debut 85
worrying 72–3, 127–8
   see also fears
writing blocks 202–4
writing skills 183–208, 218–21
   10 steps to success 189–201
   academic forms 184–5
   action plan 191–5
   assessment 187–8
   better assignments 188–9
   checklist 222
   communication 184–7

development and support 32, 201
drafts 195–8, 218–19
feedback 200
formative and summative assessment 188
free writing 206–7
learning 187–8
'leave it' 197–8, 219
plan structure 195, 218
prepare to research 189–91, 217
prompted writing 204–6
proofreading 199, 220
questionnaire 185–6
reading and information sources 218
reflective essays 210–11, 223–35
reports 236–47
review notes 195, 198, 218, 220
SWOT analysis 101–2, 124, 200, 221
   see also essay writing